The Illustrated
Encyclopedia of
Succulents

The Illustrated Encyclopedia of
Succulents

Gordon Rowley

Consultant: Charles Glass. Editor of Cactus and Succulent Journal of America

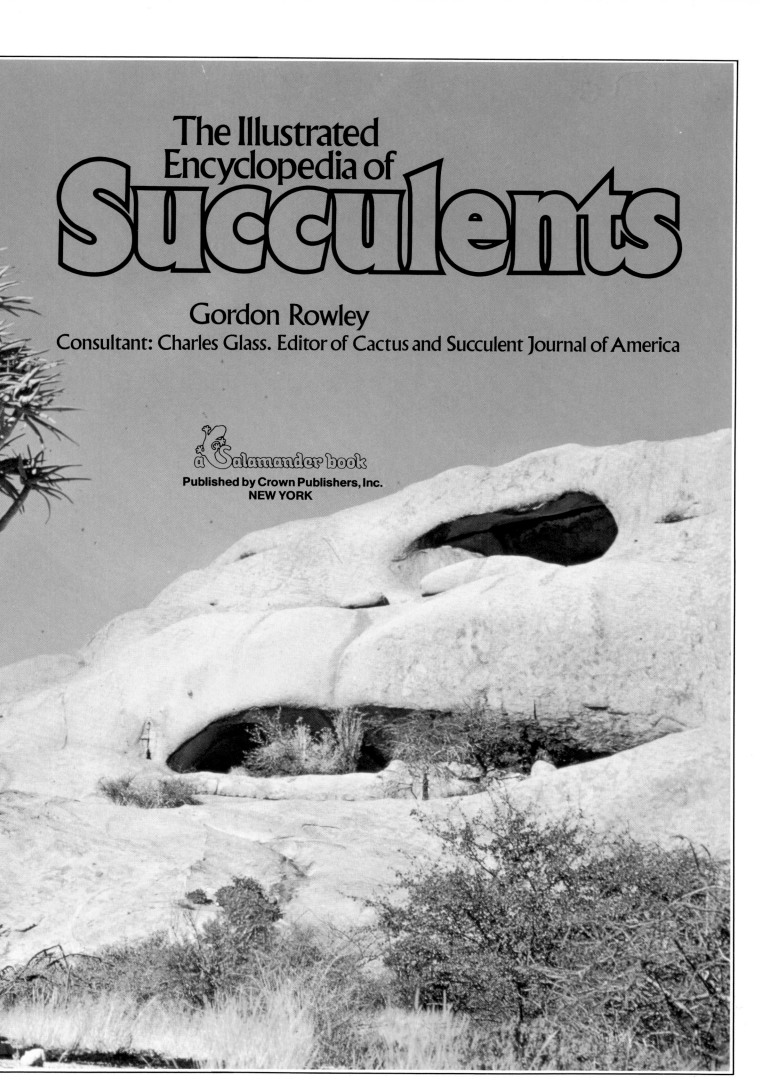

a Salamander book
Published by Crown Publishers, Inc.
NEW YORK

A Salamander Book

First published 1978 in the United States by
Crown Publishers Inc.,
One Park Avenue,
New York, New York 10016,
United States of America.

Published in Canada by General Publishing Company Limited.

First published in the United Kingdom in 1978 by Salamander Books Limited.

© Salamander Books Ltd 1978
Salamander House,
27 Old Gloucester Street,
London WC1N 3AF, United Kingdom.

Library of Congress Cataloging in Publication Data
Rowley, Gordon.
  The illustrated encyclopedia of succulents.
  Includes index.
  1. Succulent plants.   I. Title.
SB438.R682   582'.13'04'61   77-16555
ISBN 0-517-53309-X

All correspondence concerning the content of this volume should be addressed to Salamander Books Ltd.

Credits
Editor: Geoff Rogers
Designer: Carol Collins

Illustrations:
Max Ansell
June Baker
Pat Lenander

For full credits see page 256.

Filmset:
Modern Text Typesetting, Essex, United Kingdom

Color reproduction:
Bantam Litho Ltd., Essex, United Kingdom.
Colourcraftsmen Ltd., Essex, United Kingdom.
Paramount Litho Co., Essex, United Kingdom.

Printed in Belgium by Henri Proost et Cie,
Turnhout, Belgium.

Distributed in Australia/New Zealand by Summit
Books, a division of Paul Hamlyn Pty., Sydney,
Australia.

Endpapers: White-flowered variant of
Mammillaria zeilmanniana, *a popular and
easy-growing cactus ideal for beginners.*

*Half-title (1): Succulents on the Mediterranean
coast—one of many spectacular vistas in the
Jardin Exotique at Monaco.*

*Title page (2/3): Succulents come in all sizes,
from no larger than a pea to tall trees, like this*
Aloe dichotoma *in the Namib Desert.*

*Left: All succulents flower, some in more
spectacular fashion than others. This is*
Adenium obesum *from East Africa.*

*Below: Geometrical patterns and a high
degree of symmetry are a feature of most
succulents. This is a leaf rosette of* **Agave.**

Contents

Left: Young shoots of **Opuntia** *bear scale leaves; the adult stems are leafless.*

Below: Crowning glory of a cactus, the blooms on a barrel cactus offer nectar and abundant pollen to prospective pollinators.

Foreword

Some ten thousand species of flowering plants are included beneath the umbrella-name of succulents—three or four percent of all known species, and representative of about twelve percent of all recognized Families. They possess certain features in common which catch the eye and evoke immediate reactions of admiration or distaste as do no other plants. They are diversified by seemingly endless variations in pattern and adornment, texture and colour, making them an ideal subject for collectors and enthusiasts. Their solidity and statuesque pose give the illusion of timeless immutability, but the observant cultivator finds delight in watching their continual changes throughout the seasons.

An encyclopedia is defined as a "literary work containing extensive information on all branches or one particular branch of knowledge . . ." I quote this lest anyone should be disappointed at not finding here an alphabetical catalogue of all the known species. For them, there are already handbooks by Jacobsen, Backeberg, Rauh, Haage and others, as cited in the refences starting on page 247. Most of the extensive literature on succulents, apart from strictly scientific monographs, is concerned with just two aspects: describing species, and expounding cultivation. Here the aim is different. It is to take an overall view of succulents as one element of the world flora, noting their distinguishing features in structure, mode of life, habitat, reproduction and survival, their evolution and

their sytematic classification. In this last, the emphasis is on the higher categories from genus upwards; individual species are mentioned not so much on their own account as for the tendencies and characteristics that they illustrate.

Over the centuries botany has developed its own terminology: a beautiful and precise language that enables a plant to be exactly characterized in a few telegram-style sentences instead of a whole page of normal prose. Words like "cactus" and "desert" have a special meaning, and it is a pity that current usage so often misapplies them. Each chapter in this book introduces some of these terms, familiarity with which will open the doors on a wealth of other reference books. Every term is defined where it first occurs and, should the reader miss this, he will find a glossary on page 249.

I am grateful to Charles Glass and to colleagues at Reading University who have read sections of the book and helped with ideas and criticisms from their own fields of expertise, to Geoff Rogers of Salamander Books for the meticulous care he has taken in seeing this book through the press, and to all those owners of copyright material who have permitted their work to be reproduced or adapted. A full list of acknowledgments will be found on page 256.

Below: Longest established of the large open-air plantings of succulents in North America: the Huntington Botanical Gardens.

PART ONE

The World of Succulents

"There is a great diversity in plants in respect of number and fewness, largeness and smallness, and in respect of strength and weakness."

It is not merely the tensions and uncertainties of everyday life that drive us more and more to take an interest in natural history. Certainly there is solace in the silent world of plants: a greenhouse is an ideal retreat from the cacophony of the city, and the popularity of books and documentary films on wild life bears witness to this familiar need to escape. No aspect is too obscure to be of interest — indeed, there is a strange lure in subjects off the beaten track, which would lose appeal if they became over-familiar. But equally potent in turning people's attention to the living world is the realization that it is steadily being driven back by man's increased use of the land and oceans. Succulents, more so than many other plants, are disappearing fast in their native homes, and unless steps are taken soon, many will be extinct before they have even been adequately classified, let alone tested for possible uses.

Both these themes — the quest of knowledge and the need to conserve — are dealt with in the first part of this book: an introduction to the natural history and cultivation of one very special group of plants that excels in colonizing arid and inhospitable terrain. What are these succulents, these surrealist vegetables of the

wilderness? How do they differ from other plants, and how do they flower, propagate and survive? The secret of their success touches upon many disciplines, including physiology, ecology, genetics and evolution. Surprisingly, despite much study, we still find gaps in our knowledge. In the search for new leads, we often discover that the bare truth is more beautiful than any of the gaudy myths with which the subject has been so generously draped for public display.

Technical terms are defined in boxes set in the text area and again in the Glossary, which begins on page 249.

Illustrations are cross-referenced in the text by the chapter and photograph (or diagram) number that appears in brackets at the beginning of each caption. Thus (9.3) refers to illustration 3 in Chapter 9.

"Succulents" is used throughout the book in its correct botanical sense to include cacti, unless otherwise stated.

The quotations used as chapter headings come from "De Plantis" in the collected English edition of Aristotle's works Vol. VI edited by W. D. Ross, 1913 — perhaps the oldest surviving treatise on botany and attributable, at least in part, to Aristotle (B.C. 382–322).

Below: Not all that looks like a cactus is one. This **Tavaresia barklyi** *belongs to the Periwinkle Family. The differences lie in the flowers and fruits.*

The Succulent Lifestyle

*"We must consider what the ancients have said on these
points, and examine the works written upon them."*

The earliest reference that I can trace to succulents is in a rare book of the early seventeenth century[1] by a Swiss botanist who lists a number of plants with fleshy leaves, and notes their ability to survive on stored water long after uprooting. An Englishman, Richard Bradley, who was the first Professor of Botany at Cambridge (1724-1732), includes both leaf and stem succulents in his book[2] and defines them as plants 'that are not capable of an *hortus siccus'*—that is, cannot be pressed to make presentable specimens for the herbarium for systematic botanical study.

Misers for water

Succulence is more than just an expansion of stems and leaves as water stores —"plants with middle-age spread" as a revered botanist once described them to me. A storeroom for water is of no use if it lacks a door to prevent the contents from escaping. The external features that distinguish succulents from other plants are discussed in the next chapter. Internally, the succulent tissue has a distinctive look (1.3, 2.5), with large, thin-walled cells and conspicuous air spaces, suggestive of a sponge. These large, watery cells are further distinguished by being highly *polyploid*—that is, containing up to 16 times the normal number of chromosomes (page 62). The sap is slimy and bitter to the taste. So much for the legend of the life-giving cactus, discharging cool, refreshing water to the thirsty traveller! Far from being cool, the inside temperature of a cactus is several degrees above that of

the air outside, and the survival of such plants is in part due to the ability of their cells to endure temperatures 15 to 20 degrees C (28 to 36 degrees F) above those that would damage other plants. Another feature of these storage cells is their ability to collapse gracefully following water loss and to expand again without bursting, which would be fatal. An extreme example of succulence is reported[3] for the South African genus *Muiria* where the plant body encloses a mass of large cells like frog spawn, each up to 2mm ($1/12$in) in diameter and able to remain plump in a dry room for up to ten days before collapsing.

Unusual pathways of life

The observant Romans are credited with having been the first to notice that certain fleshy herbs such as the stonecrop *(Sedum acre)* taste more bitter when picked in the morning than in the evening. You can easily repeat the test to your own satisfaction. Herein lies the germ of the discovery that succulents differ fundamentally from other plants in certain of their life processes, notably by accumulating acid during the night and using it up again during the day. To understand how this comes about, let us briefly review, with the aid of the diagram (1.2), the key events whereby a mesophyte manufactures its food from air, water and salts in solution in the presence of light and *chlorophyll* "leaf green". The process, known as *photosynthesis,* takes place in the green surface tissues of leaves (or stems) during the hours of

sunlight. The chlorophyll is contained in lens-shaped bodies, *chloroplasts,* scattered throughout the cell sap. Water and salts in solution enter the plant through the roots and are conveyed upwards to the photosynthesizing tissues. Air enters through special valves or pores called *stomata* (2.11), which control the flow by opening or closing, rather like the automatic sliding doors of an airport. The nitrogen and oxygen of the air are not directly usable in gas form by plant life; only the carbon dioxide, a mere 0.03 percent of the total, is extracted and used.

The daily cycle of a mesophyte is summarized in 1.2. The stomata open by day and close at night. Light energy from the sun combines water and carbon dioxide in the presence of chlorophyll to form sugar, a complex organic compound classed as a carbohydrate. A by-product of this reaction is oxygen, which is released to the air. By night there is no sun, hence no photosynthesis.

Chemical energy, as distinct from light energy, is also needed for maintaining the vital processes of plants, and this comes from a process called *respiration,* which reverses photosynthesis, breaking down rather than building up carbohydrate. Respiration goes on all the time, but

Right (1.1): High light intensity and evaporation are problems for this aloe in South West Africa. The leaves are thick and fleshy; dead, dry leaves form a protective sheath up the stem.

Below (1.2): Daily cycle of photosynthesis in non-succulent and succulent plants.

Plant types

Mesophytes ("middle plants") are adapted to moderate water requirements.
Xerophytes ("dry plants") are adapted to survive less-than-average water supply. Structural devices that prevent water loss, such as a reduction of surface or a covering of hairs, are known as *xeromorphic* characteristics.
Succulents store water in specially enlarged spongy tissue. All succulents are more or less xerophytic, but not all xerophytes are succulents.

A cactus (plural cacti) is a member of the botanical Family Cactaceae (Chapter 16). All cacti are more or less succulent but not all succulents are cacti.

Succulents are universally known under their scientific names, the few common names being national rather than international.

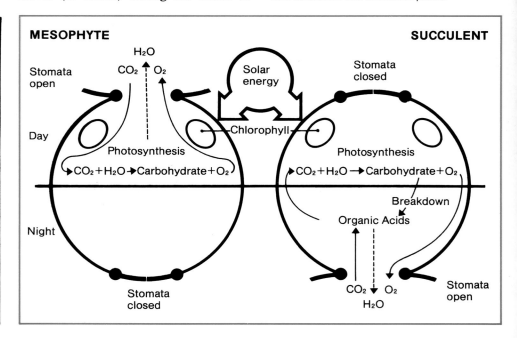

MESOPHYTE · SUCCULENT

Stomata open · Day · Night · Stomata closed

H_2O · CO_2 · O_2 · Solar energy · Stomata closed

Chlorophyll

Photosynthesis · Photosynthesis

$CO_2 + H_2O \rightarrow$ Carbohydrate $+ O_2$ · $CO_2 + H_2O \rightarrow$ Carbohydrate $+ O_2$

Breakdown

Organic Acids

CO_2 · O_2 · Stomata open

H_2O

1: INTRODUCTION

during the day is masked by photosynthesis. Part of the carbohydrate is broken down to give water and carbon dioxide, and oxygen is used up as in the burning of fuel.

The daily cycle in succulent plants is not the same. Here, the stomata remain closed by day and open only at night, when intake of air occurs and its carbon dioxide is extracted and fixed by organic acids produced from the partial breakdown of carbohydrate. During the day these organic acids (malic and isocitric mainly) break down into carbon dioxide and water, which are taken up direct and used in photosynthesis, as in a mesophyte. This daily cycle was first noted in a member of the Crassulaceae Family in 1813[4] and hence bears the name Crassulacean Acid Metabolism, or CAM for short. Recently, two other deviations from the mesophytic cycle have been given the symbols C_3 and C_4, because they involve the formation of 3- and 4-carbon carboxylic acids. They are mentioned here because there is a strong correlation between the distribution of CAM and C_4 systems and that of succulence throughout the flowering plants. Fig. 1.6 makes this clear. It seems as if succulence could evolve only in company with a change in the "normal" respiratory cycle. Now why should this be? The most likely answer is that it is one of many strategies that enable a plant to minimize water loss. When stomata open, as they must in order to allow gas exchanges to take place, they also allow precious water vapour to escape. In mesophytes this is rarely harmful, because more moisture can be drawn in from the soil. Evaporation is much less in the cool night air, and succulents in general adopt the cycle of closing stomata by day and opening them only after dark.

But they can do this only if they have evolved a way to filter out and fix the necessary carbon dioxide at night and use it by day for photosynthesis.

Origin and diversity

How succulence originated is not yet clearly understood, although we know that it has happened independently in widely dissimilar groups of plants, as Fig. 1.6 shows. Experiments have shown that iron starvation can increase succulence in *Tradescantia* by causing the cells in the leaf to elongate vertically, and a similar enhanced fleshiness can be induced in *Kalanchoe* by reducing the day length by periodic shading[5]. Not all succulents are comparable in habitat and behaviour. We find one type of succulence in plants of the seashore and salt marsh. A familiar example of these *halophytes* ("salt plants") is the glasswort or marsh samphire, *Salicornia* (1.5), which, unlike the xerophytic succulents, has a high rate of transpiration and wilts when allowed to dry out. But the same is true of *Glottiphyllum* (11.13), from the hot dry karroos of South Africa, so there are exceptions to most attempts to define a succulent.

A classification into succulents and non-succulents helps the field botanist to

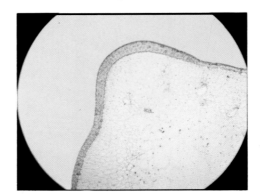

distinguish one element of the flora from others, and certainly aids the gardener by grouping together plants of similar cultural needs, general aesthetics and collector appeal, just as he makes parallel groupings for alpines, epiphytes and aquatics. But botanists universally adopt a classification based on all characters of the plant, not just the degree of fleshiness, because it brings related kinds together and gives the maximum retrieval of information about them. This is the basis of Fig. 1.6, and of the layout of Part 2.

Difficulties of defining a succulent make the limits of our subject somewhat elastic. Some would include the halophytes, and some the yuccas, which show fleshiness of a sort in their stems although many are hardy enough to withstand frost. Others would include orchids (several of which qualify on all counts) and bromeliads — members of the pineapple Family now so popular as house plants. To include such plants would broaden the scope of this book considerably, and these two large and highly individual Families are more suitable for specialist treatment by themselves.

Another Family, the Zygophyllaceae,

Left (1.3): Cross-section of an aloe leaf highly magnified. The large spongy central cells are protected from water loss by a tough surface layer, stained yellow here.

Right (1.4): Leaf and stem succulents representing several different Families from both New and Old Worlds growing happily side by side in similar soil and cultural conditions in an English glasshouse.

*Below (1.5): **Salicornia**, the glasswort, a native halophyte on an English seashore. The soft, green, erect stems are succulent, but wilt if dried, and the plant is an annual.*

Life processes

Metabolism is the collective term for all the chemical changes that go on within a living organism.

Photosynthesis ("light synthesis") is the manufacture of plant food (carbohydrate) from carbon dioxide and water in the presence of light and the green pigment *chlorophyll*. Oxygen is given off.

Respiration reverses photosynthesis: complex organic matter is broken down to carbon dioxide and water, releasing energy essential to plant growth. Oxygen is used up. The process goes on at all times, unaffected by the presence or absence of light.

The loss of water by evaporation through the breathing pores (*stomata*; singular *stoma*) of the plant is called *transpiration*.

One cubic metre of air consists of approximately

4/5 nitrogen	N_2
1/5 oxygen	O_2
300 cubic centimetres of carbon dioxide	CO_2

1: INTRODUCTION

Which plants are succulent?

(1.6) Takhtajan (1966) divides the flowering plants into 73 Orders of Dicotyledons and 21 Orders of Monocotyledons, as shown here, arranging them to show increasing levels of structural complexity. Among these the Families including succulents have been printed in black. Succulence of a sort has been evolved independently in more than a quarter of all known Orders. In some instances, however, the degree is slight and the Families are not mentioned further in this book.

The codings indicate the distribution of three basic biochemical features, as described on Page 14:–

CAM ▲ C₄ ● Betacyanin ■

Note that succulence and CAM usually go together; succulence and C₄ sometimes; and Betacyanin is confined to one group of succulents.

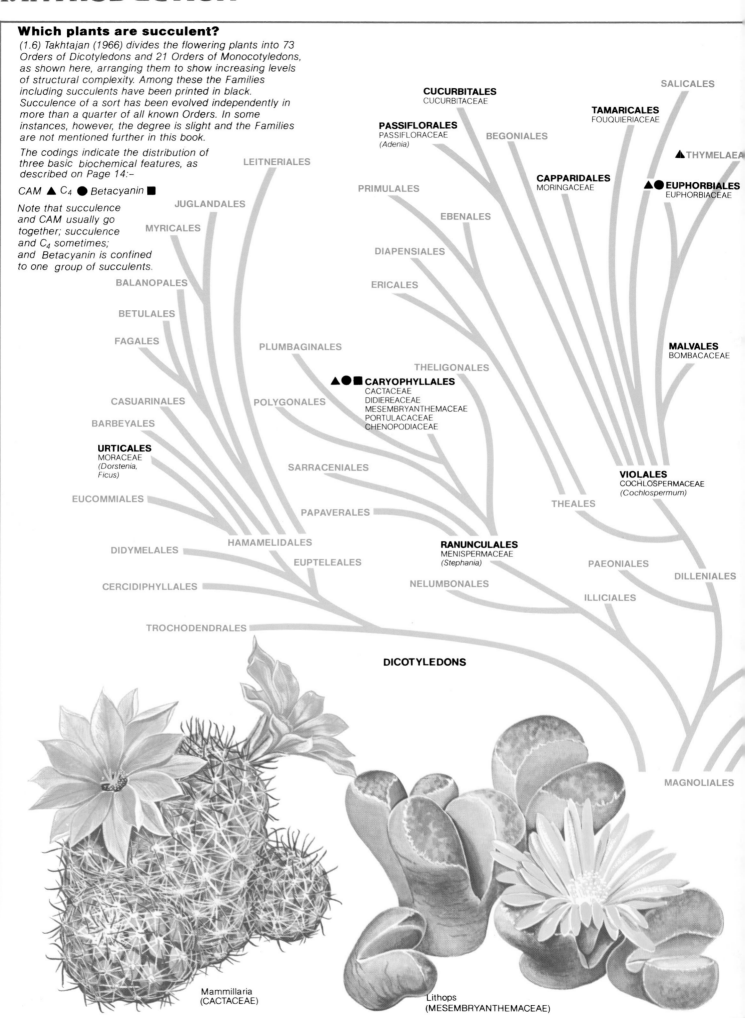

CUCURBITALES
CUCURBITACEAE

SALICALES

PASSIFLORALES
PASSIFLORACEAE
(Adenia)

BEGONIALES

TAMARICALES
FOUQUIERIACEAE

LEITNERIALES

PRIMULALES

▲THYMELAEA

CAPPARIDALES
MORINGACEAE

▲● EUPHORBIALES
EUPHORBIACEAE

JUGLANDALES

EBENALES

MYRICALES

DIAPENSIALES

ERICALES

BALANOPALES

BETULALES

FAGALES

PLUMBAGINALES

MALVALES
BOMBACACEAE

THELIGONALES

▲●■ CARYOPHYLLALES
CACTACEAE
DIDIEREACEAE
MESEMBRYANTHEMACEAE
PORTULACACEAE
CHENOPODIACEAE

CASUARINALES

POLYGONALES

BARBEYALES

URTICALES
MORACEAE
(Dorstenia, Ficus)

SARRACENIALES

VIOLALES
COCHLOSPERMACEAE
(Cochlospermum)

EUCOMMIALES

PAPAVERALES

THEALES

DIDYMELALES

HAMAMELIDALES

RANUNCULALES
MENISPERMACEAE
(Stephania)

PAEONIALES

DILLENIALES

EUPTELEALES

CERCIDIPHYLLALES

NELUMBONALES

ILLICIALES

TROCHODENDRALES

DICOTYLEDONS

MAGNOLIALES

Mammillaria
(CACTACEAE)

Lithops
(MESEMBRYANTHEMACEAE)

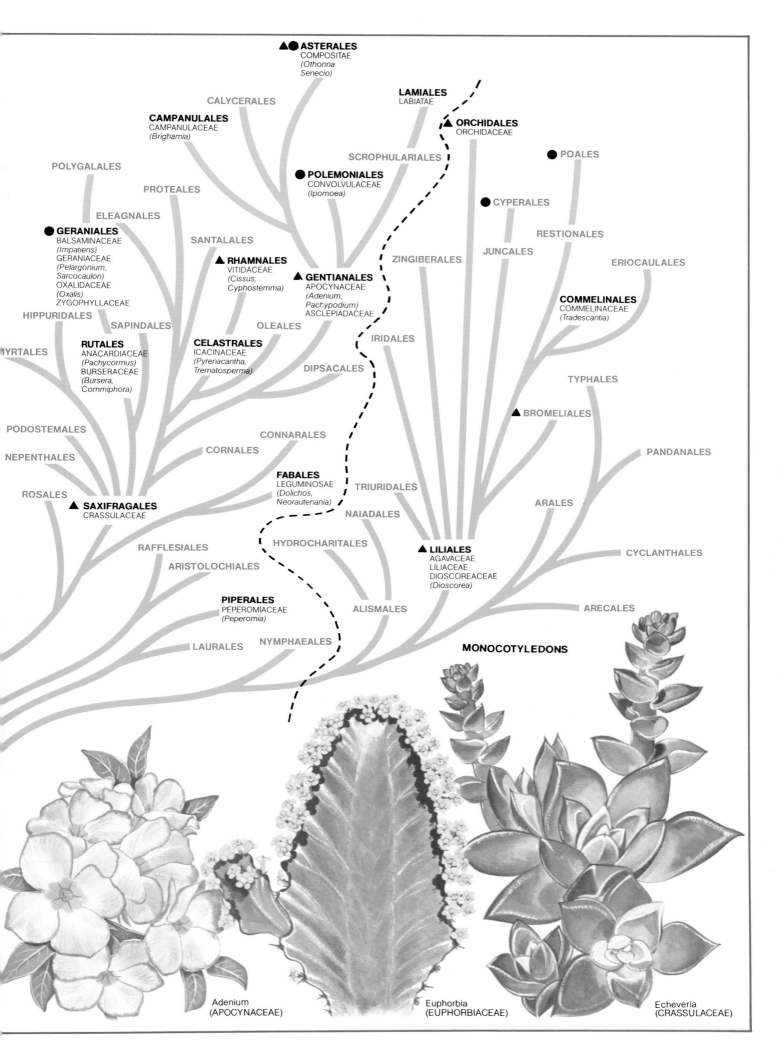

ASTERALES
COMPOSITAE
(Othonna
Senecio)

CALYCERALES

LAMIALES
LABIATAE

CAMPANULALES
CAMPANULACEAE
(Brighamia)

ORCHIDALES
ORCHIDACEAE

POLYGALALES

SCROPHULARIALES

POALES

PROTEALES

POLEMONIALES
CONVOLVULACEAE
(Ipomoea)

CYPERALES

ELEAGNALES

RESTIONALES

GERANIALES
BALSAMINACEAE
(Impatiens)
GERANIACEAE
(Pelargonium,
Sarcocaulon)
OXALIDACEAE
(Oxalis)
ZYGOPHYLLACEAE

SANTALALES

JUNCALES

RHAMNALES
VITIDACEAE
(Cissus,
Cyphostemma)

GENTIANALES
APOCYNACEAE
(Adenium,
Pachypodium)
ASCLEPIADACEAE

ZINGIBERALES

ERIOCAULALES

COMMELINALES
COMMELINACEAE
(Tradescantia)

HIPPURIDALES

SAPINDALES

OLEALES

MYRTALES

RUTALES
ANACARDIACEAE
(Pachycormus)
BURSERACEAE
(Bursera,
Commiphora)

CELASTRALES
ICACINACEAE
(Pyrenacantha,
Trematosperma)

IRIDALES

TYPHALES

DIPSACALES

PODOSTEMALES

CONNARALES

BROMELIALES

NEPENTHALES

CORNALES

PANDANALES

ROSALES

FABALES
LEGUMINOSAE
(Dolichos,
Neorautenania)

TRIURIDALES

ARALES

SAXIFRAGALES
CRASSULACEAE

NAIADALES

RAFFLESIALES

HYDROCHARITALES

LILIALES
AGAVACEAE
LILIACEAE
DIOSCOREACEAE
(Dioscorea)

CYCLANTHALES

ARISTOLOCHIALES

PIPERALES
PEPEROMIACEAE
(Peperomia)

ALISMALES

ARECALES

LAURALES

NYMPHAEALES

MONOCOTYLEDONS

Adenium
(APOCYNACEAE)

Euphorbia
(EUPHORBIACEAE)

Echeveria
(CRASSULACEAE)

17

1: INTRODUCTION

is omitted for a different reason. Over large areas of South Africa *Zygophyllum* is a common sight, its plump watery foliage resembling that of the so-called ice-plant Family, the Mesembryanthemaceae, with which it shares company. Yet who has ever seen any of its 100 species in cultivation? The reasons for its absence are easy enough to find. Transplants fail to establish, cuttings blacken and quickly perish, and seed, if it can be made to germinate at all, produces seedlings that languish and die. Such intractable plants pose problems for the conservationist, as explained in Chapter 7.

By now it will have become apparent that all cacti are succulent, but not all succulents are cacti. The single Family Cactaceae is of distinctive appearance but is confined to the New World (although naturalized elsewhere) and is only one of three major Families of succulents, each with over 1,500 species. There are also about 33 other Families in which succulence has evolved independently in one or more species— representatives of some 600 genera in all. Faced with such diversity, we are not surprised to find that succulents range in size from tiny annual weeds to towering trees, and that they occupy a vast range of habitats. Some require more heat than others, some partial shade; some are extremely sensitive to too much water, others tolerate it; growing seasons differ according to local conditions and to whether they live north or south of the equator. Thus anyone wishing to cultivate them must remember that they cannot all be treated alike in one glasshouse.

Uses of succulents

If succulents have contributed little to human welfare to compare with the major agricultural crops, the catalogue of their uses is nevertheless long and varied. In regions where they are the dominant vegetation we find, not surprisingly, that they are locally exploited for all manner of uses: food, medicine, fibre and—in the case of tree-like species—wood.

Crops and food plants. The nearest to conventional crop plants are the agaves *(Agave)* and the prickly pears *(Opuntia)*. The massive tough foliage of *Agave sisalana* contains long fibres that are extracted by shredding and made into ropes and twine, carpets and sacking. The best fibres are creamy white and rank second only to manila hemp in strength and durability. Brazil and Africa continue as the main sources of supply, despite competition from synthetic fibres. *Agave* is also the source of intoxicating drinks. One is obtained by decapitating the flower stalk as it arises and collecting the sticky sap that oozes freely from the stump. This contains 12-15 percent of sugar and is fermented to produce a

rough brew called "pulque". Tequila is made by distilling the hearts of certain dwarf species of *Agave*.

Of edible succulents, first place goes to the prickly pear. The popular name refers to the fruit, which is like a large plum or pear in appearance (1.7), full of sweet pulp and black seeds but covered with formidable spines. A celebrated American plant breeder, Luther Burbank, set out at the start of the present century to select some for larger, less pippy and smoother fruits, and others for lack of spines so that the plant itself could be fed to cattle. Some of his large-fruited strains are grown commercially today in parts of California and Mexico and the fruits are eaten raw or made into jam, jelly and other confections[6]. Young stem sections stripped of their spines and diced can be eaten raw in salads or cooked and served as "nopalitos". As cattle fodder the prickly pear did not make the desert rejoice and blossom to the extent that Burbank hoped. It needed fencing to prevent the cattle from grubbing up whole plants, and proved to have a lower food value than other grazing plants for dry areas. But wild prickly pear still finds favour in times of famine, when the spines can be cut or burnt off and the juicy green stems fed to cattle.

Medicines and drugs. In the Old World the aloes have a long history of economic use parallel to that of *Agave* in the New World. Here the interest is in the bitter, slimy sap that oozes from cut leaves. It contains aloin, and when dried becomes the "aloes" of medicine. Taken internally it induces purging. *Aloe* leaves have long been credited with healing properties. They were sliced and laid on the skin to relieve itching and heal burns—a use that is occasionally revived today for the treatment of radioactive burns. The European houseleeks, *Sempervivum,* are said to have similar virtues.

Modest fame has recently come to the elephant's foot, *Dioscorea elephantipes* (21.8), and its allies by the discovery that the huge swollen caudex (basal storage organ) manufactures a precursor of cortisone.

No account of the uses of succulents would be complete without mention of the peyote or peyotl *Lophophora* (16.34), the sacred cactus of Mexico. For over 2,000 years this has featured in ritual ceremonies of the Mexican Indians, who suck and swallow the dried tops of this dwarf, spineless cactus ("mescal buttons"). The resulting state of euphoria and colour visions are described in detail in a number of books, of which the best-known is Aldous Huxley's *The Doors of Perception*. The active ingredient is the alkaloid mescaline, but at least 14 other alkaloids have been identified in the same plant. In some countries possession of

Lophophora plants has now been made illegal because of this narcotic effect.

Other uses. In addition to food and medicine, other uses are many and varied. Columnar cacti, euphorbias and others make excellent hedges (1.8), impenetrable to anything but a bulldozer, and rampant creepers such as *Carpobrotus* (3.11) are good sand binders and have been planted to consolidate dunes in the South of England and elsewhere. They can likewise clothe fire breaks in forests. The virulent sap of some African species of *Euphorbia* is used as arrow and fish poison, and *E. paganorum* has ritual uses in West Africa, where it is planted around shrines.

Succulents in cultivation

Horticulturally, succulents are more popular today than ever before. Periods of intense interest on the part of cultivators have in the past alternated with total neglect, during which time the

stage has been occupied by orchids, ferns, palms and other novelties as fashion dictated. Now, however, there are succulent plant societies (usually burdened with the tiresome tautonym "Cactus and Succulent Society of . . .") in America, Europe, South Africa, Australia, New Zealand and Japan. The demand for plants keeps many nurseries, large and small, in business—indeed, the drain upon habitats to supply imported plants has caused so much alarm to the conservationist that many countries now have strict legislation regarding the export and import of succulents. To the nurseryman and private grower this provides greater incentive to raise from seed, a topic I shall discuss in more detail in Chapter 7.

Right (1.7): Fruits of **Opuntia,** *the prickly pear one of the few cacti of economic value and raised commercially in America and S. Africa.*

Below (1.8): Ocotillo, **Fouquieria splendens,** *used as a hedge in Arizona. Cut stems are merely planted and watered until established.*

Succulent Designs

"The differences of plants are recognized in their parts, their form and colour and sparseness and density and roughness and smoothness, and all their incidental differences of taste, their inequality of size, their numerical increase and decrease, their largeness and smallness."

Broadly speaking, there are three types of succulents, according to where the water storage tissue is located in the plant (2.9). Each represents a different life form — that is, the overall habit of the plant as determined by its ecological requirements. There is some overlap between the three groups.

Leaf succulents are plants with enlarged, fleshy, water-storing leaves, as distinct from those where the bulk of storage is concentrated in stems or roots.

Stem succulents are those in which the fleshy tissue is developed mainly in the stems, which are green (at least when young) and are the main photosynthetic centres in the plant. Leaves are often absent, or very small, flat or awl-shaped, and deciduous; only rarely are they persistent and somewhat fleshy. Many succulents in this group have the stems conspicuously ribbed or covered in tubercles, and commonly they may be constricted into joints.

Caudiciform ("root") succulents form the third group. 'Root' is included in inverted commas because the swollen storage organ may be all root, all stem, or root below and stem above. Hence a better term is *caudex* (adj. *caudiciform*), a neutral word for any massive basal storage organ of whatever origin. This distinctive life form is characterized by a division of labour between the short-lived, aerial photosynthesizing organs — thin leaves, shoots or flowering stems

(inflorescences) — and the perennial, non-photosynthesizing storage organ at or below ground level. Further distinguishing the caudiciforms from stem succulents is the fact that the caudex is almost never green or regularly jointed, ribbed or tuberculate. *Bowiea,* a curious plant of the lily Family whose bulb goes green if planted above ground, is included here for convenience also.

The growth of a seedling

The tough, black seed coat splits, cells divide, water swells the contents, and a new seedling breaks forth into the world The miracle of life resurgent is so familiar that we tend to take it for granted. And succulents are no different from other plants in the conditions they need for germination or the stages whereby a mature specimen unfolds from an undifferentiated blob of cells (6.19).

The primary root of a seedling heads downward in response to gravity and moist soil beneath; the stem thrusts upward to the light. The first appearance of green tissue is usually in the seed leaves (cotyledons), which may number one or two. The flowering plants divide into two major groups: Monocotyledons (*monocots* for short) with one seed leaf, and Dicotyledons (*dicots* for short) with two. Even plants that have no leaves at maturity, such as cacti, have at least the rudiments of seed leaves recognizable as two bumps on the seedling.

The anatomy of roots

Not all underground organs are roots, nor do all roots grow in the soil. Some stems grow underground. The surest distinction between stems and roots lies in their internal anatomy, but a more obvious

Right (2.1): **Ferocactus diguetii,** *giant barrel cactus of Lower California. This specimen is nearly 2m (6½ft) tall. Note the ribbed stem.*

Below (2.2): The rosette habit, as in this **Echeveria,** *is common in plants growing in adverse habitats. The leaves shade one another, and dead outer leaves protect the growing point during severe drought.*

Study of studies

Morphology ("shape study") is concerned with form and development of parts. *Anatomy* deals with their microscopic structure.
Ecology ("house study") deals with organisms in relation to their environment.
Anthecology ("flower ecology"), or flower biology, covers the functioning of flowers and their pollination mechanisms.
Cytology ("cell study") concerns the individual cells, and in particular their chromosomes.
Genetics is the science of heredity.
Physiology ("natural produce study") is the study of life processes within an organism. *Biochemistry* deals with the chemical processes involved.
Pathology ("disease study") is the science of diseases.

difference is that roots never bear buds or leaves along their length as do stems. The first root developing from a seed is called the *radicle;* if this continues strongly in a downward direction it is called a *taproot* and its side branches are *laterals.* If thin, radiating laterals predominate and the taproot remains short, the root system is said to be *fibrous,* as in most species of the Familes Crassulaceae and Mesembryanthemaceae. In *Peniocereus* and *Fockea* (21.2) the taproot becomes greatly expanded and may weigh several kilograms when full grown, whereas in *Wilcoxia* it is the laterals that enlarge to form a dahlia-like cluster of tubers. A swollen conical taproot is common to many dwarf globular succulents (2.3) and the astute gardener growing such plants allows extra sharp drainage, knowing that the soft bulky tissue is prone to rot if the soil becomes waterlogged.

Old roots develop a central woody core, which gives them great strength longitudinally while allowing them to flex a little as the trunk is rocked in the wind. In addition to providing anchorage, roots absorb water and food materials in dilute solution. Storage of water, or elaborated food, or both, occurs in roots that may become enlarged and succulent. Absorption from the soil takes place through the *root hairs* — special elongated cells from the surface — which are short-lived and continuously replaced as the roots grow. During periods of drought, a succulent can to some extent reverse the flow of water up the stem and transfer some downwards to keep the roots, which have no xeromorphic features, from dying back too much. Even so, conditions in nature are never as severe as in a small pot in a glasshouse left in the burning sun, where there is no large volume of soil below to buffer against rapid water loss, and no cool rock beneath which the roots can insinuate, as in the wild. Many plant losses in cultivation are due to ignorance of this big difference.

In general, roots are much more uniform and stereotyped than the other parts of a plant. If you were to plant a mixed collection of succulents upside down, with the stems concealed from view, they would look much alike and not obviously different from any other sort of plant. Because of this, roots are normally described in textbooks or cited in classifications only where they offer some rare distinction, such as the fleshy laterals of some haworthias, or the sausage-shaped tubers of *Senecio hallianus.*

Roots that arise from stems, leaves or aerial parts of the plant, not from existing roots, are called *adventitious.* All cuttings grow by means of adventitiously developed roots, and may or may not eventually duplicate the same peculiarities (as tubers, for instance) of the parent plant.

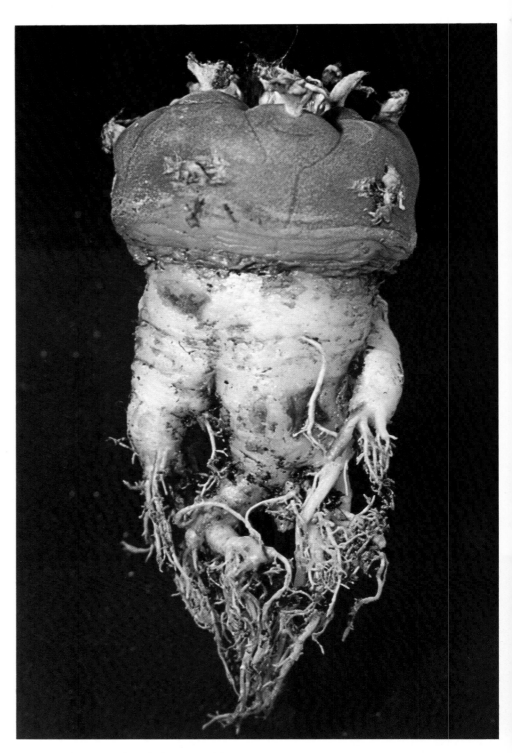

Above (2.3): Enlarged conical taproot of the peyote cactus, **Lophophora williamsii***: an underground food and water store. Plants with soft, fleshy underground organs need extra sharp drainage and care with watering.*

Below (2.4): A section of the woody skeleton of a cactus, showing the hollow cylinder and open network of woody fibres. A similar anatomy has been independently evolved in Euphorbia, Fouquieria *and other succulents.*

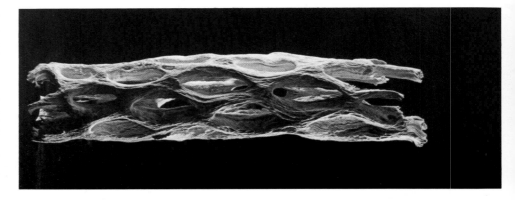

When repotting any succulent with thick branching roots or tubers, it is tempting to cut off pieces and see if they can be induced to generate new plants. Sometimes they do, sometimes they don't. I have found *Pachypodium succulentum* one of the easiest to propagate this way. Any piece of root down to pencil thickness can be planted like an ordinary cutting.

Further considerations of root forms will be found in the introduction to caudiciform plants, Chapter 21.

Succulent stems

Whereas a leaf succulent, on the one hand, bears thin, woody, leafy shoots, a leafless stem succulent has photosynthesis and the other functions of leaves transferred to the green stems (2.1). Between the two extremes there are all manner of intermediates (2.9), showing different degrees of leaf reduction and location of water storage. In stem succulents such as cacti, stapelias and euphorbias, normal cork formation takes place as the stems age, so that the green tissue is confined to the youngest shoots. This is a natural process and cannot be halted, although it worries some growers, who resent seeing a favourite show specimen age visibly. Ultimately the succulent

Below (2.5): Cross-section of Mammillaria bocasana. *The central pith contains purple betacyanin and is surrounded by a ring of conducting tissue with further water storage cells between that and the tough epidermis.*

tissue is largely replaced by a woody core, so that the trunk of veteran cacti and euphorbias becomes externally indistinguishable from that of normal trees. A hollow, net-like cylinder is the characteristic form of the wood (2.4): light and open in structure and mechanically ideal for supporting the weight—up to several tons—of the crown of water-filled branches.

This sort of woody skeleton has evolved independently in cacti, euphorbias, *Fouquieria* and other tree-like succulents. The wood is not very exciting to the carpenter or cabinet maker, except for producing trinkets and novelties for souvenir hunters, but it is locally used for fencing and simple kinds of building.

Wherever a stem is thickly cylindrical or approaches a sphere in shape, we find that the surface is folded into ribs or broken up into protuberances (tubercles). This permits expansion and contraction without damage. Thus, in some of the giant cacti of Arizona it has been shown[1] that the bulk of the plant alters considerably with water content, swelling after rain and shrinking during drought. The volume change is accommodated by concertina-like expansion and contraction of the ribs (2.1). Without them, the tissues would split open. This does actually happen to some stem succulents in cultivation, if grossly overwatered.

Epiphyllum, Schlumbergera and related cacti, and certain euphorbias, have flat, leafless, green shoots that look

and function like leaves (2.8). Non-botanists may call them "leaves", but the technical name for a flattened stem is "phylloclade", or "cladode". Their anatomy, and the presence of buds that grow into flowers or further phylloclades, leave no doubt as to the true nature of such organs.

As I have suggested, the line of separation between leaf and stem succulents is often hard to draw. Similarly there is a gradual transition from stem to caudiciform succulents where the photosynthesizing organs are usually shed as leaves or whole shoots during the resting season and the main food and water store is at or below ground level.

Variety of leaf forms

The leaf of a typical mesophyte (2.9) has a thin, flat, expanded green area (the blade or *lamina*) supported on a stalk *(petiole)* from whose base on the upper side there is a bud. Additionally, there may be two small lateral outgrowths at the base of the petiole, one on either side (the *stipules)*. The arrangement of leaves on a stem *(phyllotaxy)* is spiral, or alternate, or opposite in pairs, or sometimes whorled—three or more in a ring, as in *Peperomia galioides. Gasteria* (13.8) shows the leaves clearly in two series and alternating. Where successive pairs of opposite leaves are set at right angles up the stem, as in *Crassula arborescens* (2.19), they are said to be decussate. Foreshortening of the main axis converts

spiral leaves into a rosette *(Echeveria* 2.2) and decussate leaves into a square column *(Crassula teres, C. columnaris* 2.7). The rosette habit is common in leaf succulents, as it is in alpines and many persistent weeds such as daisies and plantains. *Greenovia* and some other rosette succulents close up like a bulb when dried out, the dead outer leaves effectively protecting the bud in the centre.

Leaves in succulents vary in size from microscopic scales to those of some agaves, which reach 2m (6½ft) or more in length, 0.5m (20in) in width at the base and a proportionate thickness. With their sharp terminal prickle and saw-like margins they present a formidable defense (2.16). Some species of *Anacampseros* show a curious specialization (12.3) in which the tiny, scale-like green leaves are completely enveloped by the white papery stipules—an effective means of lessening evaporation and reflecting some of the light.

Numerous unrelated succulents display translucent stripes or patches on their foliage. In *Pilea* each tiny leaf has a transparent underside as if a droplet of water hung from it. *Peperomia dolabriformis* has a clear ridge along the top of each vertically compressed leaf, and various haworthias have translucent leaf tips, best seen when the plant is held up against the light (2.6). The most advanced "windows" occur in some Mesembryanthemaceae *(Fenestraria* 11.21, *Frithia* 11.22, *Conophytum, Lithops),* in *Haworthia maughanii* and *H. truncata* (13.12) and in *Bulbine mesembryanthoides.* Here the leaf rosette is naturally buried in the ground with only the clear windowed tips exposed. The chlorophyllous tissue is restricted to an area near the leaf surface below ground, and the plant seems to have a crude optical system that permits incident light striking the window to be diffused by crystals of calcium oxalate on to the green area beneath.

Leaves of deciduous succulents—notably the caudiciform types—may look little different from those characteristic of mesophytes. Because the leaf drops at the onset of drought, measures to limit transpiration are unnecessary. However, most leaves of succulents are strongly xeromorphic: simple in outline, hardly ever finely divided like those of a fern, and often *sessile* (without a stalk). The stipules, if developed at all, are often modified into protective structures: hairs in *Portulaca,* spines in some euphorbias, *Jatropha* (21.15) and *Pereskia aculeata* (page 178). A sphere has the minimum surface in relation to volume, and thus the ultimate surface reduction is found in plants with spherical leaves *(Senecio rowleyanus)* or spherical leaf pairs *(Conophytum* 11.29). In consequence of the fleshiness, veins are rarely perceptible. *Sempervivum montanum* and species of

Psammophora have the leaves covered in sticky resinous glands that pick up windblown particles of soil and sand. This "mudpack" is not an aid to beauty but makes the plants less conspicuous and doubtless reduces transpiration.

Some succulents have leaves of two distinct types: we say they are *dimorphic.* In *Mitrophyllum* (11.11) and allied genera, leaves of the resting period expose less surface for evaporation than those at the height of the growing season. Another type of dimorphism occurs in *Gasteria,* where juvenile foliage is so unlike the leaves on adult shoots that it is hard to believe both belong to the same species.

A little water goes a long way

Succulence by itself would be of little use to plants facing drought conditions without special adaptations for retaining such

Above (2.6): *"Window leaves" of* **Haworthia**, *viewed against the light. Each transparent leaf tip is the size of a little finger.*

Below (2.7): **Crassula columnaris** *has decussate leaves so tightly packed that only the margins are exposed to lose water.*

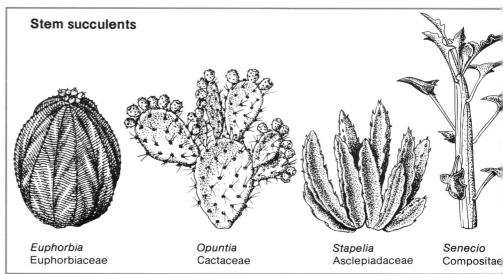

Stem succulents

Euphorbia
Euphorbiaceae

Opuntia
Cactaceae

Stapelia
Asclepiadaceae

Senecio
Compositae

water as is collected. Many of the peculiarities of form and structure in succulents can be interpreted in this light. The following list includes a selection of these *xeromorphic* modifications.

Surface reduction. The surface of a succulent may be reduced to as little as $\frac{1}{300}$ of that of a comparable mesophyte. Leaves are the first to go, or at best are simple in outline and only very rarely pinnate or lobed. When leaves are present they are commonly overlapped in rosettes or like rows of roof tiles, whereby only part of the surface is exposed to drying winds. Often leaves develop only in response to watering *(Senecio articulatus*

Below (2.8): Similar function from different organs: the five on the right are all leaves; the five on the left are modified stems (phylloclades).

15.2, *Euphorbia milii* 20.6) and drop as soon as drought ensues.

Twin-purpose stems. Where foliage is reduced, the stems are green and take over the role of leaves in photosynthesis.

Breath control. Water escapes from plants as vapour through the breathing pores *(stomata),* or directly through the walls of the surface cells *(epidermis).* The former is checked by the unique cycle of many succulents, in which, as already explained, the stomata open only at night, when evaporation is less. The number of stomata is also reduced, and they are commonly localized in shaded areas (the leaf undersides, the angles between ribs) or are overlaid with hairs, spines or other surface appendages. When stomata are sunken in pits (2.11), a column of still air

retained above the pore has a similar effect. Transpiration through the epidermis is also kept down by a thick waterproof surface layer *(cuticle)* or the development of a whitish wax surface that also reflects some of the light (10.5).

Super-efficient roots. Many succulents have wide-spreading roots that never go far below the soil surface (3.10). These are especially suited to the rapid absorption of water after rainfall, and of moisture from the heavy night dews.

Telescoping of organs Many special features of succulents are explicable as a superimposing of organs that in a mesophyte are spread out on elongated growths. The cactus *areole,* a characteristic organ of the Family, is a contracted lateral branch, rather like the spur shoot

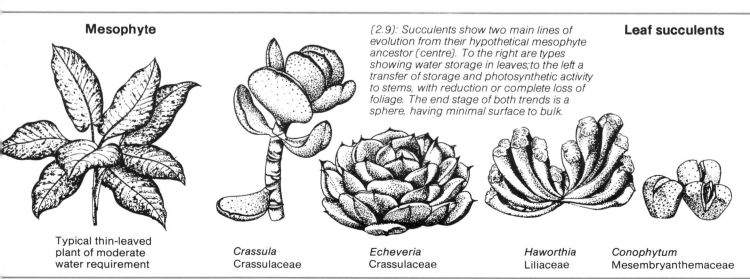

Mesophyte

(2.9): Succulents show two main lines of evolution from their hypothetical mesophyte ancestor (centre). To the right are types showing water storage in leaves; to the left a transfer of storage and photosynthetic activity to stems, with reduction or complete loss of foliage. The end stage of both trends is a sphere, having minimal surface to bulk.

Leaf succulents

Typical thin-leaved
plant of moderate
water requirement

Crassula
Crassulaceae

Echeveria
Crassulaceae

Haworthia
Liliaceae

Conophytum
Mesembryanthemaceae

2: MORPHOLOGY

of an apple or cherry, with many growing points coincident at one level and leaves reduced to spines. The "fruit" of a prickly pear (1.7) is similarly an ovary sunken within a modified shoot. In *Conophytum* the ovary remains protected within a pair of leaves, and in *Calymmanthium* we have the most extraordinary development of all: the whole flower is engulfed by the stem and has to break its way out (2.10). Foreshortening of the main axis may lead to the leaves originating direct from the crown as in *Lithops* (2.12) or even to the entire plant being reduced to a flat flower head as in *Crassula pageae*.

Flower economy. The opening of a flower in a desert is like turning on the tap: precious water is lost unless economy is practised. Large flowers, such as those of *Echinopsis* (16.1), usually open at night and most have already wilted by the following morning. Small flowers are less of a drain on the plant's resources, but even for these the period of opening may be very limited (*Anacampseros* 12.5). A type of xeromorphy, where the petals are leathery and fleshy, is found in the Stapelieae (Chapter 19) and enables these blooms to remain open for several days without wilting.

Not all succulents possess all the above features, just as there are non-succulent xerophytes that have many such features but without the succulence. Annuals survive the dry season as seeds; hard-wooded desert shrubs such as the mesquite *(Prosopis)* and the creosote bush *(Larrea)* root deeply. There are indeed many strategies for combatting water shortage; what might be called "the

Below (2.10): flower of **Calymmanthium substerile,** *which demonstrates an extreme example of xeromorphy. Notice how the petals have to tear their way out of a solid green bud.*

succulent syndrome" is only one of them.

Succulent armature
Prickles, thorns and spines are conspicuous features of many xerophytes (2.13).

Right (2.11): Surface view and vertical section through a stoma of aloe. This breathing pore controls gas interchange by expansion or contraction of the guard cells.

Below (2.12): A plant of Lithops *comprises a single leaf pair united into a conical body that dries up annually as a new leaf pair arises from the centre.*

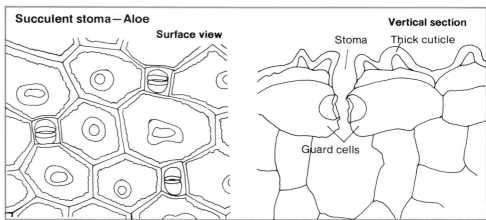

Succulent stoma—Aloe
Surface view
Vertical section
Stoma   Thick cuticle
Guard cells

Indeed, the spines of a cactus may be the first contact one makes with it, and the experience is often memorable. Each of the three terms has a special botanical meaning, and it is better to use a neutral word such as "arms" or "armature" in referring to them collectively.

Prickles are non-woody outgrowths of the surface that are not in direct contact with the conducting tissues (vascular system) of the plant. Familiar examples are the prickles of a rose or blackberry, which snap off cleanly when pushed. Examples among succulents are the leaf margins on some agaves (2.16) and aloes, and the randomly scattered prickles of *Euphorbia milii* (20.6).

Thorns are modified branches, woody and with their own vascular system. As evidence of their stem origin, traces of leaves and lateral buds can often be seen on them. Hawthorn and gorse provide well-known examples of thorns. In succulents, we find a great diversity of thorns in *Euphorbia,* some of which are obviously persistent inflorescences (20.4),

Below (2.13): Types of armature. Left to right: prickles in Euphorbia milii, *leaf prickles in agave, thorns in* Euphorbia schoenlandii, *spines in a cactus and in* Pelargonium spinosum. *The presence of some form of armature is characteristic of many xerophytes.*

others more advanced and distinct from the flowering shoots (20.12).

Spines are modified leaves, where the blade is undeveloped and the leaf stalk or stipules are stiff, woody and pointed (2.14). One special type of spine is the *glochid,* found in *Opuntia.* This is small, readily detached and barbed like a bee sting. Although no succulents have poison stings, these glochids are most irritant and discomforting, and the experienced cactophile always has forceps handy to remove them as soon as their presence is felt. In addition to the Cactaceae, the Didiereaceae and *Sarcocaulon* have spines, and there is a special sort (in *Fouquieria* and *Pelargonium spinosum* 2.13) where a leaf blade develops but soon drops, leaving its stalk to harden as a spine.

The above terms can be used precisely only if the origin of the armature is known, and that is not always the case. There is also much diversity of opinion on why so many plants of dry places are heavily armed. First it must be stressed that an organ need not have a function: so long as it does not impede survival of the organism it may remain, just as does the human appendix. Thus one school of thought regards the armature as a mere relic—all that persists after streamlining the surface areas. Cactus spines are often

rich in crystalline deposits (calcium oxalate, silica), and it has also been suggested that the armature might serve as a garbage dump for the waste products of the plant's metabolism.

Others see the armature as protective. Fat, juicy succulents would soon be eliminated in habitat by grazing animals if the plants had no means of defense. It is true that in times of drought some hoofed animals can kick open barrel cacti and devour the contents, and opuntias may also be grazed, but the glochids cause terrible inflammation of the mouth and stomach lining. Support for the view that armature is a defense mechanism comes from the revelation that among the many unarmed succulents, other deterrents are present: a milky irritant latex in *Euphorbia* and alkaloids in *Lophophora, Ariocarpus, Echinopsis pachanoi, Selenicereus* and the Stapelieae.

Hooked spines occur only in the cacti, and can be a means of propagation in smaller mammillarias where offsets detach readily and can become entangled on fur or feathers. Cylindrical-stemmed opuntias achieve the same result by shedding their spiny terminal joints: the dreaded jumping cholla (16.6) has the reputation of seeming to jump at you as you walk near it.

A good dense mantle of spines or bristles covering the stem of a cactus

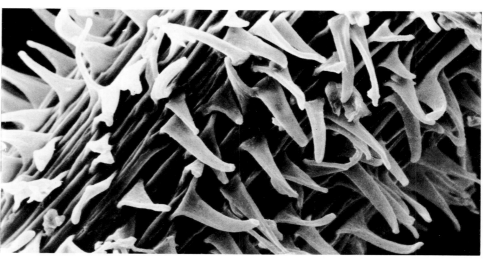

Above (2.14): Armature of a **Mammillaria**: many white, spreading radial spines surrounding two brown, inclined, stouter centrals, the whole arising from each areole.

Above (2.15): A central spine of **Mammillaria** seen under the scanning electron microscope, magnified 200 times. Forms and patterns differ from species to species.

maintains still air around the stomata and lessens evaporation. If the spines are white, some of the incident light will be reflected also.

Physiologists have suggested that the sharply pointed organs on xerophytes may act as nuclei for the condensation of night dews. Water droplets condensed on cactus spines run down to the felted areole, which soaks them up like a sponge. Whether or not actual reabsorption directly into the stem takes place is, I think, unresolved as yet, but isolated experiments using markers added to the water suggest that it does. Otherwise, the water will run down to the soil at the stem base, where plentiful surface roots take it in. Reabsorption of water through the surface has been demonstrated in leaves of *Crassula*.

So far as the average cactophile is concerned, the function of the armature has never been in doubt. It is the crowning glory of any cactus, put there for his special delight as a mark of distinction from lesser vegetation. The seemingly endless variety in shape and form, texture and colour, provide him with the stimulus to collect. There are straight spines and hooked, plain and multi-coloured, bearded and plumed, often several types at one areole, and most of them going through a cycle of colours as they age. In ferocacti the colours itensify dramatically after the spines are wetted. Bearing in mind the fact that cacti flower for only a few days, or at most weeks, every year, their popularity depends to a large extent on the beauty and bounty of the armature.

Flowers, fruits and seeds

The way in which flowers function is the subject of Chapter 4; here we are concerned with establishing their structure and the names of the various parts (2.18). For the full story, there is no scarcity of

Left (2.16): Leaf prickles in agave. The stout marginal and terminal prickles make these plants formidable to handle, and well protected against grazing animals.

29

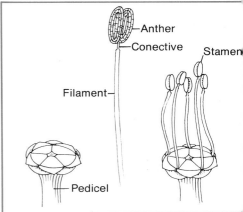

Top (2.17): A halved flower of one of the epicacti, and (left) a closer view of the ovary and ovules. Pollen alighting on the style must grow down a tube several cm long to reach the ovary.

*Right (2.19): The starlike bloom of **Crassula arborescens,** with five each of sepals, petals, stamens and carpels, may be taken as a model by which to interpret other more complicated flowers.*

Ovaries

A female unit of a flower is the **carpel** containing the *ovules,* which eventually mature as *seeds.*
Carpels are **free** when standing separately in the centre of the flower; **united** when fused together.
The one or more carpels, free or united, collectively constitute the **ovary.**
An ovary is **superior** when standing above the level of insertion of the floral envelope (sepals and petals); **inferior** when immersed in the axis with the floral envelope on top. Such flowers are referred to as *hypogynous* and *epigynous* respectively, or *perigynous* if halfway between.

popular primers on botany; my present aim is merely to define those terms most commonly used by the botanist in describing succulents, and essential to an understanding of the systematic accounts of them in Part 2.

Unlike the vegetative features, which contribute a highly individual "desert facies" to succulent plants, the reproductive organs have changed little during the advance into dry habitats and show few features that we can point out as typical of succulents. Each retains the characters of its Family, as set out in Chapters 9-21. I should like to stress one overall truth about succulents; they all flower, regardless of what the prophets of doom would have us believe after having tried to grow the wrong sorts under the wrong conditions. If they did not bloom and set seed, they would have disappeared from this earth long ago.

Botanists interpret a flower as a transformation of a shoot in which the *calyx* (sepals), *corolla* (petals), *androecium* (stamens), and *gynoecium* (carpels) are derived from modified leaves. The order of parts is always constant, with the female organs at the centre surrounded by males and then the protective outer whorls of petals and sepals that make up the *perianth*. The whole arises from the more or less flattened tip of the axis, which is known as the *receptacle*. Pollen from the anthers is required to reach the surface of a stigma, where a pollen tube grows down into the ovary and the pollen nucleus enters an ovule and effects fertilization (2.17).

Following pollination and fertilization, the sepals, petals, stamens and styles wither and usually drop off, leaving the ovary to enlarge and form a fruit — a dry capsule (2.20), or a juicy berry (2.21), or rarely something half way between, as in several cactus genera. The tiny ovules ripen into seeds, which may be minute and dust-like *(Dinteranthus, Crassulaceae)* or larger than peas *(Jatropha)*. Cactus fruits are peculiar in often containing areoles on the outside, and appear to have originated from an ovary sunk in a modified shoot. In opuntia and some pereskias the unripe fruits proliferate to grow further flower buds and eventually even whole chains of fruits, one suspended from the other. In certain opuntias such a chain eventually drops off and roots to form a daughter plant beneath the parent.

Flower colours in succulents cover most of the spectrum except blue, which is curiously absent from all except *Sedum coeruleum,* a handful of semi-succulent Labiatae, and *Cyanotis.* The dazzling reds, magentas and pinks of those Families included in Caryophyllales (see page 130) are due to betacyanin (2.5), a nitrogenous pigment that differs chemically from the anthocyanin found in all other plant Orders.

Some succulents flower in a few weeks from seed: the annual portulacas (5.3, 12.1) and *Dorotheanthus* (11.10), for example. Many popular dwarf cacti *(Mammillaria)* and Mesembryanthemaceae bloom in the second year from seed or even sooner. Some take many years to attain maturity; the tree cacti, Didiereaceae and *Agave* (14.1), for example. The name "century plants" for the last is an exaggeration: seven to 70 years is more typical of the lifespan. Then the rosette rapidly puts up a huge inflorescence, after which it dies, to be replaced by seedlings, offsets, or viviparous buds falling from the old

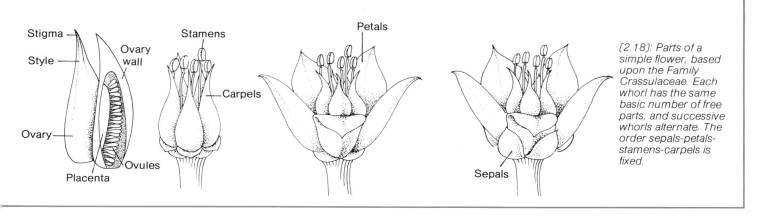

(2.18): Parts of a simple flower, based upon the Family Crassulaceae. Each whorl has the same basic number of free parts, and successive whorls alternate. The order sepals-petals-stamens-carpels is fixed.

inflorescence. In *Melocactus* the onset of flowering after perhaps ten years of vegetative growth is the development of a *cephalium,* or crown of wool and bristles (16.28), after which the plant is fully mature and ceases to grow vegetatively. The name 'Turk's Cap' is descriptive of this large central cephalium. Other cacti produce cephalia laterally *(Espostoa)* or lopsidedly *(Cephalocereus).*

Most flowers are more complicated than the simple *Crassula* (2.19), with its ring of free parts in fives. But it is always possible to relate them to the same basic plan through transformations such as the fusion or splitting of parts, or alterations in number or function. In place of radial symmetry like the spokes of a wheel *(actinomorphy)* a flower may be symmetrical about one vertical plane only *(zygomorphic* 9.1).

A special subject by itself is the form of pollen grains, seeds, spines and other plant surfaces as revealed under the microscope, especially the recently developed scanning electron microscope (SEM), which enables us to obtain superbly three-dimensional pictures at a wide range of magnifications (2.15). Every species is found to have its own peculiar patterning and shapes, which, like finger-prints, can be a valuable means of identification. A whole new field of study has opened up, and taxonomists are increasingly using characters of pollen and seed in their classifications.

Above (2.20): Immature fruits of **Agave.** *Eventually each will ripen to a dry, brown capsule which sheds its flat, winged, black seeds through three vertical splits.*

Right (2.21): **Cyphostemma juttae,** *a relative of the vine, with its bunches of small, inedible grape-like fruits. The plant grows to a height of about 75cm (30in).*

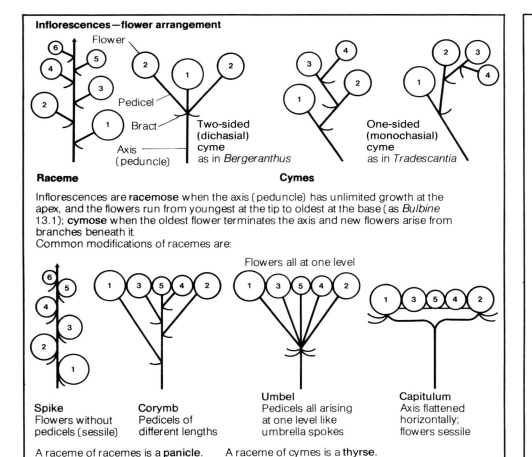

Inflorescences — flower arrangement

Flower
Pedicel
Bract
Axis (peduncle)

Raceme

Two-sided (dichasial) cyme as in *Bergeranthus*

One-sided (monochasial) cyme as in *Tradescantia*

Cymes

Inflorescences are **racemose** when the axis (peduncle) has unlimited growth at the apex, and the flowers run from youngest at the tip to oldest at the base (as *Bulbine* 13.1); **cymose** when the oldest flower terminates the axis and new flowers arise from branches beneath it.
Common modifications of racemes are:

Flowers all at one level

Spike
Flowers without pedicels (sessile)

Corymb
Pedicels of different lengths

Umbel
Pedicels all arising at one level like umbrella spokes

Capitulum
Axis flattened horizontally; flowers sessile

A raceme of racemes is a **panicle**.   A raceme of cymes is a **thyrse**.

Fruits
A fruit consists of the seeds and their enclosing ovary, plus external accessory organs such as the areoles on a prickly pear. Fruits can be fleshy or dry at maturity. **Dehiscence** is the spontaneous opening of a fruit, releasing seeds.

Fleshy fruits
The **berry** of *Cissus* (15.5) and *Cyphostemma* (2.21) is grape-like and derived from a simple, superior ovary. In Cucurbitaceae, the berry is a miniature gourd derived from an inferior ovary, hence including tissue of the supporting axis also in the outer walls.
In Cactaceae the same is true — even vegetative areoles may be present on the berry (1.7).

Dry fruits
A **follicle** is a fruit derived from a single carpel that splits longitudinally, as in Crassulaceae, Asclepiadaceae (19.8) and Apocynaceae.
A **capsule** consists of two or more carpels united in a ring. In Liliaceae and Agavaceae it dehisces by vertical splits; in portulacas by a circular lid. A very special type of capsule with valves actuated by water is described in Chapter 11 for Mesembryanthemaceae.
A **schizocarp** is a capsule that breaks up at maturity into part-fruits (mericarps) — three in euphorbias (4.16).

2: MORPHOLOGY

Novel forms of growth

As if succulents were not curious enough already, they are more prone than most other plants to an abnormal type of growth known as *fasciation:* the growing apex of the stem broadens to form a crest, so that the normally cylindrical stem expands to become fan-shaped (2.23). Subsequent growth may contort the fan into irregular, brain-like masses. Such plants are referred to as *crests* or *cristates* (Latin *cristatus*). An allied phenomenon is the production of multiple growing points, creating an effect like the heart of a cauliflower, termed *monstrous growth* (Latin *monstrosus*).

Temporary fasciation or monstrosity may result from mechanical injury or the effects of chemical weedkillers, but other types are more or less permanent, and in some rare cases may even be inherited, the crests bearing flowers and the seedlings showing similar growth. Such growth changes arise in the first place from seed, or as a sport *(mutation)* on a normal plant; the cause is often impossible to ascertain. In the wild, cristate and monstrous plants are at a disadvantage and are eliminated in time, but in cultivation they can be perpetuated by cuttings or grafts, and because of their comparative rarity are much sought after by some collectors. A few of the more striking are worth including in any collection to add variety.

Among other growth changes that occur from time to time are spiralled ribs, absence of spines, disorganized ribs and proliferating flower buds. Such abnormalities fascinate many growers, but there is not much that one can say to explain them beyond the recognition that hormonal imbalance can cause a flower bud to proliferate into a shoot or vice versa, and virus infection is responsible for the cancer-like outgrowths that sometimes disfigure normal plants.

Spots and stripes

Another source of horticultural novelty is *variegation* (Latin *variegatus*). This results from a local absence of the green pigment chlorophyll. The tissue affected appears white — or yellow or pink if these other pigments were masked by the green (2.22). Not all such striping or mottling is stable: some may be caused by temporary nutritional maladies (calcium deficiency, for instance), and even the best variegated plants may throw occasional reversions. All-green reversions are best removed, because they are more vigorous and will in time outgrow the other shoots and take over. Stems entirely without chlorophyll, or with too little to manufacture sufficient food, can never lead an independent existence, but they can be kept going as grafts (6.27), as long as the stock remains green.

Above: (2.22): Variegated **Kalanchoe fedtschenkoi,** *in which the uppermost leaves have lost their chlorophyll, and hence draw all their nutriment from the lower leaves.*

Right (2.23): Fasciation in a cactus (**Lemaireocereus**). *Only some stems on this large shrubby specimen are affected; normal growth can be seen in the background.*

Succulents on Home Ground

" Of plants which grow in dry places, some grow on mountains, others in the plain; some plants grow and flourish in the most arid districts . . . and increase there better than anywhere else. A plant changes very much with a difference of locality, and such variations must be taken into consideration. "

A map of the world distribution of succulents is better left to the imagination than attempted on paper: the spread is so uneven. For instance, Australia is a continent almost without native succulents: just a handful of not particularly fleshy and mostly cosmopolitan weeds. More species of succulents of the type attractive to collectors could be found in one square meter of parts of South Africa than in the whole of Australasia.

Patterns of distribution

To portray such a range of concentrations would require an enormous map and many fine shades of colouring, and to the best of my knowledge nobody has yet attempted one. If there were such a map, the heaviest shading would come around the horse latitudes, 30°N. and 30°S. of the Equator, and it is certain that South Africa and subtropical North and South America would score highest for numbers of species as well as for density of populations. America is the home of the cactus Family (Cactaceae) and the century plants *(Agave),* various Crassulaceae (Echeverioideae), some Portulacaceae (*Lewisia, Talinum,* etc), Euphorbiaceae and others. South Africa, the home of the widest range of all, lacks only indigenous cacti among the major Families, although even these are to be seen in the form of semi-naturalized prickly pears, originally planted near farms as emergency cattle fodder, and the widespread *Rhipsalis.*

Outside these heavily shaded areas of our map, much of the world's land surface, except the colder areas toward the poles, would have paler shadings. Crassulaceae occur wild in all five continents, notably as the tiny, moss-like annual crassulas *(Tillaea),* of minimal interest to succulent collectors but the most widespread of all. The native European succulents—*Sedum* (3.1) and *Sempervivum* mainly—have a special interest because they are almost the only succulents known to classical writers and hence featured in ancient literature.

Within the tropics, fewer succulent species occur, although even in the rain forests a few rather less fleshy types are to be found. Most conspicuous are climbers such as *Hylocereus, Selenicereus* and *Epiphyllum* in the Western Hemisphere, *Cissus quadrangularis* in Africa and *Hoya* in Southeast Asia, and epiphytes such as *Aporocactus, Rhipsalis* and *Schlumbergera* in Mexico and *Dischidia* in Southeast Asia. The epiphytes live as do the orchids and bromeliads, perched on the branches of trees or sometimes supported on rocks, but not as parasites: they derive their nutriment from humus transported by wind or rain. Their inbuilt stores of water profit them in times of drought. The tropics are also the home of certain relicts that seem to have been left behind in the advance into drier, more exposed habitats. They remain as "living fossils" that suggest an evolutionary link with the past: *Pereskia* (16.4) in Central America, for instance, or the leafy *Caralluma frerei* (19.5) in India. Some large and adaptable genera such as the euphorbias, aloes and kalanchoes have many representatives within the tropics.

Recently much interest has been shown in types of succulents occurring in unlikely and isolated places such as oceanic islands. These are often curious caudiciforms with massively thickened *(pachycaul)* stems: *Impatiens* in Sumatra, *Brighamia* in Hawaii, *Jatropha* in Panama and *Pelargonium* in St Helena.

Man the distributor

So far we have been considering indigenous succulents—that is, those growing wild before the arrival of man. The natural distribution patterns of succulents have been greatly upset by man's activities in transporting them from continent to continent. *Rhipsalis,* the wandering 'Mistletoe Cactus', has already been mentioned: it is found today in Africa (4.18), Madagascar and Sri Lanka, and is the only cactus genus apparently wild outside the New World, but it could well

Right (3.1): Native European succulents: pennywort, Umbilicus rupestris, *and stonecrop,* Sedum reflexum *growing on a stone wall in South-west England.*

Below (3.2): This seemingly desolate wilderness adjoining the Hol River in South Africa is one of the richest hunting grounds for miniature succulents in the world. New discoveries often come to light.

Distribution patterns

Widespread distribution is one that is larger than average, eg *Cissus quadrangularis* (15.5) from tropical Africa through Arabia to India; *Crassula* almost worldwide.

Discontinuous or **disjunct** distribution is occurrence in two or more separate areas, eg *Pachypodium lealii* (18.4) in South West Africa and Natal; *Portulaca* (5.3) in Africa and South America.

Endemism is occurrence in a smaller than average area, eg *Talinum guadalupense* (15.4) on Guadalupe Island; Didiereaceae in southwest Madagascar.

have been an early introduction by man. The few succulents credited with medicinal or other uses have been carried around for so long that their original habitats—if indeed they had one, and are not ancient hybrids—are no longer known to us. *Aloe barbadensis,* the medicinal aloe, is one such (page 18), and purslane *(Portulaca oleracea),* long in use as a potherb, another.

The great adaptability of some succulents led to their becoming naturalized far from their native homes. Although it has few native succulents, Australia has the right climate for them, as was shown by the dramatic spread of certain species of *Opuntia* (16.7), introduced as ornamentals from the eighteenth century onwards. Over 1,500,000km²(60,000,000 acres) of agricultural land were overrun before control measures began to take effect. The dreaded prickly pear proved resistant to normal methods of cutting or spraying, and success at curbing its spread was achieved only by biological control by the moth *Cactoblastis cactorum,* whose larvae feed exclusively on the stems of *Opuntia.* Even today the danger of spread is not entirely past, as other species of cacti are unaffected by the predator.

Succulents in habitat

My first encounter with cacti in their native habitat shattered some preconceived ideas about them gained from years of tending potted specimens in a London glasshouse. It took place on the slopes of the Rocky Mountains near Denver, Colorado, to which I had been led by a friend with the enthusiasm of so many American cactophiles, who love to show off their unique flora. However, the site seemed so unpromising that I wondered who would ever go cactus hunting in this sort of terrain? It looked more like a rough English meadow than the anticipated desert of Western movies. But,

sure enough, many cacti were there nestling in the grass, and so hidden that one almost tripped over them before seeing them. So two illusions were dispelled at once: succulents do not grow alone in solitary possession of the desert, and the smaller ones (those dearest to the heart of the connoisseur), although so conspicuous in a pot, are often very well camouflaged in nature.

These facts are true not only of the American cacti but of many South African Stapelieae, haworthias and other genera. Further surprises were in store. The most frequently encountered soil type turned out to be a form of weathered granite, quite unlike anything a conscientious gardener weaned on commercial potting mixes would consider fit to bring inside his glasshouse. Although the soil appears to be short of organic matter, analysis shows that there is usually no lack of the elements essential for growth. Water, which makes the nutrient salts available for absorption, is the limiting factor, and its sparsity slows down the decay of humus. It would be a mistake to collect soil along with the plants and assume that it would be the ideal medium for their cultivation. Succulents grow where they do often because competition excludes them from other habitats, not because conditions are ideal there.

Natural variation. But the most far-reaching of all revelations on studying succulents in their natural environment is their variability (5.1). In cultivation we see little of this: every plant of one species in collections may even be the same

Right (3.3): **Aloe dichotoma** *on level ground in South Africa forming an unusual type of forest. The plants reach 9m (30ft) in height and their wood is light and fibrous.*

Below (3.4): **Aloe macrocarpa** *growing in Northern Ghana. The roots find anchorage and sustenance in the rock crevices.*

individual derived by repeated vegetative propagation from a single import. This gives us a stereotyped image of what that species looks like, so that when we see a slightly different fresh import we jump to the conclusion that it is a new species. Field collectors further distort the picture by tending to go for anything that looks different, sampling the extremes of the population rather than average specimens. Thus the collector can get a narrow and totally false picture of the species. A species is not one individual, whether living or preserved on a herbarium sheet. It is the sum of all its populations, and may be as full of minor variations as is the human species, *Homo sapiens.*

A succulent paradise. In a few places in South Africa, almost the only plants to be seen are succulents (3.2), from the tiniest of annuals to tree aloes and euphorbias that may dominate the landscape (3.3). I have wandered bemused in parts of the South African Richtersveld and Little Karroo, which together form the ultimate paradises of the succulent addict, trying to assimilate all the species as one after another comes into view, some familiar to the point of being taken for granted, others excitingly new. Instinctively my hand lifts the branches of shrubs as I walk by. Hiding under them I have found up to ten different species of dwarf succulents, representative of several unrelated plant families. Photographs, regrettably, do scant justice to such floral surfeit. Time stands still as you attempt to overcome human limitations and take it all in. To anyone reared on the relative poverty of the flora of Great Britain the wealth of such areas is unbelievable.

Semi-deserts. That "cacti grow in deserts" is a favourite piece of dogma. The word "cacti" is misused to cover anything from a prickly pear to a carrion flower, and "desert" also needs careful defining. For this we turn to the ecologists, who arbitrarily define a desert as an area that averages less than 25cm (10in) of rain a year. Now the life forms of succulents, with their closely guarded internal store of water, are ideal for conferring upon them a camel-like disregard for periodic droughts. But to store water they must receive water in the first place, and periodic drought is not the same as perpetual drought. The succulents most popular with collectors flourish in areas where the annual precipitation may be quite a bit more than for true desert, as defined above. Indeed, some get as much as 50 to 80cm (20 to 32in). Hence it is more precise to speak of these as semi-desert plants.

Mountain slopes, screes and rough rocky places generally are favourite locales for succulents. Inclines and precipices are especially favoured by

Above (3.5): Chaparral-type vegetation in the Mojave Desert, California made up of **Opuntia** with yuccas and smaller xerophytes. Note the wide spacing and absence of ground cover.

Below (3.6): Fog belt vegetation in Northern Chile. In the absence of rainfall, plants can survive if they make use of atmospheric condensation as fog rolls in from the sea.

Fog zone vegetation

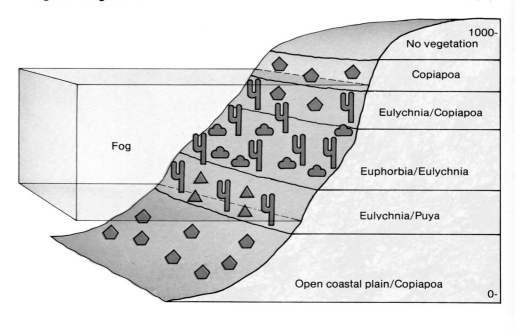

rosette types such as *Aeonium* and *Aloe* (3.4), which if planted with the rosette horizontal in a pot will often grow over sideways to face the light. The mountaineering skill of the would-be collector, nil in my case, is tested to the limits. More obliging species inhabit level ground, particularly those hot, dry plains and mountain plateaux, sparsely dotted with thorny shrubs, that are known as *chaparral* in Mexico and the American Southwest (3.5) and *veld*[*t*] in southern Africa. They utilize every bit of shade,

and species that grow out in full sunlight, such as *Ariocarpus* and *Lithops,* are commonly half buried in the soil. The immensity of such areas makes one realize how much there is yet to be explored. It is not surprising that new species are coming to light every year.

It must be remembered that, unlike the aerial parts of the plant, the roots of succulents have little protection against water loss, and if roots dry out beyond the threshold of survival, plant growth is checked until new roots form. Hence there is a tendency for roots to insinuate into clefts in rocks where water collects, making the plant impossible to remove without damage. Anyone who has tried to dig up a caudex-forming *Pachypodium* from its bed of compacted rock chippings will realize the enormous pressure exerted by the turnip-like expanding root, which sometimes reaches one metre (39in) in length. In cultivation such plants not infrequently burst their pots. Seedling succulents require a measure of shade, and it is probable that all species in the wild begin life under the protection of rocks, other shrubs or the parent plant.

Incidentally, there are other sorts of desert than those typified by the Sahara and Gobi. The icy, barren wastes toward the Poles are also deserts, because water is withheld from plants by being frozen. No' succulents have ventured into these areas. Another kind of desert exists on the western slopes of the Andes, in Chile and Peru, where precipitation is negligible but heavy coastal fogs provide just enough moisture to foster the growth of

xerophytes[1] (3.6). Under these conditions grow *Oroya* (16.17), *Borzicactus* and other dwarf globular cacti. Collectors cherish such plants because they are easy to adapt to normal glasshouse culture away from their habitat—another instance of how needless it is to attempt to duplicate the habitat in glasshouses, even if it were practicable to do so. A very similar environment to that of the Andes is found at lesser altitudes along the Atlantic coast of southern Africa in the Namib Desert, where a unique succulent flora has built up in the narrow coastal belt within reach of dew-laden onshore winds.

Temperate habitats. Although succulents are a less conspicuous feature of the flora outside semi-desert areas, some compete well with non-succulents and their inbuilt store of water allows them to colonize specialized habitats. Thus in the mountains of Europe and Asia rosette succulents such as *Sempervivum* and *Rosularia* are at home in alpine regions

alongside saxifrages and other xerophytic non-succulents. The high evaporation rate during alpine winters when the soil is frozen needs some form of water conservation. Lewisias occupy similar niches in western North America. A few succulents even compete in moister habitats: the annual *Sedum villosum* inhabits fresh-water marshes, and at least one *Crassula* can grow wholly submerged in water, although it flowers only when the branches break the surface. A native of New Zealand, *C. helmsii* has become a popular, if invasive, aerating plant for pools and aquaria. Indeed, there are few environments from which succulents are completely absent. Ironically, instead of calling them desert plants, we should be almost nearer the truth to say that deserts are the one place where they do not grow.

Below (3.7): Vegetation of the lower slopes of the Andes. The tall columnar cactus is **Eulychnia**; *among the shrubs is a semi-succulent* **Oxalis**. *Similar scenes are typical of the semi-deserts of N. America and S. Africa.*

3: DISTRIBUTION AND ECOLOGY

The influence of climate
As we have seen, the habitats of succulents are exceedingly diverse. The only features they have in common are periodic drought and temperatures generally above freezing. Even freedom from frost is not universal; cacti in the high Andes, the northern USA and southern Canada freeze annually, though protected from the lowest temperatures

Below: Over an area as large as South Africa, climatic factors vary widely and influence our ideas on cultivation. Top map (3.8): Rainfall areas of South Africa. Bottom map (3.9): Expected annual rainfall in South Africa.

by a blanket of snow. A glance at rainfall maps of South Africa[2] (3.8, 9)—the centre of maximum diversity and density of succulents—reveals big differences in the season when rain is expected and in the total amount, from almost nil to more than the annual average for the British Isles. (Note that the seasons are reversed relative to the Northern Hemisphere.) If we are seeking cultural assistance from the homeland, then, it is not sufficient merely to know that a plant comes from South Africa. Closer localization is needed for us to decide how much rain it normally receives and, equally as important, at which time of the year.

Life forms and survival
Many dwarf perennial succulents are especially adapted to pass the dormant season underground, and are hence to be seen only during the often brief rainy periods, or when in flower. Indeed some, such as *Albuca unifoliata* (page 158), are so retiring that their existence was unsuspected for decades, even in well-worked areas. Bulbs and caudices are ideally suited to tide plants over long periods of desiccation. *Haworthia* and *Bulbine* afford examples of plants with *contractile* roots —that is, roots whose strong fibrous core shrinks during drought and draws the crown of the plant deeper into the ground.

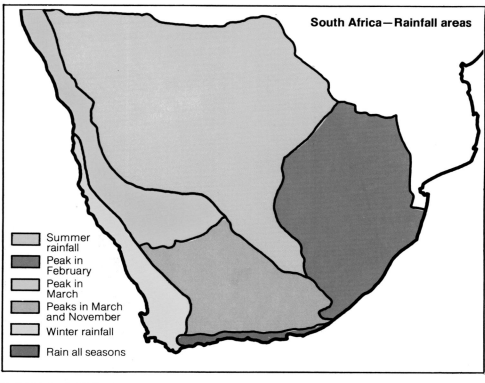

South Africa—Rainfall areas

Summer rainfall
Peak in February
Peak in March
Peaks in March and November
Winter rainfall
Rain all seasons

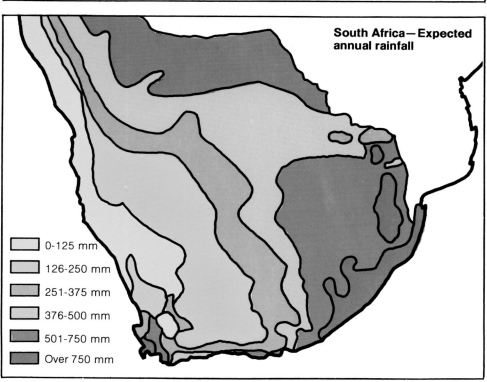

South Africa—Expected annual rainfall

0-125 mm
126-250 mm
251-375 mm
376-500 mm
501-750 mm
Over 750 mm

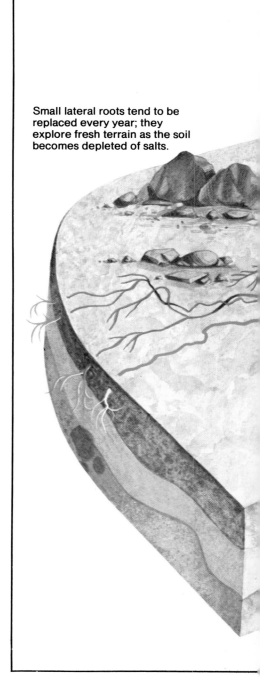

Small lateral roots tend to be replaced every year; they explore fresh terrain as the soil becomes depleted of salts.

Flat-topped mammillarias and neoporterias achieve the same result by shrinkage of their turnip-like taproots; they may disappear from view completely as windblown sand and humus piles on top of them. In cultivation, such plants tend to grow much taller (16.43), although the shrinkage and retraction when dormant may still be evident. The difference shows up dramatically if the same plants are photographed during summer and winter (6.4, 5).

From rather limited samplings of root systems of succulents in the wild in America and Africa, the same general pattern emerges for cacti, euphorbias,

aloes, carallumas and others. The taproot is little developed, but the laterals radiate to considerable distances all around (3.10). A saguaro *(Carnegiea)* only 1.2m (4ft) high was found to have a spread of lateral roots up to 5m (17ft) from the main trunk. These laterals are never far from the soil surface: 2 to 8cm (¾ to 3¼in) in *Opuntia arbuscula,* 1.5 to 3cm (⅗ to 1¼in) in *Echinocactus*[3]. Root studies of succulents in East Africa[4] revealed that the fine feeding roots that grow out from the laterals sometimes turn upwards and approach still nearer to the surface, thus reversing the rule that roots all grow downwards. The roots of succulents are

specialized for rapid absorption of whatever rain may fall, and they also utilize the heavy dews that condense overnight as a result of a sharp drop in temperature after dark. Profuse root development is noted near the crown of the plant—that is, in the area on which drips fall during rain. All this is in contrast with non-succulent xerophytes, whose roots generally run deep in the soil.

Succulents are usually only one component of the flora, sharing the habitat with other non-succulent xerophytes that have developed different ways of combatting drought (3.5, 7). Some are trees or shrubs, often spiny, with hard wood,

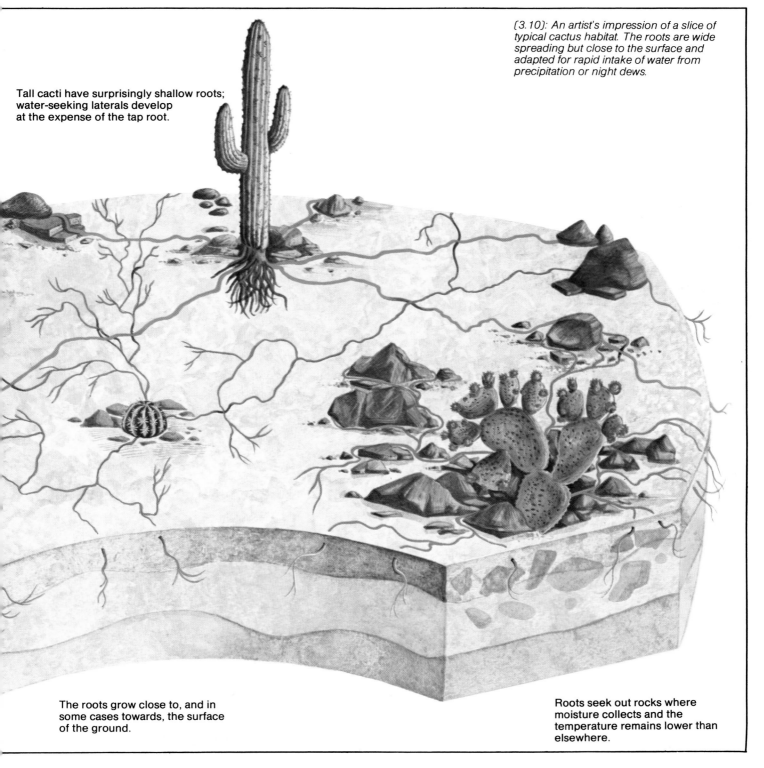

(3.10): An artist's impression of a slice of typical cactus habitat. The roots are wide spreading but close to the surface and adapted for rapid intake of water from precipitation or night dews.

Tall cacti have surprisingly shallow roots; water-seeking laterals develop at the expense of the tap root.

The roots grow close to, and in some cases towards, the surface of the ground.

Roots seek out rocks where moisture collects and the temperature remains lower than elsewhere.

3: DISTRIBUTION AND ECOLOGY

deep roots and leaves either early deciduous or small and leathery. They have developed to a high degree the art of wilting gracefully. Quick-growing annuals (drought evaders) pass the dry season as seed and burst rapidly into growth and flower as soon as the rains come. A few denizens of the semi-desert show hardly any xeromorphic features and nobody has yet satisfactorily explained their secret of survival. It has been shown, however, that certain small herbs, although not parasites in the sense of forming organic union with other plants, grow their roots close to those of cacti and imbibe water from the sheath of moisture surrounding the cactus root. When soil moisture falls below a given level, a cactus can reverse the flow and pass water down to the roots from the store in the stem.

Habitat as a guide to cultivation

What can we learn from a study of succulents in the wild that will help us in their cultivation? The most obvious lesson is: don't attempt to imitate the natural environment. The much-repeated story of the lady who telephoned the weather bureau in Mexico City and watered her cacti only when told it was raining there may be apocryphal, but there are nevertheless many growers with exaggerated faith in trying to copy nature. Bedding displays of tall *Cereus, Euphorbia, Ferocactus* and *Gasteria* may be the grower's ideal of "a slice of desert", as may the troughs of mixed *Lithops* neatly arrayed among matching pebbles, but these are pure works of art and have no counterpart in the wild. As sunlight passes through glass it loses much of its ultra-violet radiation (supposedly the reason why plants in glasshouses may burn during a heatwave), and the best-ventilated structure does not match the free air circulation out in the open. Yet none of this need discourage the cultivator, who can supply the basic needs of nutrition in other ways, knowing that a cactus is little different from a cabbage or a carnation in this respect. European-grown seedling cacti may never grow spines to match those of wild plants in size or colour intensity, but they can surpass them in shapeliness, freedom from pests, diseases and scars, and regularity of flowering. Some are unlikely to reach flowering size when pot-grown; others compensate by the splendour of their annual profusion. The only note of caution that should be sounded is to botanists who might be tempted to rely on garden-grown specimens in their systematic studies. Changes due to cultivation may be considerable (7.3), especially if the plants are grafted, and one must make allowance for increased size, reduction of protective devices and a less xeromorphic look.

Without attempting to imitate habitats in a glasshouse, however, the cactophile does well to know something about how his plants fare in the wild, particularly in relation to how much rain they may receive and when they receive it. Despite contrasted climates and growing seasons, most South African succulents adapt quite happily to glasshouse culture, whether in Europe or in New Zealand, and grow when they are watered and rest when kept dry. For obvious reasons one encourages them to grow in summer, when light is at its maximum, and to rest in winter, when both light and heat are limiting factors. A few—mainly dwarf Mesembryanthemaceae—resist this treatment and grow out of character or die if watered at the wrong time (6.2). These test the skill of the specialist grower, but mostly respond to a correct watering routine. They are certainly worth the extra effort, because they include some of the most bizarre succulents.

Mean annual rainfall may be linked to ease of cultivation, too. It has long been recognized that certain globular cacti of North America are notoriously difficult to transplant, rarely surviving long as imports in Europe, and seed raising is equally difficult. *Pediocactus* (16.39) includes several examples. Recently it has been shown[5] that the "difficult" cacti all come from areas that have less than 25cm (10in) average annual precipitation—that is, they are true desert cacti. The readily adaptable species are from regions of higher rainfall, although the intervals between rain may be long and erratic. Whether the same rule holds good with African succulents I do not know, although I suspect that it does, recalling the problems we have with *Welwitschia, Zygophyllum,* some stapeliads and dwarf Mesembryanthemaceae from South West Africa. But there are crassulas from the same area that acclimatize readily, visibly changing their

form and structure in the process. Indeed, there can hardly be any one genus in all flowering plants with greater adaptability than *Crassula,* ranging from the limits of desert colonization to marsh and aquatic species, all within a single genus. Comparison of a "wild" and cultivated plant demonstrates how the adaptation takes place; internodes elongate, and leaves originally packed into a sphere draw apart and expose greater surface to the air. The resulting plants are atypical, and would draw a frown from a botanist and show judge, but they give an interesting insight into the close links between plant structures and the environment.

Right (3.11): **Carpobrotus** *is one of the few Mesembryanthemaceae of economic value. It is widely planted to consolidate sand dunes, some species thriving in temperate climates.*

Below (3.12): A coastal scene at Buffels Bay in the Cape Nature Reserve, South Africa. The succulent carpeting the ground is a species of **Carpobrotus** *(Mesembryanthemaceae).*

From Flower to Seed

*"The most important and appropriate subject of inquiry
which arises in the science of botany is that proposed by
Empedocles, namely, whether female and male sex is found
in plants, or whether there is a combination of the two sexes."*

The terms "male" and "female" as used in classical writings about plants bear little resemblance to present-day usage, for they were applied only by vague analogy with the animal kingdom. A clear understanding of the true function of stamens as the male organs and bearers of the pollen, and of egg cells *(ovules)* as the female organs, had to await discovery until the late seventeenth century, and further progress was possible only after the invention of the compound microscope.

Unlike animals, plants usually have both sexes in a single individual, which is referred to as *hermaphrodite.* Flowers are the means whereby a species perpetuates itself through sexual reproduction. Seed set involves the transfer of pollen from anthers, usually recognizable by the golden dust covering them, to the stigmas, the receptive tips of the styles down which a pollen tube must grow to fertilize the ovules in the carpel below. Following fertilization, each ovule ripens into a seed, and the ovary becomes the dry or fleshy fruit. Other parts of the flower, having fulfilled their attractive function, normally wither and fall off. The seed must then be dispersed away from the parent plant to take its chance of landing in a locale suitable for growth. We shall discuss these functions of flowers—pollination and dispersal—in turn.

Self- and cross-pollination

At first sight it seems a needless complication to attract insects or other visitors to the flower as unconscious carriers *(vectors)* of the pollen. Why not self-pollination? As many gardeners can testify, "selfing" is quite possible in many succulents when only one plant is in bloom. Some even set full pods without any outside agency at all. The first to supply an answer to this question was

Above (4.1): In this **Opuntia** flower the anthers have shed copious pollen, but the stigmas are still tightly closed and unreceptive. Later they will spread out and become sticky.

Right (4.2): Anthophorid bee on a flower of **Opuntia**. Most of the pollen has gone, but note the yellow grains adhering to the green stigmas and to the body of the bee.

Charles Darwin, who found by experiment that when primroses were forced to self-pollinate, they produced a lower set of seed and weaker progeny than when pollen came from another individual of the same species. "Inbreeding depression" is the term that plant breeders have for the ill effects of continued self-pollination. Very few succulents self-pollinate regularly in the wild. Annuals such as *Portulaca* and *Dorotheanthus* do so to some extent, but not exclusively; they are attractive to insects and a measure of *outcrossing* (pollination from other individuals of the same species) takes place. Selfing tends to produce a stereotyped, true-breeding population that loses the ability to vary and hence to evolve. As a short-term means of increasing the population, it may have advantages, especially for annuals, but in the long run it is an evolutionary dead end.

Two extreme instances of self-pollination in succulents are encountered in *Anacampseros* and *Frailea.* The *Anacampseros* flower—the most ephemeral of all succulents—opens for only an hour or so, and sets an abundance of seed in

isolation without any insect visitors (12.5). In *Frailea,* we find a further stage: fruits gravid with fertile seeds ripen without any sign of an open flower at all. We call such behaviour *cleistogamy,* and there are many isolated examples among flowering plants. *Frailea* seems to get the best of two worlds: the cleistogamous fruits assure mass-production of individuals, whereas occasional fully expanded flowers set no seed with their own pollen and are adapted to outcrossing.

At the opposite extreme are the dioecious succulents, such as *Euphorbia obesa* (20.10), where two plants of opposite sex are needed in order to obtain seed. Those with yellow anthers are male, and those with greenish three-lobed stigmas

---

Sex distributions

Hermaphrodite flowers are bisexual—that is, having both functional male organs (stamens) and female ones (carpels), eg almost all cacti.
Unisexual flowers have organs of one sex only, although rudiments of the opposite sex may persist.
Monoecious plants bear separate male and female flowers, eg *Kedrostis africana,*
Dioecious plants bear only male flowers or only female ones, eg *Euphorbia obesa, Sedum rosea.* ♂ signifies male, ♀ female and ☿ or ⚥ bisexual.

4: POLLINATION AND DISPERSAL

Below (4.3): A flower of **Monanthes muralis** 8mm (⅓in) in diameter, showing the large, yellow, spoon-shaped nectaries between the linear petals and carpels. Although tiny, the flowers are clustered and the nectar drops sparkle in the sun.

Above (4.4): A white-bellied sunbird sipping nectar from the hanging flower of **Aloe chabaudii** in the Transvaal, South Africa. Bird flowers are commonly red or yellow, robust, and secrete copious nectar.

Mating patterns

A plant is said to be **self-compatible** (less accurately, *self-fertile*) when it sets viable seed with its own pollen, and **self-incompatible** *(self-sterile)* when it does not. All descendants by vegetative propagation of one plant count as the same individual. Collectively they are all genetically identical, and constitute a **clone**.

A flower that sheds pollen before the stigmas are receptive is said to be **protandrous** (such as *Echinopsis* 16.1); one that ripens stigmas before pollen is **protogynous** (such as *Weingartia lanata*).

---

are female. *Dioscorea,* the 'Elephant's Foot' (21.8), is also dioecious.

The sex-change flowers

Many bisexual flowers are constructed and function in such a way as to discourage self-pollination. A fairly common arrangement is that shown by many cacti. When the flower first opens it is functionally male (4.1), the stamens brimming with yellow pollen but the stigma lobes held high and dry above them. Next, when most of the pollen has been shed, the stigmas open star-like and become receptive, making the flower effectively female. The stigmas provide an obvious landing place for insects attracted by the scent, colour or general form of the flower, and these will inevitably deposit on the stigma any pollen they carry. Finally, as the flower wilts, differential growth or shrinkage draws the stigmas level with the brush of stamens, where they can pick up any residual pollen. When two kinds of pollen meet on the same stigma, the "selfed" pollen usually grows a pollen tube more slowly than the crossed and is hence less likely to effect fertilization. Many plants have independently evolved this neat and efficient mechanism, which encourages outcrossing but, as a last resort, ensures seed set if the flower is unvisited. The interested observer can learn much from a study of the blooms that open in his collection, especially if he looks at them daily with a pocket magnifier.

Attracting the pollinators

Sprengel, a rector in Spandau in the late eighteenth century, was the first to study the devices whereby flowers attract potential pollinators. He noticed the baits offered: surplus pollen and nectar. He observed the form and design of the flower, and the way contrasted areas of colour *(nectar guides)* pointed the way to the source of food. Such guide lines in red can be seen on the petals of *Pelargonium fulgidum* (4.5). Some visitors—bats, for instance—eat not only pollen but whole stamens. In flowers that produce no nectar, pollen provides the sole attraction.

Nectar. Where nectar is developed, it is secreted near the centre of the bloom, sometimes from conspicuous glands called *nectaries* (4.3). Certain plants also have nectaries other than those in the flower (*extrafloral* nectaries). *Coryphantha* and *Ferocactus* species can secrete nectar from the areoles, where an unsightly black mould that develops on the sugary liquid is an indication of the presence of an extrafloral nectary. Nectar is very attractive to ants, and the extrafloral nectary may be nature's decoy to avoid losing the precious fluid within the flowers to ants.

Nectar contains several substances in

dilute solution, but the chief one is sucrose. The copious watery nectar of *Aloe arborescens* (13.2), a bird-pollinated species, contains 13 percent of sugar and averages 54.5mg per flower[1]. Bee-pollinated flowers produce less, but more concentrated, nectar; the higher the sugar content, the more the bees like it.

Scent. Sweet scents, "the swift vehicles of still sweeter thoughts" to the poet, bring delight to the gardener and bafflement to the botanist who struggles to describe them. But they are the stock-in-trade of the biochemist, who labels them as aliphatic terpene alcohols, aldehydes and so forth. And they are vital to those flowers that produce them as their main enticement, in the absence of showy display and colours—*Neohenricia,* for example. Not only are scents hard to describe, but human noses often disagree when comparing them. *Euphorbia caput-medusae,* which smells intolerably rank and musty to me, was praised as all sweetness and serenity by another grower. It has been shown that an ability to discriminate among different-coloured freesias by their scent is genetically controlled, and no amount of training or

Above (4.5): Flowers of **Pelargonium** **fulgidum,** *each 8mm (⅓in) from top to bottom. The corolla is zygomorphic, with clear red nectar guides on the two uppermost petals. Such flowers typically have only one pollinator—one of the more intelligent insects responsive to set patterns.*

perseverance can alter heredity.

Among the most powerful fragrances in succulents (indeed, in any flower) is that of the night-flowering cerei (4.11), whose often large, white blooms of matchless purity and delicacy have justly earned them the title 'Queen of the Night' ever since the day when Marie Antoinette summoned Redouté, the celebrated Belgian flower painter, to the Temple where she was kept prisoner to immortalize the bloom of her favourite *Selenicereus* at midnight, witnessed by the assembled court and royal family. The perfume varies from one species to another, those visited by bats (4.6) having a musky, acid aroma. Brought into the home, a single bloom will fill the house with a pleasing fragrance, perceptible many metres away, but close up the effect is overpowering, as if the nose is surfeited.

Although opinions differ over the scents of some crassulas and euphorbias, there is complete unanimity about one group, the so-called carrion flowers (4.7). These Stapelieae are the classic example of flowers adapted for attracting flies and bluebottles, and in varying degrees they simulate carrion not only in form, texture and colour but also in scent. So successful is the ruse that even in cultivation flies often lay their eggs on the corolla, although there is no food supply for the larvae and they die in consequence. Despite their "bad breath", the Stapelieae are popular with collectors for the remarkable form and diversity of their flowers, which range from less than 1cm (⅜in) to over 30cm (12in) in spread.

The pollinators

To the best of my knowledge no succulent is reliant on the wind for pollen transfer *(anemophilous)*, as are the grasses and many catkin-bearing trees and palms.

Most depend on the visits of insects *(entomophilous)* or birds *(ornithophilous)*, although bats (4.6) appear to be the main pollen vector in such nocturnal cacti as the giant saguaro. But we have few accounts of pollinators observed visiting succulents in the wild. Field workers are usually too intent on seeking new species to bother. Who wants to sit in the blinding sun all day beside a *Ceropegia*, hoping to catch sight of the one tiny fly whose visit sets a whole pod of feathery seeds? Another problem is that you need to be an expert entomologist as well as a botanist in order to identify the insect visitors, and the days of the all-round naturalist — such grand pioneers as Sprengel, Müller, Kerner and Knuth — are no more.

Although we have only a few isolated records, we can often predict the type of visitor to a flower from its form and colour, symmetry and food source. Thus Vogel[2], in studying flower form in African Aloineae, contrasted *Aloe ferox* (with pendent, red, bird-pollinated flowers) with *Aloe (Guillauminia) albiflora* (with white bells pollinated by bees) and *Aloe (Leptaloe) minima* (with narrow-tubed, slightly oblique whitish blooms attractive to butterflies).

Bees. Of all visitors to flowers, bees are the most efficient pollinators (4.2) because of their constancy and their ability to work mechanisms such as those of a snapdragon *(Antirrhinum)* or an orchid. Honeybees *(Apis mellifera)* have been

closely studied, and we now know that they can recognize and memorize patterns and shapes of flowers (is "intelligence" too strong a word?) as well as communicate information to one another. When flowers are scarce in early spring, bees can be seen foraging for a good source of pollen or nectar. In a glasshouse a bee will go from *Haworthia* to *Crassula*, then perhaps to *Rebutia*. But once it finds a plentiful food source it will return to the hive and alert other bees by means of a special "bee dance", giving indications of the direction and distance of the newly discovered food source.

Bees recognize flowers by their combination of colour, patterning, shape in three dimensions and scent, scanning the edges first on making their approach. Their colour vision extends to the ultra-violet, so that some blooms that look plain to the human eye register to a bee as patterned in light and dark. Their scent perception also extends beyond ours: they have been noted taking the characteristic flight pattern that follows reaction to scent on approaching flowers that are odourless to the human nose. Truly they

Right (4.6): A bat attracted to the white nocturnal bloom of a columnar cereus. Nectar, pollen and whole stamens are equally acceptable. Note pollen on the bat's head.

Below (4.7): Flies on Stapelia ambigua, one of the carrion flowers. Eggs are commonly laid near the centre of the bloom, but the larvae die for lack of food.

are remarkable creatures. As taxonomists, bees can distinguish fine shades of difference, as between two allied species of snapdragon *(Antirrhinum)* grown in a mixed plot, and rarely mistake one for the other.

In the semi-desert regions characteristic of succulent habitats, solitary bees are commoner than social bees. These tend to be more restricted in their habits, foraging on a few or even a single species, and hence limited in activity to the flowering season of that species. This synchronization can be amazingly fine: for instance, the rise in temperature needed to open the buds on a cactus may be the same as that required to awaken activity by the bees.

Butterflies and beetles. Other insects are less "intelligent" and less faithful in their attentions to a single species. Some

are quite random in their visits, and thus of minimal significance for cross-pollination. Pollen robbers such as flies and beetles (4.8), which visit flowers erratically to feed but rarely pollinate them, are positively excluded from the more specialized flowers by devices that, for example, restrict access to the stamens or hide the nectar at the base of a long tube that is accessible only to an insect possessing a suitably long proboscis. The proboscis length in honeybees is up to 6mm (¼in); in bumble-bees 8-16mm (⅓-⅔in); and in butterflies and moths up to 15cm (6in) or more. On the other hand, hoverflies have a proboscis length of only 2-4mm (¹⁄₁₂-⅙in), although one or two

exceptions reach 12mm (½in). They feed on both nectar and pollen.

The special case of carrion flowers, pollinated by blowflies and dungflies, is discussed further below.

Birds. Like butterflies (4.9), birds respond particularly to the red range of colours, and to the presence of nectar, which needs to be in large supply to satisfy the thirst of a bird. Among succulents, the tubular, red or yellow blooms of many aloes (13.10) are typical bird flowers, although equally accessible to bees. If there is no landing stage for the bird it hovers beneath the bloom probing upwards with its bill. In their natural habitat

Below (4.8): Primitive insects on a primitive flower. **Acmaeodera** *beetles on a flower of Ferocactus. Beetles are inefficient pollinators; they roam at random and eat the pollen.*

Below (4.9): **Vanessa urticae,** *the Small Tortoiseshell butterfly, on flowers of* **Sedum spectabile.** *This is commonly planted in temperate region gardens to attract butterflies.*

in Africa some species of sunbirds visit aloes (4.4), but when these aloes are grown in California humming-birds are equally attracted.

Flower form and function

Flowers can be arranged in an evolutionary series starting with those that attract many and varied visitors up to those admitting only a single type—the "right" one to effect pollination. The former, primitive, pattern produces an abundant food supply but is wasteful of pollen. The flowers are radially symmetrical and conspicuous, with easy landing and access to the banquet. Examples among succulents are *Portulaca* (5.3), the Mesembryanthemaceae and the Cactaceae, all of which produce numerous stamens—in the saguaro (16.12), over 3,400 in a single bloom, the largest number on record for

any plant. It is surprising to find in cacti simple, spiralled flowers with many parts at such a low level of specialization, side by side with the extraordinarily advanced vegetative habit.

Another great Family of succulents, the Crassulaceae, also has simple, radially symmetrical flowers, but although they are individually small, the blooms are massed together in flattish or domed heads *(corymbs)*, which makes them collectively as conspicuous as a single large flower (4.10). Small and large insects find an easy landing ground, and nectar is accessible to the shortest proboscis. In biting stonecrop, *Sedum acre*[3], the five erect outer stamens shed pollen first, then the inner five rise up and take their place, prolonging the effective life of the flower. The stigmas mature late, but sufficient pollen is still around to

permit self-pollination as the flower wilts, if no insect visitors have called.

Timely flowering. Large, flat, open flowers in the desert sun are a great drain on the plant's water reserves, and we find that they are usually short-lived, or open only at set hours during the day, presumably when the right pollinators are active. In 1794 Haworth[4] suggested making a floral clock using different species of Mesembryanthemaceae, which, he noted, have specific times for opening and closing. The largest cactus flowers open only at night (when evaporation is much less intense) and are pollinated by moths or bats. Because pollen is spoilt if wetted, many cacti and Mesembryanthemaceae close their flowers rather rapidly when the sky clouds over—a fact soon discovered by would-be photographers of

these flowers, to their annoyance.

Another phenomenon to be seen in certain cacti and Mesembryanthemaceae is sensitive stamens. If, for instance, you touch the filaments of an *Opuntia* flower fully expanded on a hot sunny day, they rise up smartly and form a brush around the style, gradually returning later to the original position. This is no doubt effective in dusting the underside of a large insect visitor with pollen.

Once pollination has taken place, there would be no advantage in a flower staying open and losing precious water. In an experiment with *Mammillaria* flowers, those pollinated by hand were found to close two days in advance of those left unpollinated. To prolong the life of flowers in captivity, you would therefore be wise to avoid pollination unless you want seed.

Complex pollination systems. More specialized flower types are the zygomorphic blooms of *Haworthia, Coleus* (9.1) and *Pelargonium* (4.5), which are symmetrical about one vertical plane only and tailor-made in three dimensions to fit one type of visitor—typically a bee,

although five different pollen vectors have been reported for different species of *Pelargonium*[2]. Nectar is concealed at the bottom of a narrow tube, and the mouth of the flower has a characteristic lobing and colouring that advertise the way in, often by means of converging lines or nectar guides.

Most highly developed of all pollination mechanisms in succulents are those of the Asclepiadaceae: Stapelieae and Ceropegieae *(Brachystelma* and *Ceropegia).* The pollen of these, instead of separating as grains, remains stuck together in a mass, one from each of the two anther cells, linked together by a yoke to form a *pollinium* (19.5, 7). The complete pollinium is transferred from one flower to another on the hairs of the leg or proboscis of a species of fly. On crawling over another flower the fly deposits the pollinium on the stigmatic surface near the centre. Recent observations on a *Caralluma* in bloom in a Johannesburg garden showed that its only visitors were tiny fruit flies *(Drosophila),* which transferred the pollinia from flower to flower; this was the first recorded instance of a flower reliant on fruit fly as pollen vector.

Below (4.10): **Sedum telephium,** *like* S. **spectabile,** *has tiny flowers, but their massing together in corymbs makes them more conspicuous and a landing stage for a great diversity of insects.*

Right (4.11): Nocturnal flowers are economical in a desert: they lose less water than during the heat of the day. Most are large and white, with a powerful scent, as in this night-blooming cereus.

4: POLLINATION AND DISPERSAL

In the related genus *Ceropegia* the corolla is developed over the essential parts of the flower into a long tube with an oddly ornate top that may resemble a lantern, canopy or umbrella (4.14). This acts as a trap for tiny flies or midges, in much the same way as does the common arum *(Arum maculatum)* of European hedgerows. The insects are attracted by the faint but specific scent and the garish patterns on the top of the canopy, which often includes vibratile hairs. The walls are slippery, and the insect soon finds itself trapped in the swollen belly of the corolla tube, prevented from escaping by the smooth walls or sometimes by downward-curving hairs. Although the tube is dark, the belly is light, often from translucent "windows" that direct light onto the pollinia. In darkness the insects (tiny midges, *Ceratopogon,* in *Ceropegia woodii)* would become inactive, but in the light they buzz around, pick up pollinia and finally escape when, in a day or so,

the flower inclines from vertical to horizontal and any obstructive hairs wilt. Flies and midges have short memories and repeat the process before long, thus effecting pollination[5].

Flowering communes. The Compositae and Euphorbiaceae stand apart from the succulents already reviewed in producing, not a single large flower, but an aggregation of many tiny blooms (4.12, 13) surrounded by a protective envelope so that overall the appearance is that of a single large bloom. The structure of these is further described in Chapters 9 and 20. A compound head of flowers such as this has certain biological advantages over a single flower of the same bulk. The florets open serially over a long period of time, prolonging the working life. It is more or less weatherproof, and the outer covering of bracts gives added protection to the developing seeds. In a single large ovary, biting or chewing insects have only to

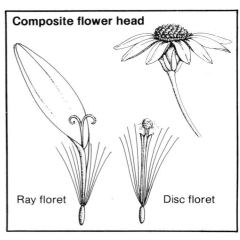

Composite flower head

Ray floret   Disc floret

Above (4.12): The inflorescence of Compositae is made up of two different kinds of small flowers (florets): radially symmetrical disc florets in the centre, and zygomorphic ray florets around the outside.

Below (4.13): A composite flower with white rays and yellow pollen on the outer disc florets.

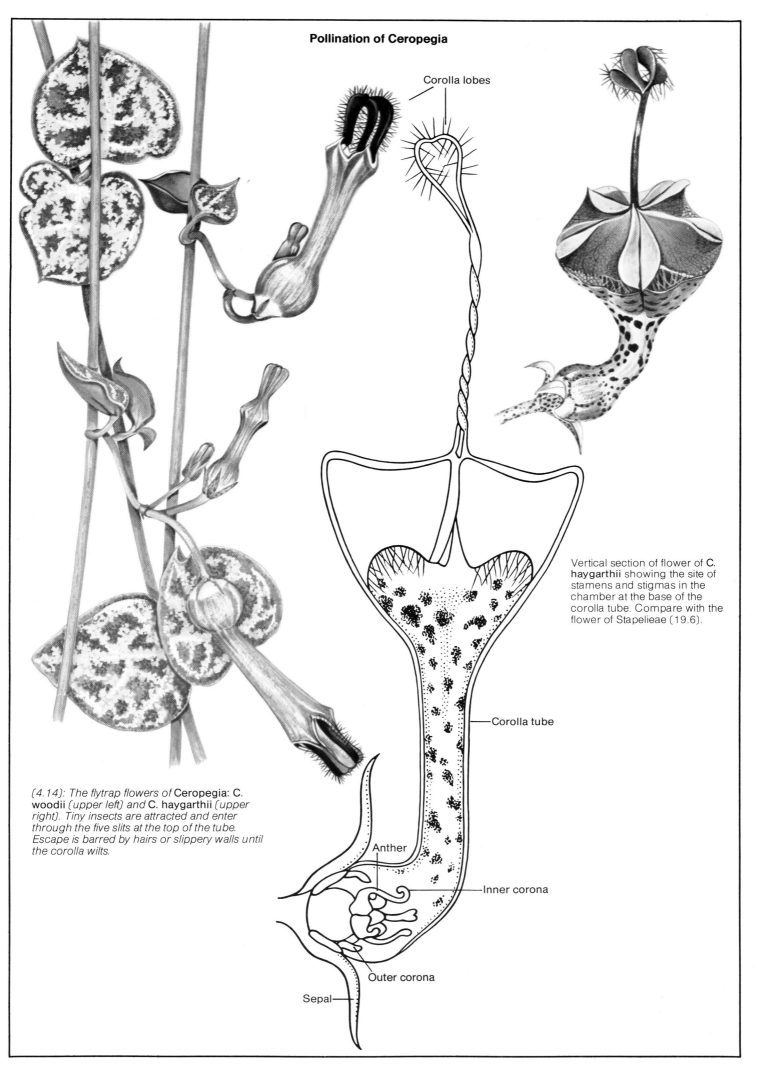

Pollination of Ceropegia

Corolla lobes

Vertical section of flower of **C. haygarthii** showing the site of stamens and stigmas in the chamber at the base of the corolla tube. Compare with the flower of Stapelieae (19.6).

Corolla tube

(4.14): The flytrap flowers of **Ceropegia: C. woodii** *(upper left) and* **C. haygarthii** *(upper right). Tiny insects are attracted and enter through the five slits at the top of the tube. Escape is barred by hairs or slippery walls until the corolla wilts.*

Anther

Inner corona

Outer corona

Sepal

penetrate once and all the contents are theirs for the taking, but in a large compound head, each seed is individually protected. It is hardly surprising, then, that these two Families are among the most widespread, diverse and successful of all flowering plants.

Dispersal

The second function of flowers, following cross-pollination and fertilization, is the dissemination of seed. Efficient dispersal requires that daughter plants grow up sufficiently far from the parent to avoid direct competition, but not so far away as to lessen chances of cross-pollination. Long-distance dispersal provides the means of founding new populations and increasing the range of a species.

Dispersal mechanisms have been classified under five groupings[6]: wind, water, mechanical means, animals and man. As we examine these insofar as they relate to succulents, it will be convenient also to mention vegetative means of dispersal as well as seeds.

Wind. The globular, easily detached offsets of the houseleek *(Sempervivum* 10.19) provide us with an example of what is called a *tumble-weed,* detaching and being caught up in the breeze to roll

around and root where and when conditions are favourable. This is a simple means of establishing daughter colonies, and in flat country surprisingly large distances can be covered.

Many succulents bear capsules that dry and split open at maturity, allowing the seeds to fall out or catch in the breeze (Aloineae; *Agave* 2.20). Such seeds are often winged, shaped like a sail or covered in sail-like outgrowths. A refinement is the development of something akin to a pepperpot. In *Anacampseros* a basket-like structure remains after shedding the floral parts, and by swaying in the breeze it releases a few seeds at a time (4.17). *Pterocactus* and *Dioscorea* have seeds with conspicuous wings, and the large winged seeds of *Welwitschia* (not strictly a succulent, but a unique desert inhabitant) are about 3cm (1¼in) across. Despite the bulk of these seeds, I have seen clouds of them blowing around in the strong onshore winds that sweep their level habitat in South West Africa.

Plumed seeds or fruits are common in succulents and highly efficient for transport, being found in some of the most widespread genera: *Senecio,* whose parachutes float over all five continents; the Stapelieae, which extend from India to the Cape of Good Hope; *Ceropegia,* which

Above (4.15): Seed dispersal in **Pelargonium carnosum.** *The style is just splitting, each awn carrying one seed with its own parachute.*

Below (4.16): The three-lobed capsules of euphorbias (this is **E. virosa)** *fly apart with an audible crack when ripe and shoot the three seeds a distance of some metres.*

has reached the Canary Islands from Africa; *Pachypodium* (18.3-5); and *Adenium* (18.1,2) whose seeds have two parachutes, one at each end, and whose range includes East Africa and Socotra. A special type of plumed dispersal organ is produced by *Pelargonium* (4.15). The long style in the centre of its bloom splits into five springy strands *(awns)* at maturity, and each curls up like a spring, carrying part of the ovary with a single seed. The plume of hairs assists in wind transport. On falling to the ground, the spiral awn responds to changes in humidity, curling this way and that, and effectively screws the seed into the ground.

Equally efficient for long-distance dispersal are tiny dust-like seeds, as shown by the wide distribution of the Crassulaceae. Although richest in genera and species in South Africa, this Family occurs in all five continents, and *Crassula* has reached isolated islands as well: the Azores, the Prince Edwards, and Kerguelen. Its tiny seeds are also carried on the fleeces of sheep, and plants turn up in dock areas where wool is imported.

Below [4.17]: Stages in the developing fruit of **Anacampseros**, *from wilted bloom (left) to a basket of fibres (right), from which seeds are intermittently blown by the wind.*

Water. The classic example of seed dispersal by water is in the Mesembryanthemaceae. A few genera have capsules that open when dry, and *Carpobrotus* has a fleshy berry, but the remainder have capsules with 4, 5 or more valves that open star-like in response to water and usually close again as the fruit dries out, repeating the process several times. The open capsule has an almost flower-like appearance, giving a novel look to the plants in a collection after they have been watered. At the base of each valve is special hygroscopic tissue, which expands when wetted and causes the valve to open. The biological significance of this is plain: the seed is released at the one time when there is water enough for germination, and the seedlings become established before the next drought. It has been observed that the open capsules are what we call "splash cups"—that is, they are so designed that raindrops striking the conical centre flush out the seeds from the chambers below. In this way seeds may be shot 1.5m (5ft) or more from the parent plant.

Conicosia capsules open once only on wetting and do not close again. The loose seeds are then shaken out over a period of time as from a pepperpot. Subsequently the light, buoyant capsule breaks off and rolls along the ground, scattering further seeds over greater distances. Finally it decomposes into segments, each composed of a wing-like membrane that divided the cell chambers. In this are two tiny pouches, each trapping a single seed. These seeds have a long viability (I have had good germination after five years) and so they ensure perpetuation in time as well as space. Three different dispersal mechanisms from one fruit must constitute something of a record; indeed, the fruits of Mesembryanthemaceae are among the most complicated structurally of any plant.

Mechanical means of dispersal . Under this heading we can include "expansive dispersal" in which plants send out long runners or stolons *(Crassula sarmentosa)* or creep and root along the ground *(Sedum lineare, Ceropegia woodii),* so that a single individual spreads and, after its death, survives as daughter colonies. Some kalanchoes (such as *K. suarezensis)* dip their long leaves to the soil and produce new plantlets from the tip; others, the familiar 'Mother of Thousands', *K. daigremontiana* (6.23) and *K. tubiflora,* develop adventitious buds along the leaf margins, and these drop off and generate new plants all around the parent—rather

4: POLLINATION AND DISPERSAL

too readily for comfort in a crowded glass-house. Some agaves achieve a similar local spread by dropping bulbils from the inflorescence. The inbuilt water reserves of succulents make them especially well adapted for mass propagation by detached portions of the plant body, even by single leaves.

Turning to seeds, we find explosive mechanisms well-developed in *Euphorbia* and *Dorstenia*. When the three-lobed capsule of a *Euphorbia* has ripened, it bursts into three part-fruits, each containing a single seed. The bizarre flat green receptacles of *Dorstenia* are covered in many minute unisexual flowers and edged with tentacle-like bracts (4.19). Each female flower ripens a single seed, which is shot out some distance from the receptacle by differential contraction, much as the soap slips from one's hand in the bath. In the process, the cup-like hollow housing the fruit turns inside out, so the bumps perceived on the surface of the receptacle are not seeds, but evidence that the seed has already gone. Collecting seed from these plants is a problem. The best way is to isolate the specimen before its fruits are ripe and to screen it with a glass shade or fine net—a lady's stocking is ideal.

Dispersal by animals. Just as many flowering plants rely upon animals for transfer of the pollen, so do many depend on animals for transport of their seeds, either externally or internally. Fleshy berries are the predominant fruit type in cacti, ranging from the tiny mistletoe-like berries of *Rhipsalis* (4.18) to the massive, highly coloured fruits of *Hylocereus,* as big as oranges. Sometimes the fruit becomes even more conspicuous by splitting and offering a soufflé of seeds mixed with white or coloured pulp. *Opuntia* produces the edible prickly pear (1.7), attractive to many wild creatures as well as to man. Once prickly pear had been introduced to South Africa, baboons and lemurs ate the fruits and rapidly spread it. In Arizona over 50 species of birds have been recorded as eating the fruits of the giant saguaro *(Carnegiea).* The seeds of all these plants are small and thick-skinned, so that they pass undamaged through the digestive system and end up germinating on a ready-made compost heap. Some seeds, indeed, do not germinate readily fresh from the fruit, and if they do not pass through an animal's digestive system they need chipping or chemical treatment with acid to assist. *Cissus* (15.5) and *Cyphostemma* (2.21), relatives of the grape vine, have large pips, and these are probably not swallowed but rejected in situ, or stick to the bill of a bird and are wiped off some distance from the plant that bore them.

The minute fruits of *Peperomia,* borne on long green spikes (9.2) are sticky and probably transported on the wings of birds. This would account for the wide dispersal of this large genus, centred in South America but reaching many islands of the tropics.

Dispersal by man. Man, by far the most disruptive of all influences on the natural distribution of plants, spreads them throughout the globe in a number of ways, intentionally and unintentionally. Seeds travel from one place to another attached to clothes and cartwheels, trains and aeroplanes. Others become mixed in with seed crops, drugs, bird seed, fodder, vegetable packing and fibre, wool, ballast and road-building material. Human activity has altered the range of some species for so long that it is no longer possible to be certain where they originated. But by carrying plants to new environments we at least ensure their survival if the original habitat is destroyed.

Right (4.18): **Rhipsalis baccifera,** *here growing in Ghana as a tropical forest epiphyte, is the only cactus found apparently wild outside the New World. Tiny flowers give way to juicy white berries.*

Below (4.19): A vertical section through the flattened inflorescence of **Dorstenia,** *showing flowers and the fruits sunken in pockets.*

Variations on a Theme

"Empedocles said that plants had their birth when the world was yet small and its perfection not attained, while animals were born after it was completed."

Genetics is the science that deals with heredity: the mechanism whereby offspring come to share characteristics of both parents, and the physical basis responsible for this inheritance. The descent of the individual naturally leads us to consider the descent of succulents from their non-succulent ancestors— evolution in the Darwinian sense. Both subjects have their practical side, and an understanding of them is essential for the plant breeder.

The chromosome blueprint

To begin at the beginning, we must first look at *chromosomes*. If we take the tip of a root or stem that is actively dividing, and look at single cells, suitably stained, under a high enough magnification, we can see the chromosomes—a constant number of dark, sausage-shaped bodies in each nucleus (5.2). In most cacti, for example, there are 22, 11 derived from one parent and 11 from the other. Each set of 11 chromosomes contains the genes in linear sequence, and by their interaction with the cytoplasm they control the expression of every heritable character of the plant. In the simplest case, one gene controls one character—flower colour, for example. Genes are liable to *mutate* (that is, to change permanently), and to these *mutations* we owe the diversity of plants as seen today.

Cell division

Cells multiply by the process of *mitosis,* in which each chromosome divides to form two identical daughter chromosomes; these separate into two clusters and a cell wall forms between them. In this way each of the millions of cells forming the body of a plant contains exactly the same set of genes, barring rare accidents.

Cells and cell division

Plants are composed of **cells**, each with a **nucleus** surrounded by **cytoplasm**.
The nucleus contains a fixed number of rod-like bodies, the **chromosomes**, each of which contains the **genes** (transmitters of inherited character) in linear sequence.
Cells of the plant body divide by **mitosis**, each of the two daughter nuclei receiving an identical full set of chromosomes.
Prior to reproduction a special reduction division called **meiosis** halves the number of chromosomes transmitted to the egg cells and pollen grains. Fertilization again restores the full quota.

As a prelude to the development of reproductive cells *(gametes),* the chromosomes undergo a special type of division, *meiosis.* First they form up in pairs, each chromosome of one set of 11 pairing up with its partner in the other set. At this stage an exchange of genetic material takes place, so that when the chromosomes separate, those derived from parent A have some genes from parent B, and those derived from parent B have corresponding genes from parent A. There follows a reduction division in which only half of the overall *(diploid)* number of chromosomes passes into each pollen grain or egg cell. These are *haploid* (that is, containing the halved or basic number of chromosomes). Fertilization restores the original number of 22 in a cell, and a new plant develops from the seed with the same overall number as both parents but with uniquely shuffled arrangement. It is a feature of sexual reproduction that, by the laws of chance, no two individuals will be identical (5.1).

What chromosomes tell us

Looking at chromosomes under the microscope is, in a way, like looking at the blueprint of life: the architect's plan rather than the finished building. This is not the place to enter deeply into the chemical and physical properties of chromosomes: a subject that attracts intense interest and research, stimulated by the ever-present desire to learn more about the origin of life. Here it must suffice to give a few simple examples to show how investigation of the number, form and pairing behaviour of chromosomes helps the classifier, the evolutionist and the plant breeder.

Many wild plants are *polyploid,* having two or more times the basic set of chromosomes in each cell. Diploidy is the ancestral condition; polyploidy a later derivation. Sometimes even within one species polyploidy may occur, as in the widespread *Rhipsalis baccifera* (4.18), which is diploid with 22 chromosomes in Brazil, Paraguay and Bolivia, tetraploid with 44 chromosomes in Mexico, Costa Rica, Cameroon, Kenya and Madagascar, and octoploid with 88 chromosomes in Madagascar also. Polyploidy has been observed within one single plant even.

Right (5.1): Seedling variation in a population of **Echinocereus reichenbachii.** *This picture demonstrates better than words the folly of trying to define a species from a single plant.*

5: GENETICS AND EVOLUTION

The large watery cells of succulent tissue in some Mesembryanthemaceae contain up to 16 times the basic chromosome number. But these cells are not concerned with reproduction, and the plant produces normal haploid pollen and egg cells.

Chromosomes differ not only in number but also in form. Thus, in the Aloineae the basic number n=7, each set being made up of four long and three short chromosomes. Even more marked size differences are to be found in the Agavaceae. *Agave* and *Yucca* were originally classified in separate Families (see Chapter 14), but both genera have a unique make-up: five large and 25 minute chromosomes in each set. Such a novel feature is hardly likely to have evolved twice, and this confirms the close relationship between the two genera.

In true species, the chromosomes pair regularly at meiosis, each with its corresponding partner. This pairing and subsequent uniform separation is essential for the production of good pollen and functional egg cells. In a hybrid, the two sets contain different genes, or a different order of arrangement, and pairing takes place with difficulty or not at all. In the ensuing tangle, many of the pollen grains and egg cells may contain odd numbers of chromosomes and be non-functional. This sterility of hybrids has long been recognized (the mule is a classic example), and it plays an important role in nature by deterring random crossing between allied species growing together. But few hybrids are completely sterile, and a persevering plant breeder can often persuade seeds to set if he tries hard enough. Crosses with an odd number of chromosomes—a triploid cactus with 33 chromosomes, for instance—could obviously never form an exact number of pairs at meiosis. A plant breeder ignorant of this could waste much time trying to hybridize, say, *Mediocactus coccineus* with the epicacti. The former is tetraploid, the latter are diploids, and therefore the progeny would be sterile triploids.

Most standard botanical works of reference—monographs and floras—now cite chromosome numbers for species, if they are known.

How inheritance works

To see how the chromosome cycle functions, let us take the simplest of examples: the red- and yellow-flowered *Portulaca grandiflora* (5.3). Red flowers are governed by gene R, yellow by gene r. A true-

Top right (5.2): The 14 chromosomes of **Bulbine alooides**, *magnified 1900 times. Note size variation and the apparently clear constriction dividing each into two arms.*

Right (5.3): **Portulaca grandiflora**, *showing the flower colour variation in cultivated strains of this popular annual bedding plant. Flower doubling is also to be seen.*

Chromosome numbers

The basic set of chromosomes, as present in pollen grains and egg cells, is **haploid** (n). Thus, in Aloineae n=7, in Mesembryanthemaceae n=9, in succulent euphorbias n=10, in Cactaceae and Stapelieae n=11 and in *Agave* n=30.
Each cell of the plant body contains a double (**diploid**) set of chromosomes, half coming from each parent.
Higher multiples of the basic number are called **polyploid**. Thus:

Ruschia impressa	has 2n=18	Diploid
Ruschia nonimpressa	2n=36	Tetraploid
Ruschia uncinata	2n=54	Hexaploid.
Haworthia tessellata	2n=14, 28, 42 or 56 in different populations.	

Odd numbers (broken sets) are referred to as **aneuploid**. Thus:
x *Gastrolea nowotnyi*   2n=20   (7 x 3 − 1).
("x" before a name indicates hybridity).

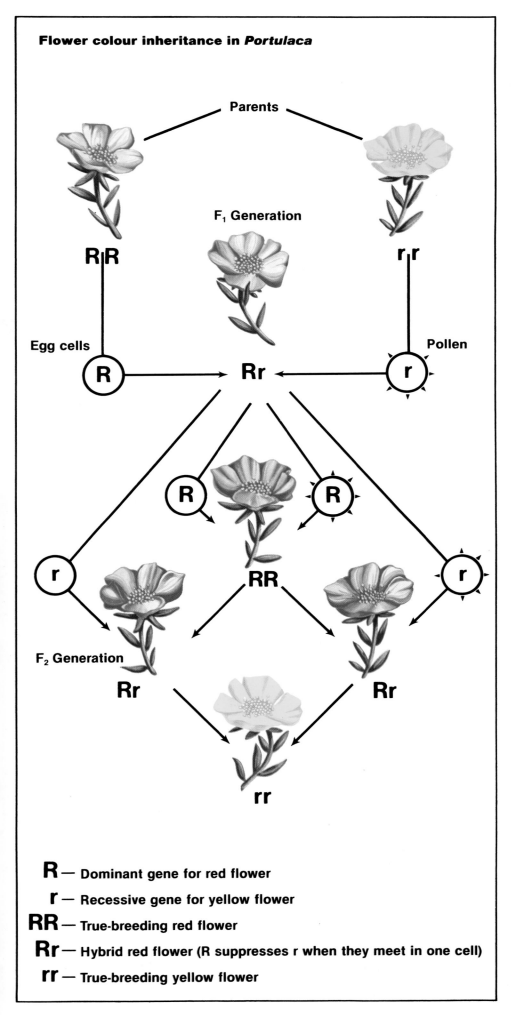

Flower colour inheritance in *Portulaca*

Parents

F₁ Generation

R R

r r

Egg cells

Pollen

(R) → **Rr** ← (r)

F₂ Generation

(R) (R)

(r) (r)

RR

Rr

Rr

rr

R — Dominant gene for red flower

r — Recessive gene for yellow flower

RR — True-breeding red flower

Rr — Hybrid red flower (R suppresses r when they meet in one cell)

rr — True-breeding yellow flower

breeding red *Portulaca* will have the constitution RR, with two R genes at identical sites on the two corresponding chromosomes, one received from each parent. A true-breeding yellow *Portulaca* will have only genes for yellow, rr. In the red plant, all pollen grains and egg cells carry the single factor R; in the yellow one all carry the factor r. If we now cross a red plant with a yellow one (5.4), all the progeny will be Rr, no matter which was the male and which the female parent. This first generation, called F₁ for short, will be found to have red flowers exactly like the red parent. This is because R is *dominant* and r is *recessive:* that is, when the two meet in one cell, R suppresses the action of r.

Not all pairs of genes behave in this way: sometimes the F₁ shows characters intermediate between the two parents. The main point to realize is that in a hybrid the characteristics do not mingle like ink and water: each gene retains its identity and, although undetectable in one generation, may manifest itself in the next. This we shall see if we now cross our F₁ red portulacas among themselves. Now we have gametes of two kinds, half R, half r. From chance combinations of pollen and egg cells, three types of progeny are possible: RR, Rr and rr. Of these, both RR and Rr will bear red flowers, and only those lacking R will bear yellow ones. By the laws of chance, then, red plants will outnumber yellow in the ratio 3:1. We call this a Mendelian ratio in tribute to Gregor Mendel, an Augustinian monk of Brünn (now Brno in Czechoslovakia), who first published the mathematical basis of inheritance in 1865[1]. Note that all our second-generation (F₂) plants with red flowers will look alike, and only a further crossing experiment could separate the one RR from the two Rrs. If R were incompletely dominant to r, we should be able to distinguish them visually, and we should expect the ratio 1 red : 2 orange : 1 yellow.

The science of genetics grew up at the start of the present century with the rediscovery of Mendel's work, which had been totally overlooked since its first appearance in print. His laws were found to apply universally to plants and animals, although not always in as simple a form as that set out above. One character can be governed by a number of genes *(polygenes)*, an example being rib number and degree of white flecking in *Astrophytum*. One gene may control more than one character, and instead of two there may be three or more possible states *(multiple alleles)* at the one site on a chromosome. If two pairs of characters

Left (5.4): Flower colour inheritance in **Portulaca**, *demonstrating a simple 3:1 Mendelian ratio. Knowledge of the inheritance mechanism enables the breeder to plan his crosses and forecast results.*

are considered together, four possible combinations will appear in the F_2 in the ratio $9:3:3:1$—always assuming that a large enough number of seedlings is raised to allow for the chance meeting of gametes. Rarest will be the double recessive, only one in 16 of the population.

How succulents evolved

The story of the evolution of plant life on this planet is the story of the conquest of dry land. From microscopic beginnings beneath the sea, of which the seaweeds (algae) are modern survivors, plants evolved the means to become independent of a continuous water supply for at least part of their life cycle, and were thus able to colonize the land. Mosses and ferns are still usually plants of moist shady places; conifers show a marked advance, as well as possession of a woody skeleton. Finally came the flowering plants, latest and most successful of all major groups, with improved adaptability and efficient reproduction by seed. The coal that we mine is a reminder of some of the less successful competitors in the struggle to survive.

The missing evidence. Our only direct evidence on which to reconstruct the past comes from fossils, which put the origin of flowering plants somewhere in the early Cretaceous period, 115,000,000 to 100,000,000 years ago, before the continents as we know them today had completely separated from the one united landmass. A rapid increase in the late Cretaceous made them the dominant land plants. Unfortunately the fossil record for flowering plants is very scanty, and for succulents nothing at all. Hot, dry climates are not, apparently, conducive to the formation of fossils. Among the earliest flowering plants that can be recognized are magnolias and catkin-bearing trees (all mesophytes), and it is logical to assume that xerophytes, including succulents, were among the latest developments. But the occurrence of related succulents in areas widely separated today, such as *Sedum* in North America and Asia, and *Portulaca* in South America and Africa, suggests a common origin before the continental landmasses began to drift apart. So we need a lot

more evidence before attempting to construct an accurate chronology of events in the evolution of succulent plants.

Evolutionary trends. The chart on pages 16-17 reflects one person's ideas on which Orders are primitive and which are more specialized in plants living today. But one should not read too much into such family trees. Anyone can arrange the Mesembryanthemaceae, for instance, into a series showing progressive xeromorphism, beginning with a leafy shrub such as *Aptenia,* scarcely succulent at all, and progressing through intermediate stages of condensation and surface reduction— shrubby *Lampranthus* (11.2) and *Ruschia* (11.9), stemless *Cylindrophyllum* and *Bergeranthus*—to the ultimates of compaction such as *Pleiospilos* (11.4), *Argyroderma* (11.24) and *Conophytum*

Below: Convergent evolution in succulents. The "Medusa head" habit evolved in a South American cactus, Opuntia tephrocactoides *(left, 5.5) and in a South African spurge* Euphorbia caput-medusae *(right, 5.6).*

(11.26). But to suggest that one evolved from the other would be quite unwarranted. For one thing, their fruits are diverse in structure and show them to belong to different subtribes of the Family. For another, we must take into account the phenomenon of *convergence*. Succulents show this in a high degree. An American cactus may look superficially so much like an African *Euphorbia, Pachypodium* or *Hoodia* that one has to look closely to spot the difference (5.5,6). It is small wonder that the layman calls them all cacti! Yet we know all these to be poles apart in ancestry, and their flowers and fruits show them to belong to different Orders. Many similar examples of convergent evolution could be cited. It seems as if conditions in regions of intense sunshine and periodic drought are so rigorous that very few life forms can endure them, and the cactiform habit has arisen independently over and over again.

The direction of evolutionary trends is often difficult to ascertain. Are the ribs on a cactus derived from the fusion of rows of tubercles, or did ribs come first and divide up into tubercles later? Doubtless both trends have occurred; we may never be sure. But we can be certain of one thing: organs evolve independently of one another in response to different stimuli. One organ may advance to a high level of specialization while another remains little changed over long periods of time. Thus, all cacti show extreme advancement of the vegetative body, but retain primitive, spirally arranged flowers that have been little modified above the level of the magnolia or water-lily. Among the cacti, *Pereskia* (16.4) stands out as primitive in having thin, deciduous leaves, little succulence and unspecialized flowers and fruits. Yet it has fully formed areoles—a highly advanced feature.

Occasionally the direction of an evolutionary trend is indisputable. For example, it would be hard to imagine the spineless astrophytums (16.31) as suddenly growing spines where none existed before: it is far simpler to regard them as secondary derivatives from spiny cacti by the suppression of armature. This is supported by the observation of fine spines on the seedlings. Seedlings tend to be conservative and to retain features not present in the adult plant. Thus, leafy seed leaves may be noted in species where adult plants develop no expanded leaves at all.

In general, therefore, it is dangerous to be dogmatic about the ancestry of succulents. A study of only living plants tells us no more about their past history than a study of a crowd in a football stadium would help us to sort out the blood relations of the spectators. As far as drawing up a genealogical tree of succulents is concerned, we see only the tips of the branches: the stems and trunk are forever hidden from view.

How species evolve

Although the origin of succulents remains veiled in the past, the origin of species is more open to direct analysis. We can create species to order. In nature, new species arise from old ones either suddenly or gradually over long periods of time. Sudden origin comes from a chromosomal change that is passed from cell to cell,

and eventually to succeeding generations via sexual reproduction. The best-known and most easily definable examples are those associated with hybridization followed by doubling of the chromosome number. Let us suppose that two related diploid species have genetic constitutions AA and BB. The letters refer to the two haploid sets of chromosomes possessed by each. The F_1 hybrid will be AB, because it has received one A set from one parent and one B set from the other, regardless of which was pollen donor or egg donor. The two sets work happily side by side in each cell throughout the life of the plant, producing something that usually shows characteristics of both parents or is intermediate between the two. But a problem arises at meiosis: the A set of chromosomes cannot pair with the B set. As explained earlier, there is a breakdown and functional pollen and egg cells cannot form.

Suppose now that by some accident of cell division a plant arises with a doubled chromosome constitution: a tetraploid with AABB. Here, at meiosis, each A chromosome can pair with its own A partner, and each B with a B. Fertility is restored, and the mechanism can repeat itself. Further, the seed breeds true and the plant is isolated from its parents,

because backcrosses would result in sterile triploids AAB or ABB. By definition, a new species has been born.

But how does such chromosome doubling occur? In the laboratory it can be brought about by interfering with the normal division of cells in the growing tip of a stem or germinating seed. The classical method uses *colchicine,* a very poisonous and expensive alkaloid extracted from the autumn crocus, *Colchicum.* This retards the growth of a new cell wall following division of a nucleus, so that a tetraploid nucleus results. An example is *Kalanchoe vadensis,* a new man-made species produced by doubling the chromosome number of the diploid cross *K. blossfeldiana* × *K. grandiflora*[2]. In nature, such tetraploids can arise spontaneously from seed, or as sports (mutations) on single branches.

The gradual origin of species in the wild takes place undramatically and is harder to study, though no less potent in enriching the flora. A plant population, or part of it, may become isolated, either by migration to new terrain, or by developing internal breeding barriers so that it is cut off from gene exchange with its fellows. Its slow divergence in appearance from neighbouring populations in response to a new environment may eventually lead a

botanist to recognize it as a separate new species. Ultimate isolation occurs when chromosomal divergence creates a barrier and the new species can no longer intercross with its progenitors.

The evolution of a succulent flora

Many of the habitats of succulents give indications of being active centres of evolution. These are areas of mountain and valley, with sharp daily or seasonal contrasts of temperature and rainfall, and with different soil types and different exposures. Stimulants to change are many, from freak frosts and droughts to hurricanes, earthquakes and volcanic eruptions. In times favourable for lush growth, ranges of different species may extend and overlap, and hybrid swarms arise at the point of overlap. In the retreat following adversity, isolated survivors

Right (5.7): Survival in nature depends upon continual regeneration. The giant saguaro of Arizona (Carnegiea gigantea) *here shows all stages from seedlings to a dead adult plant.*

Below (5.8): Islands separated from the mainland are often centres of active evolution. Aeonium, *shown here, has evolved thirty-one species in the comparatively small area of the Canary Isles.*

may become the basis of new species. Seasonal variations in range have been studied for the giant saguaro in Arizona, where fluctuating minimum temperatures in winter are the limiting factor to survival (5.7). Lack of summer rainfall in California as compared to Arizona is another factor that limits the spread of the saguaro westwards over the Colorado River[3].

A clear example of an active centre of evolution is the Canary Isles, long isolated from the mainland of Africa and with a high concentration of contrasting habitats in a small area. Here we find 31 endemic species of *Aeonium* (5.8) as well as numerous interspecific hybrids between them. A similar ferment of active evolution is to be found among the Andean cacti, where species limits are correspondingly difficult to define—a situation reflected in the confusion of names and

synonyms confronting the grower of these popular succulents.

Much interest attaches to the flora of islands. How did the plants get there in the first place, and from where? And how have they changed in isolation? Darwin noted that islands are usually poor in numbers of species, as compared with equivalent mainland areas, but rich in endemics, the percentage increasing in proportion to the distance from the nearest continent. The evolution of unique, fat-stemmed succulents on remote oceanic islands has been alluded to on page 36.

Nature or nurture?

In all that I have said so far about genetics and evolution, my concern has been only with what is inherited. There are in addition changes brought about as a result of nutrition, climate or disease—

fluctuations, we call them (6.2). Red leaves may result from phosphate deficiency, yellow ones from lack of iron, stunting from general starvation. But such changes affect only the individual and are not inherited. If returned to normal growth conditions the plant will recover. The transformation that occurs in some imported succulents when they are grown in mild, moist conditions can be so startling

Below left (5.9): "Mimicry" in the Asclepiadaceae: Hoodia, *20cm (8in) high, seen against its natural rock background in South West Africa. Such plants can become quite inconspicuous at a short distance.*

Below right (5.10): "Mimicry" in the Mesembryanthemaceae: a many-headed Lithops *in habitat in South West Africa. Note how different the pattern of camouflage is from the popular idea of matching pebbles.*

as to lead the observer to believe that he has a new species.

Natural deception

One evolutionary process of peculiar fascination is that termed "mimicry": for example, a plant looking so much like a stone that it escapes detection by resemblance to its background. Mimicry is developed to a high degree in the animal kingdom, a colourful example being harmless species of tropical butterflies that escape extermination by developing similar patterns to those of butterflies that are distasteful to their enemies. "Mimicry" and "imitation" are bad words to use because they imply a conscious act of camouflage where no such motivation is involved. Any chance mutation that makes the undefended easily mistaken for the defended confuses predators and

increases the chances of survival. We see only the final, perfected "mimic", not the countless unsuccessful intermediates.

One familiar example of mimicry—I continue to use the word because I know of none better—in European plants is the dead-nettle *(Lamium* spp), which gets its name from its superficial likeness to the stinging-nettle *(Urtica* spp) but lacks stinging hairs. The two plants commonly grow together, although a glance at the flowers shows them to be quite unrelated.

The best cases of mimicry among succulents come within the leaf-succulent Mesembryanthemaceae. Many of the stemless genera are inconspicuous and seem to fade into their backgrounds: *Didymaotus* (11.18) against granite and white, incrusted *Titanopsis* (11.20) on quartz chippings. The most remarkable of all are *Lithops* (5.10) the popular

"pebble plants" and "living stones". In habitat you can stare right at them and still not see them; then, when you finally do, they are everywhere. Professor Desmond Cole of Johannesburg, the leading authority and a past master at finding the unfindable, recognizes 37 species of *Lithops*, some widespread *(L. lesliei),* some extremely local. In the course of field trips with him, I saw a little of the special mystique for *Lithops* spotting—not only in the known habitat, but in finding that habitat in the wide open spaces where landmarks and signposts are nowhere to be seen. Each of the known *Lithops* harmonizes to some extent with its background: in no known instance does the plant contrast in the way that a photographer would set it up in order to show off the subject. The colour and patterning of *Lithops* are extraordinarily diverse (11.27, 28), from plain grey or brown to intricately mottled, and one finds them associated with a corresponding range of rock formations and soils, from white quartz down to the cracked mud of dried-out river beds. And where several rock formations occur side by side, we find *Lithops* confined to places where they blend with the background; elsewhere none is to be seen.

Growers often present their *Lithops* in "natural" displays in troughs, going to great trouble to collect smooth round pebbles that match each leaf as closely as possible. This is not at all how they appear in nature, where disruptive camouflage is more usual. For instance, a *Lithops* with a grey body mottled with brown will probably be found among two sorts of rock: a grey slate or quartz and brown chippings, of granite, perhaps.

Before we jump to conclusions on the protective nature of *Lithops* markings, we need to know the answers to a number of questions. Do grazing animals have similar vision to our own? Are they as easily deceived as we are? And does *Lithops* rely on other attributes, such as a distasteful sap, to avoid extermination?

Other succulents besides the Mesembryanthemaceae resemble their natural backgrounds to some degree. In South West Africa I have almost tripped over large, robust plants of *Hoodia* because the grey of their stems and the blackish tubercles so closely match the rocks against which they grow (5.9). In America *Ariocarpus* species (16.33) are called "living rock cacti" from their resemblance to the surrounding terrain. The tiny white growths of some species of *Anacampseros* (12.3) are thought to escape detection by their resemblance to bird droppings.

Breeding new succulents

"Every plant does not produce a seed similar to that from which it is sprung; some produce a better seed, others a worse." This quote from the same ancient

5: GENETICS AND EVOLUTION

source that provides the chapter headings used here may be taken as the birth certificate of plant breeding. A hybridist can achieve in one lifetime what might take millennia if left to nature. He can speed up evolution, bringing together and crossing plants from widely separated localities, and can even open up quite new sources of variability by direct attack on the chromosomes with drugs, irradiation and other sophisticated laboratory techniques. Such methods are routine in breeding cereals and other crops, but little has yet been done with succulents. Indeed, some growers are actively opposed to the creation of novelties. Are there not enough species already? Yes, but in all spheres of horticulture hybrids eventually replace species, being better adapted and selected to suit the needs of man. By all means let us conserve the wild species of succulents, both in their habitats and in botanical gardens and specialist collections; as more and more habitats are destroyed, the onus is upon us to do so. But in private collections grown purely for aesthetic appeal, good named hybrids may have more to offer than some species, and deserve their place (8.3, 10.2). Attractive novelties such as the dwarf aloes or

astrophytums win converts at first sight, and incidentally lessen the demand for yet more imported plants from habitat.

The most spectacular results so far in breeding succulents come in the group I call "epicacti", from the fact that their ancestors are mostly epiphytic tropical forest cacti of the genera *Nopalxochia, Epiphyllum, Heliocereus* and allies. Not least remarkable here is the ease with which species of different genera can be interbred and the hybrids still retain a measure of fertility—a situation unmatched elsewhere except among the orchids. The epicacti are not much to look at as plants: their flat, green, almost unarmed stems (not leaves!) remind one more of the aspidistra than of a cactus. But during the short period when they are in bloom in early summer they are without rival (5.11, 12, 8.4). The great funnel-shaped blooms of classical simplicity and form come in white through shades of pink, orange and magenta, often enlivened with a steely blue flush—a character inherited from *Heliocereus speciosus*. They are the finest flowers in all succulents. Indeed, it would be hard to name any bloom that surpasses them in combining brilliance of display and deli-

cacy contrasting with the solid earthiness of the stems that bear them.

Other groups where great advances have been made by the hybridist are the genera *Aloe* and *Sempervivum*. Both now have their own specialist societies, with facilities for testing and recording the latest introductions.

As mentioned earlier, prospective hybridists can profit much and save useless effort by a knowledge of the genetical background to the plants on which they work. For instance, in the example of *Portulaca* given above, we saw that diversity appeared only in the second generation; all F_1 plants were identical. Thus it is desirable to go to the second generation, if that is possible, to begin to see the full potentialities of a breeding programme. Whereas many F_2 plants should be raised, only a few of the F_1 are needed because all are alike.

Epicacti: the floral glory of the cactus Family. Like orchids, they are intergeneric hybrids of complicated ancestry descended from mostly tropical climbers or epiphytic species of at least five different genera. Right (5.11) is 'Eden'. Below (5.12) is 'Carl von Nicolai'.

Growing Succulents for Pleasure

*"Some plants require someone to plant them, others do not . . .
Some plants are indoor plants, others garden plants, and
others wild . . . I think, too, that all species of plants which
are not cultivated become wild."*

There is no shortage of published guidance on how to grow succulents, both in popular handbooks and in the current journals of the various specialist societies. I shall not set out to repeat what has been said many times; rather, the emphasis will be on seeking the reasons behind such advice, because it is always better to understand principles rather than blindly accept dogma. It can be argued that cultivation is an art and cannot be taught. Even experienced growers are forever learning, and if one were to tell me he never lost a plant, I shouldn't believe him. Some books go into great detail on the niceties of how and how not to grow succulents. Comparing them reveals occasional contradictions, which is to be expected when much of what is said is based on personal faith rather than on scientifically proven facts.

There has been woefully little research on succulents, and most of the recommendations on how to meet their needs in the highly artificial environment of a glass box far removed from their native home comes from analogy with work on other, non-succulent plants — mostly agricultural and horticultural crops. In the 1930s the John Innes Horticultural Institution at Merton, in the London area, pioneered research into glasshouse construction and the formulation of standard composts. But a soil mix that suits annual glasshouse mesophytes may be less than ideal for succulents that may go two or more years without repotting, and similarly an insecticide developed for cucumbers may not suit *Crassula* and *Lithops*. Thus, although we can be thankful for a wealth of technological advances, from the polythene bag and systemics to methods of seed storage and meristem culture, we are nevertheless left to adapt these general techniques to the special needs of succulent plants.

Going back to nature

Foregoing chapters have made it clear that we can learn something about the cultivation of succulents by reference to their native habitats, notably in the cycles of wet and dry, hot and cold, that determine when the plants grow and when they rest. Although a few (mostly denizens of the humid tropics) can be kept growing all the year round, most

respond to an annual rest period, and may fail to flower unless this dormancy is observed by phasing out watering at the onset of winter, when light and temperature are limiting factors to growth. Usually this has the desired effect, and the plants can be lulled to sleep even if the seasons are reversed in relation to their natural home. A few, however, resist attempts to alter their normal annual rhythm of growth and rest: *Conophytum*, for instance, *Gibbaeum* (certain species) and some other dwarf Mesembryanthemaceae. Canary Island aeoniums tend to rest during a northern summer, no matter how freely they are watered, and to grow in late autumn. The best that can be done for such plants is a compromise: put them right up near the glass in the lightest position, and water cautiously for only as long as they indicate by growth and flowering that water is needed.

Many plants are sensitive to day length *(photoperiod)* and will flower only in response to decreasing or increasing the hours of sunlight. "Short-day plants" react to an increase in the hours of darkness, which can be achieved, for instance, by covering in black polythene. "Long-day plants" respond when the day is extended by means of artificial lighting. Both techniques are used commercially to force flowering out of season. Good examples of short-day plants are *Kalanchoe blossfeldiana* and the 'Christmas Cactus' *(Schlumbergera)*. *Sedum spectabile* and *S. telephium* are long-day plants[1]. For *Echeveria harmsii* to bloom it must have a succession of short days followed by long, whereas *Kalanchoe tubiflora, K. integra* and *Aloe bulbillifera* need long days followed by short.

Certain succulents are notoriously shy about flowering in captivity, even when mature — *Mitrophyllum* (11.11), for instance. The natural impulse is to give them extra light. However, success might come from actually shortening the day — that is, by turning lamps on for a limited number of hours each day, followed by total darkness. There is room for some important experiments here.

Right (6.1): One of the most celebrated of many outdoor gardens in southern Europe, this at La Mortola in Italy was founded by Thomas Hanbury in 1867 and has always been rich in succulents.

6: CULTIVATION

We have seen that one cannot imitate nature in a garden or glasshouse, even if this were desirable. The English sun is never that of the desert; the seasons are at variance; and the best ventilation system never allows the constant caress of the wind in the great open spaces. Above all, succulents inhabit so wide a range of contrasted habitats that the most a grower can aspire to do is to create a general environment for the majority, and either forgo nonconformist plants or segregate them for special treatment. He is helped by the fact that, far from being uniform, the conditions within a small glasshouse vary between wide limits. Apart from such obvious differences as the amount of shading at glass and floor level, there are daily and seasonal cycles, as well as fluctuations in humidity and temperature. This is easily demonstrated by watering a batch of identical pots of soil spaced out over a level staging. You will find that they dry out at different rates—those at the margins (and especially those near ventilators) first, and those near the centre, where air circulation is less, taking longer. Thus the experienced amateur is forever shifting his plants around, learning what not to put on a top shelf because of the danger of scorching, and what must go on a top shelf if he is ever to see it flower. Because light is usually a limiting factor, there is stiff competition for the brightest spots, and under the staging go the few kinds (some Aloineae, and epi-

phytic cacti) that tolerate—but do not relish—partial shade. Propagating trays can also go on the floor, although it is more difficult to keep an eye on them.

Tropical forest epiphytes need their own special treatment: a richer soil mix, partial shade from full sun, and more water and warmth.

Watering—when and how much?

If any one factor determines success or failure in domesticating wild succulents, it is watering. Many people crave to know the magic formula of how much and when, expecting a simple equation depending on the size of pot, age of plant and—maybe—the phase of the moon as well. There is no magic formula. Successful growers are those who have come to know their plants, and can tell what to do from the look of them, the feel of the soil and the weather prospects. A stem or tuber just sprouting green leaves obviously wants to grow and is asking for refreshment; flowering and fruiting are usually (though not always) the culmination of the growing season and a sign for a rest. When in doubt, it is safest not to water. It is often a matter of waiting for the plant to make the first move.

In a general collection most of the succulents can be accustomed to the typical European and American routine: grow in summer, rest in winter. This

means that, as long as they have healthy roots and are favourably situated for light, warmth and aeration, they can be given a good soaking in the summer months as often as the soil dries right out. Aim to soak all the soil: merely damping the surface encourages surface rooting. In autumn, watering should be tapered off. Thereafter, the thinner-leaved and less xerophytic species need occasional watering to prevent excessive wilting and leaf drop, but highly succulent types can be kept almost or quite dry until spring. Spraying the air to increase humidity on mild, bright days in winter is helpful, especially in electrically heated glasshouses where evaporation is high, and in centrally heated rooms. A watering can with a long, slender spout is ideal for getting the water inside the rim of small pots.

Overhead watering with tap water may leave unsightly grey markings on stems and leaves if the water is hard.

Right (6.2): The Lithops salicola *on the right is well grown and resembles the plant as found in nature. That on the left has been overfed.*

Below right (6.3): These tuberous crassulas die down to soil level for part of the year, and proper observance of a dry resting period is important.

Below: Many cacti benefit by being kept cool and dry in winter, like these natives of Colorado (top, 6.4). A month after the first watering of spring (bottom, 6.5) they are plump again. The shrinkage is normal.

6: CULTIVATION

Some cultivators prefer to use rain water, but it should be stored in a covered vessel and free of algae and other contamination. Watering from below is an excellent alternative to overhead watering, where it can be arranged. Some form of trough is needed that can be filled and then drained completely after the top soil in each pot shows damp. If the collection is small enough, each pot can be plunged separately in water to achieve the same effect. Remember, though, that this technique rapidly impoverishes the soil by washing away nutrients in solution. If annual repotting is not practicable, a programme of controlled liquid feeding must be adopted.

Some dwarf cacti shrink considerably during the winter rest, and in the natural habitat may even disappear below soil level. The contrast between the plants when dormant and after the first waterings of spring is often striking (6.4, 5). The shrinkage is normal, and one should not be tempted to water out of season — they will revive when the time is ripe.

Succulents under cover

A sunny windowsill is often the starting point for a collection, and many succulents are admirably suited to the highly unnatural conditions of directional lighting, draughts and extremes of micro-climate typical of a twentieth-century centrally heated sitting room. A site over a radiator does not suit the "desert" cacti, which pass the winter best in a cool, dry, dormant state; here the choice is better limited to tropical euphorbias (E. milii

20. 6, and allies), *Sansevieria, Peperomia* and the like.

On a windowsill that receives no direct sun the choice is even more restricted. *Gasteria* and *Haworthia* thrive if frost is excluded, but weak and untypical growth results for most other succulents. Such sills can, however, be put to good use for overwintering potted succulents that spend their summers out in the open. In Canada and the USA some collections are grown under artificial lighting to be entirely independent of direct sunshine. Some cacti can be flowered from seed without ever having seen the sun.

Keeping out the cold. In frosty areas a glasshouse — or its diminutive, a frame — is the dream of every cactophile. Where winters are not too severe, an unheated structure can cater for a modest range of cacti, agaves, echeverias, etc — the sort of plants mentioned below as hardy succulents. In some countries where winters are very cold, heating costs are prohibitive, but enterprising growers dig up the plants from their unheated glass-houses in the autumn and store them dry, wrapped in paper, in a frost-free basement during the winter. It says much for the adaptability of cacti that many of them put up with this drastic treatment and seem little the worse for it.

A glasshouse can be home-made (6.6) or purchased, free-standing or lean-to, glazed all over or on top only, and highly diverse in size, shape and construction. Every degree rise in minimum winter temperature means a bigger fuel bill, and

the grower must consider whether he really needs the delicate tropical succulents and, if so, how to house them most economically. A polythene tent in one corner of the glasshouse, directly over the heat source, is one answer. Another is to take the treasures into the home for the winter. My own 7½m (24ft) metal-framed glasshouse (6.7) is divided into three sections by glass partitions with doors: one half is kept cool (that is, with frost exclusion only) for the general collection, a central quarter is kept warmer for propagation and tropical succulents, and the end quarter has no heat, apart from what filters through from the warm section. Although drops below freezing occur, this cold section sustains a varied collection, mostly of cacti, and they respond with copious flowers after being kept dry and dormant from about October to March. In the cool section I aim to maintain a winter minimum of 4°C (40°F), although brief drops below this may occur in the coldest weather. In the central warm part the minimum is around 10°C (50°F). The large propagator is set at 21°C (70°F), with the shelf above it reserved for melocacti and discocacti.

Right (6.6): This glasshouse, built by an engineer, is glazed in plastic and can be opened in summer to admit more air. Most commercial greenhouses have too few vents.

Below (6.7): Succulents displayed in the cool section of the author's glasshouse. Guests are expected — hence the exhibits. The square plastic pots save space and are unobtrusive.

6: CULTIVATION

A second, reserve source of heat is advisable, particularly in these days of power cuts and fuel crises. A popular arrangement I have adopted in my two heated sections is an electric fan heater supplemented during the coldest months (January to March in England) by an oil lamp. As the electric heaters are controlled by a thermostat, they cut out when the oil lamps provide enough heat, and come on only during the coldest spells. Thermostatic control is also possible for oil lamps now. Natural gas, where available, has proved a reliable economical source of heat, because the fumes do not need to be ducted outside the glasshouse, as they do with coal gas. Indeed, they provide carbon dioxide, a plant food. The old-fashioned coke or coal boiler is more suited to larger collections and nurseries, but is more trouble to keep going.

Light and air. In selecting or designing a glasshouse, light and ventilation should be given high priority. Most succulent growers favour metal frames because they are narrower than wooden ones and obstruct the light less. Manufacturers tend to economize by not including enough ventilators: it pays to have extra ones fitted to allow a good through draught in summer—the best safeguard against scorching. Sheet plastic has certain advantages over glass because it is light and easy to work and transmits more ultra-violet radiation (6.6). But plastic is expensive and needs replacing

when it becomes discoloured, hazy or brittle. The polythene-covered balloon house favoured by some commercial growers is suitable for mass raising of seedlings. Many amateurs line at least a part of their glasshouses with polythene in winter. This "double-glazing" reduces heat loss and prevents drips from an old and leaking roof, although additional drips from condensation may form within. The main drawback is reduction of light at the time of year when it is most needed. A properly double-glazed glasshouse would probably pay for itself in a few years from the saving in fuel bills.

A glasshouse should preferably run east-west and be sited well clear of trees, walls and other sources of shade—a placement not easy in crowded urban areas. Painting house and garden walls white as reflectors can make up for some loss of light. A good compromise is a lean-to structure facing south.

Aims and methods. How a glasshouse of succulents is maintained depends on whether your plants are being grown for exhibition, or private amusement or for study, and how much time you are prepared to spend on their upkeep. It is possible to maintain a large and varied collection in presentable shape with suprisingly little fuss. That is why succulents are ideal for the businessman who has to be away from home for frequent short periods. Watering is by hosepipe—all or nothing—and repotting

when it cries out to be done. Automatic vents take care to some extent of daily temperature fluctuations, and an annual soaking with systemic pesticide keeps down the worst of the attackers. The busy owner may only really see his plants when taking visitors around, but the knowledge that they are there, a source of silent admiration, of escape from harsh reality and the noisy routine of city life, provides just that outlet we all so dearly need. I doubt if any other type of plant collection can offer so much in a small space and in return for so little.

At the other extreme we have the single-minded plantsman who lives for his plants, and is prepared to spend long hours grooming and caring for them. Many such devotees become experts in the more tricky and temperamental groups: the dwarf Mesembryanthemaceae, the Stapelieae, the tropical caudiciforms. It is to these dedicated folk that the conservationist turns as the hope for preserving rarities from habitats fast disappearing under the plough. For the

Right (6.8): An attractive miscellany of Monocotyledons displayed at La Mortola in Italy: small aloes in the foreground, large grey agaves behind, and for the background tall yuccas and (right) a **Dasylirion** *with oddly plumed leaf tips.*

Below (6.9): Cylindrical jointed **Opuntia** *species and columnar cerei in a large private garden on Majorca. Frosts are not unknown, restricting to some extent the choice of succulents in the open.*

6: CULTIVATION

exhibitor, watering must be done individually and repotting at least once a year, giving him the chance to weed out unsightly or malformed specimens, and discard or repropagate them. He resists the urge to overcrowd or put up too many shelves that would shade the plants below. There are a surprising number of such specialist collections around, unknown to the general public. The immaculate glasshouse of a perfectionist has to be seen to be believed.

Outdoor cultivation in warm countries

Fortunate indeed are those whose climate allows them to grow succulents without the expense of heated glasshouses. This is possible, and widely practised, in southern Europe and the southern USA, in parts of South Africa and Australia, and in the north island of New Zealand. Frosts are not unknown in many of these areas, but are sufficiently slight to allow a wide choice of the more robust succulents to thrive unprotected.

Where the summers are hot and dry, as in California, many succulents are better suited than mesophytes for garden use, and are becoming increasingly popular as their peculiar attractiveness is more appreciated[2]. The sculptural effect of the noble, stiff leaves of agaves, the organ-pipe columns of cerei and the soft, fleshy foliage of the lowly ice-plants create a landscape that is unique and compelling. Great scope for artistic design lies in blending plants and garden ornaments with the architectural background.

Your own slice of desert. Succulents can be utilized in various ways. Sloping ground or raised beds provide the ideal site for a general collection, with the free use of rocks beneath which the roots can find anchorage and moisture (6.10). The soil should be porous but nutritious—sand alone has no food value—and a top dressing of grit or shingle is advisable to prevent the plant lying on wet soil. It also helps to keep down weeds, and provides a contrasting plain background to show off the special geometry of "desert" plants. Other xerophytes, not strictly succulent, such as *Yucca, Nolina* and *Dasylirion,* fit in well with the display (6.8). Examples of landscaping with succulents can be seen on the grand scale at the Huntington Botanical Gardens in California, and in southern Europe (6.1, 8, 9, 10). For the choice of plants it is best to find a local supplier, because growth conditions vary in so many ways from one country to another.

On a smaller scale, succulents can be employed singly or in groups to fill corners too hot and dry for other plants and can be planted in decorative containers for terraces and patios. But despite their ability to withstand drought, they will benefit from watering if the summers are hot and rainless.

Ground cover and basket plants. Succulents offer a wide choice of ground-cover plants, which are especially welcome for clothing bare soil in places too parched for grass. A long list could be drawn up of shrubby Mesembryanthemaceae: they come in a variety of leaf forms and flower colours, and many are showier than the original ice-plant, *Mesembryanthemum crystallinum.* White-leaved senecios such as *S. serpens* and *S. kleiniiformis* contrast effectively with the darker foliage of creeping sedums such as *S. stahlii* and *S. spurium.* Echeverias, with their neat rosettes, are highly diverse in form and flowering.

Another use of succulents is in hanging baskets (6.16), where a lapse in watering may be fatal to mesophytes. For many kinds this is the ideal means of presentation, because it matches the way they grow in nature on cliffs and escarpments. A short list of the more obvious choices would include the rat's tail cactus (*Aporocactus flagelliformis*), *Sedum morganianum* and its hybrids, *Ceropegia woodii* and allied species, several crassulas (*C. rupestris,* for example), any of the 60 or so species of *Rhipsalis,* and *Senecio rowleyanus.*

Sunshades. For those wishing to specialize in succulents, the range of species can be extended by attention to their special needs. For instance, in much of California the fierce summer sun combined with drought upsets succulents

Right (6.10): Succulents bring a touch of the exotic to gardens at Eze on the Mediterranean Coast where they relish the frost-free climate, high light intensity and sea breezes.

Below (6.11): Cacti by the thousand in a commercial nursery in southern California. The yellow-spined plants are **Echinocactus grusonii** *,the 'Golden Barrel'; on the left, fine specimens of* **Agave victoria-reginae.**

that are accustomed to different cycles of growth and dormancy. Partial shade is the answer for these, and it can be provided in two ways. The first makes use of a natural screen by planting suitable xerophytic shrubs and grouping the more delicate succulents beneath them. The second is the lath house, with slats but no glass, which not only breaks the full force of the sun in summer but also protects against an occasional frost in winter. In moist tropical countries such as India, protective structures are also needed to keep off the excessive rains.

Where the frost bites

In countries where glasshouse culture is a necessity, collectors are intrigued by the possibility of growing succulents outdoors, unprotected, all the year round. The emphasis is on exotic and cactiform types here: the truly hardy sedums, sempervivums and lewisias come more within the province of rock garden and alpine fans. Since the war years I have annually planted out surplus succulents to test them for hardiness, first in London and later in Reading (6.12-14). Especially prepared sloping beds are used, against a white south wall. The soil is extra porous, over coarse drainage material, and rocks are used as much as possible to isolate the succulents from wet surroundings. Fog and damp are a worse enemy than low temperatures (6.14). Where a plant is valued, a duplicate of it can be kept as a reserve under glass.

The novel effect of an "outdoor desert" is well worth trying, even if some replanting is needed after a severe winter. In the trials I have made with cacti, *Opuntia robusta, O. rastrera,* (6.12), *O. polyacantha* and *O. humifusa* proved the most enduring. Globular cacti rarely last more than five years, *Lobivia silvestrii* (6.13) and *Echinocereus viridiflorus* being two of the best. Mexican agaves include a few that are hardy: *Agave parryi, A. lophantha,* and (with luck) *A. americana.* The danger is water collecting in the centre of the crown and causing rot. Of the Mesembryanthemaceae, I find *Ruschia uncinata* (6.12,11.9) by far the toughest; of the Aloineae, *Aloe aristata* (13.9). *Crassula sarcocaulis* (6.12), in its red and white forms, is highly recommended. For ground cover, annual *Portulaca* (5.3, 12.1) and *Dorotheanthus* (11.10) may be sown. Along with these true succulents can be associated borderline succulents such as *Yucca, Cordyline australis* and some species of *Dasylirion,* as well as spiky *Colletia, Eryngium, Acanthus* and others that blend well with the general "desert" effect. My choice is necessarily personal: I can speak only for those I have tried. The door is wide open for experimentation, and different areas will no doubt produce different selections of suitable plants.

As distinct from permanent plantings, many of the larger, tougher succulents may be put outdoors during the summer, either in pots or troughs, or plunged in a bedding display. The largest and spikiest plants are kept in pots for ease of handling; the smaller, unarmed species are bedded, lifted in the autumn when frosts are expected and then packed under the glasshouse staging with some earth covering the roots until they are ready for planting out again the following spring. The main problem, apart from specimens growing too massive to carry, is the danger of introducing pests and weeds into the glasshouse when the outdoor plants are brought in for the winter. But such displays look after themselves during the summer, and their novel appearance excites much comment from passers-by.

Soil or no-soil?

Soil mixtures recommended for succulents are legion. One book tabulates 25 for cacti alone. All of them are presumably based upon the author's intuition, because no experimental evidence is cited, and none in the least resembles the soil in which I have seen cacti growing in nature. The prospective newcomer may well close such a book in despair and settle for a less exacting hobby. In practice, however, most growers use a single compost throughout, with only minor modifications for epiphytes (which need an extra-rich medium) and rot-sensitive kinds (for which extra grit is added). Their success indicates that succulents by and large are not fussy: the basic needs for nitrogen (N), potassium (K), phosphorus (P) and lesser amounts of other minerals *(trace elements)* are much as in other plants. Thus we need consider only three

points in determining the medium to use: (1) it must be porous and drain freely, to permit ample aeration to the roots; (2) it must supply a correct balance of nutrients in dilute solution; (3) it must support the plant.

The choice today is between two types of more or less artificial media: a traditional loam-based compost, and an inert medium to which nutrients are added—the so-called soilless composts. Both have proved equally successful in the hands of different growers. Of the loam-based mixtures, the John Innes formulae remain unsurpassed after more than 40 years. A good loam (seven parts) is tempered by coarse sand (two parts) to improve drainage and peat (three parts) to add humus and water-retaining properties. A base fertilizer supplies N, P and K in slow-acting form, and contains enough lime (calcium hydroxide or carbonate) to ensure that the mix is just on the acid side (pH about 6.5) of neutral (pH is defined in the Glossary). Composts 1, 2 and 3 contain respectively one, two and three doses of the fertilizer, and a separate compost is available for seed raising. For rooting cuttings, a mixture of sifted peat

Three views of the author's outdoor plantings. Top right (6.12): Opuntia rastrera, *white and red-flowered* Crassula sarcocaulis *and, in between, pink* Ruschia uncinata; Agave lecheguilla *at top right.*

Right (6.13): Lobivia silvestrii *(better known as* Chamaecereus silvestrii*), the popular 'Peanut Cactus', is surprisingly hardy if it is grown in a sufficiently sheltered site.*

Below (6.14): A mantle of snow protects plants from very low temperatures. But the danger is rot from waterlogging afterwards. This Agave coarctata *survived many years without any form of protection.*

6: CULTIVATION

and coarse sand in equal parts is the norm. All the above materials are—or should be—sterile; only the loam requires special sterilization by heat or chemical means to kill unwanted pests and disease spores. English loam is rarely deficient in trace elements: where that is a problem, correctives must be added. These John Innes composts were developed primarily for non-succulent glasshouse crops, and for succulents cautious growers like to add extra grit to increase the drainage. Some sundriesmen offer a ready-made "cactus compost" adapted in this way. The greatest snag is the loam: an indefinable ingredient that varies from place to place, and is increasingly difficult to obtain in good form. Another problem is that peat is difficult to wet again once it becomes dry. A mixture of leaf mould and sand, favoured by some, may have the necessary nutrients, but varies from source to source, and needs sterilization before use.

Because of these snags, many have gone over to loam-free formulae. The UC Soil Mix, developed by the University of California, uses sharp sand and peat moss with six added chemicals to provide food initially[3]. Levington Compost has a peat basis, without sand, and with enough added nutrients for 6 to 8 weeks of normal growth[4]. For either, subsequent watering includes dissolved nutrients, which for succulents should be high in potash and low in nitrogen. Commercial brands of tomato fertilizer are adequate, and can also be used for plants in loam composts when they are overdue for repotting. But never give fertilizer to dormant succulents, unrooted cuttings, or in an attempt to accelerate weakly specimens.

Choosing a container

The act of confining a cactus in a small pot is a radical departure from its normal way of life, where roots spread widely and seek the shelter and moisture of rock crevices. Porous clay pots allow quick drying out and—if exposed to prolonged hot sun—scorching and death of the fine root tips. Plastic pots are less susceptible to this, but there is the opposite danger of waterlogging in damp, dull weather. Standing porous pots on a bed of shingle, or half plunging them, lessens the danger of baking, as does communal planting of small succulents in pans or troughs. In any glasshouse collection it is worth making at least one bed where the plants can be set out in open soil, if only to see a select few of the larger growing species at their best (1.4). Tall cerei, for instance, flower much more profusely when bedded than when kept in pots. But management of beds is more difficult, because some specimens easily become too large and smother the remainder. It is also important to leave gaps for access for removal of weeds and general clearing up.

For indoor culture, plants are commonly displayed in troughs or bowls, which can range from the plain and functional to the elaborately ornate, often costing more than the plants they contain (6.15). If the display is to be permanent, the container must be deep enough for a good layer of soil, 6-8cm (2¼-3in), plus drainage crocks, which are doubly important if there is no outlet for water.

Right (6.15): Decorative containers add much to the presentation of exhibition specimens. In this case **Sarcocaulon burmannii** *is well displayed in an attractive ceramic pot.*

Below (6.16): A veteran plant of **Haworthia batesiana** *has been unpotted, inverted, bound with plastic cord and suspended like a basket: a novel mode of presentation.*

6: CULTIVATION

Raising plants from seed

Those who buy only adult specimens for their collection miss half the fun of life with succulents. They can never know the deep satisfaction that comes from seeing the first flower on a plant of their own raising from seed. Seedlings are often unlike the adult plant and have a special charm of their own: like kittens, some are never so delightful when they grow up. Elaborate equipment is not needed for raising seedlings. Many first attempts begin on a sunny windowsill in summer, and a domestic airing cupboard over a hot-water tank can be pressed into service for germination, although light is needed when green sprouts appear.

Germination of succulents is not basic-ally different from that of mesophytes. It requires moisture and warmth, and the seedlings will need gradual acclimatization to the cruel world outside. In nature, only those seedlings that come up in the rainy season in the shade of rocks or other plants are likely to survive. Depending on the size of the seed, its stores of food are exhausted more or less rapidly, so if you sow on an inert medium such as sand, growth will be checked unless the seedlings are fed or pricked out on to a more nutritious compost.

For germination a minimum temperature of 15°C (59°F) is needed; up to 25°C (79°F) will do no harm. There are many ready-made propagators on the market, but a handyman can make his own (6.18). Some are quite elaborate, with separate heater cables above and below soil level, and these can be used for raising both seed and cuttings.

Spring is the ideal time for sowing seed (6.17), and the seedlings are best kept warm and watered throughout their first winter. John Innes Seed Compost or a peat sand mixture can be used after passing through a sieve to separate the coarse particles, which are used as drainage with the fine residue on top. Tiny seeds should not be covered; with larger ones the old rule applies, that you cover them for their own depth. Sifted grit is a good top dressing, because the particles, give support and leverage to the emerging seedlings. It is a common mistake to sow

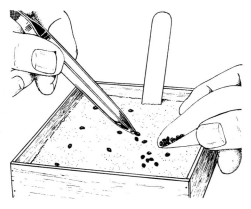

Seed raising (6.17): Plant the label first, then scatter the seeds thinly, using forceps to spread them evenly. Mix dustlike seeds with fine sand to avoid overcrowding.

Fine seeds need no covering; for others the rule is grit to the same depth as the seed diameter. Grit particles give leverage to support the emerging seedling.

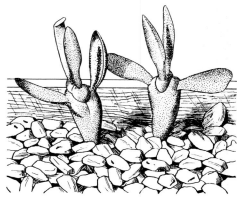

Seedlings of **Euphorbia gorgonis** ready for pricking out. Growth will suffer a check if seedlings get overcrowded. **Euphorbia** seeds are large enough to plant individually.

seed too thickly: pricking out the forest of tiny plantlets is then difficult. It is better to sow thinly so that they can be left to develop their first shoots before the need to transplant. Provided they do not starve, the fact that they come to touch one another will not matter.

To maintain an even, humid atmosphere in a seed pan, it is usual to cover it

Below left (6.18): Seed raising over a radiator. The seed pan is enveloped in a polythene bag, and watering is automatic by a wick siphon recharged from an upturned bottle.

Below (6.19): Fortnight-old seedlings of **Conicosia** *with two fleshy cotyledons and the seed coat borne at their tips. The first foliage leaf is seen on the right.*

with glass or polythene and, if exposed to direct sunlight, with paper or some other material that will diffuse the light. Gradually the glass is raised and the shading removed as growth proceeds. Some growers put their pots of seed inside sealed polythene bags and leave them for several weeks, until the plants are large enough for pricking out. As long as the pot is clean and the soil sterile, all should be well. If seedlings elongate and go pale and leggy, it is a sign that they are getting too little light and air.

Some seeds—those of Stapelieae, for instance—germinate in from two to four days under favourable conditions; any not up within a fortnight can be counted as lost. Others take longer, or appear

erratically: *Othonna* for example. A few germinate better the second season than the first. With these one must be patient and not discard the seed pan too soon. Instead, leave it to dry right out in the sun, stir up the topsoil, water it, and return it to the propagator. Erratic germination is an advantage in nature: if all seedlings came up at once, a severe drought or other natural disaster would kill every one and leave nothing in reserve.

Thus we find many mechanisms, both mechanical and chemical, that retard germination. *Opuntia* seeds, for example, have a thick, waterproof coat and usually germinate only after exposure to a cold winter. Some growers recommend refrigerating them before sowing.

6: CULTIVATION

Failures are sometimes due to the seed being old or non-viable. If in doubt, and if the seed is not too tiny, cut one open: this can be done conveniently with a pair of blade-and-anvil secateurs. The contents should be plump and white. If they are shrunken or discoloured, the answer is obvious. Another test for seed is to stir it up in water. Good seeds usually sink; any that float should be rejected. Freshly harvested seeds from your own plants usually germinate better than packaged seeds, especially if these are old.

Vegetative propagation

Although the only practicable way to propagate a few succulents (*Ariocarpus, Astrophytum, Frithia, Euphorbia obesa*), is from seed, most lend themselves more or less readily to vegetative multiplication by division (6.20), offsets, suckers, cuttings (6.21), adventitious buds or grafting. Having their own internal water store, they suffer less than most plants from the temporary interruption to water intake. Vegetatively propagated plants have a head start over seedlings, and are genetically identical with their parent. For hybrids that are sterile or do not come true from seed, these are the only means.

To begin, all that is needed is a pan of "cuttings mixture": sifted sharp sand and peat in equal amounts. This should be put in a warm but slightly shaded part of the glasshouse. If extra heat is not available, the warmer months of summer are the best time; with bottom heat one is less dependent on the season. Before planting, a cutting should be left on an airy, light shelf until the wound has sealed itself with a protective callus layer. If set directly in moist soil it would probably start to rot. According to the size of the cut area, three to four days' drying in summer will suffice for most, but longer does no harm, and a degree of wilting predisposes some to root. In autumn or winter it is sometimes best to leave the cuttings until spring before planting. It pays to have patience and avoid rushing things. Many growers recommend dipping the cut surface in hormone rooting powder.

When planting a cutting, it is wise to avoid burying the base too deeply. If the cutting is top-heavy, it should be supported by a small stick or stone so that only the base comes in contact with the rooting medium (6.22). Rooting ability varies widely, even within one genus. Where difficulty is encountered, one should experiment with cuttings of different sizes and taken at different times of the year. *Euphorbia,* for instance, is more trouble than most cacti and rots if overwatered. One should wash off all traces of the milky, irritant sap and allow ample time for callusing before inserting it in the rooting medium.

Single leaves of most of the Crassulaceae will regenerate plants, and so will leaves of some haworthias (those with softer foliage) and most gasterias; aloes and Mesembryanthemaceae hardly ever. But any broken portion of a succulent is worth a try. One of the many delights of the hobby is experimenting to find new ways of raising rarities, so that you have continuous stocks for replacement and sharing. And in the process you will endear yourself to the conservationist.

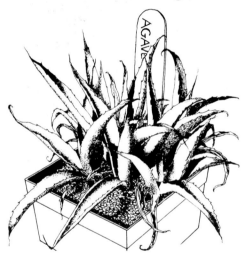

Repotting sequence (6.20): This neglected agave is potbound and unsightly. Repotting is best undertaken at the start of the growing season, and with the soil on the dry side.

Tap the plant out of its pot either by banging with a trowel handle, as shown, or by inverting and thumping the rim of the pot on a table edge while supporting the plant.

Tease away weeds and old soil and trim back any dead roots. Remove offsets if desired, for propagation purposes. Remove withered leaves or trim back with scissors.

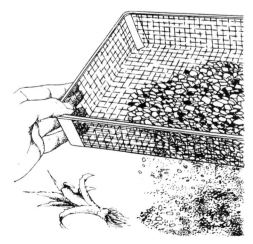

Screen fresh potting compost through an 8mm (1/3in) sieve and put the coarse residue in a clean pot to act as drainage material. Compost should be moist, not dust dry.

Spread the roots evenly and dribble the soil in, thumping the pot at intervals and using fingers or the trowel handle to firm the soil. But do not ram it down too solidly.

The final result: a smart, presentable agave and spare plants to pot up or give to friends. Do not forget to include the label: a name lost may be hard to replace.

Taking cuttings

(6.21): Some suggestions for propagating succulents by taking cuttings. Often the shape of a plant can be improved, and cutting off tall stems encourages basal growth and a bushy habit.

The red lines show where the cuttings should be made.

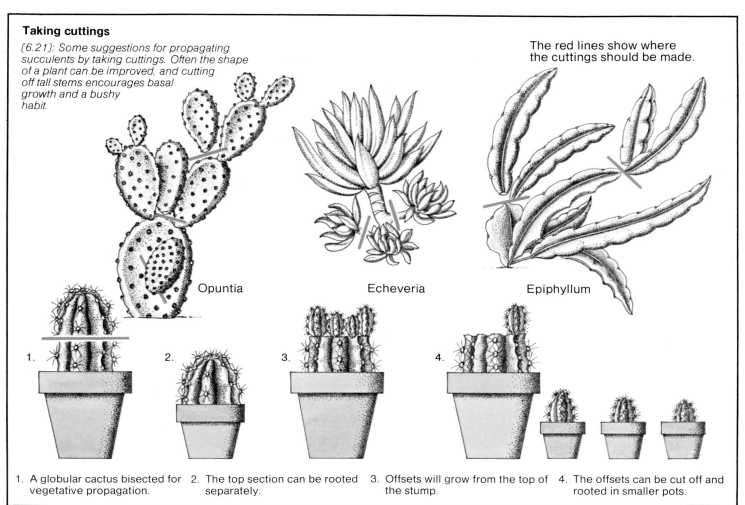

Opuntia   Echeveria   Epiphyllum

1. A globular cactus bisected for vegetative propagation.

2. The top section can be rooted separately.

3. Offsets will grow from the top of the stump.

4. The offsets can be cut off and rooted in smaller pots.

Rooting cuttings

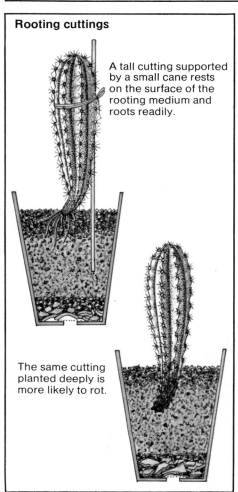

A tall cutting supported by a small cane rests on the surface of the rooting medium and roots readily.

The same cutting planted deeply is more likely to rot.

Left (6.22): Stem cuttings should be allowed to heal over the cut surface before planting in rooting medium. A pot three-quarters full of soil topped by sand and peat can be used.

Below (6.23): Some succulents are easy to propagate. Kalanchoe daigremontiana *produces adventitious buds on leaf margins that drop off and generate daughter plants.*

6: CULTIVATION

Grafting

The technique for making one plant grow on the roots of another has been known at least since the time of Aristotle, in whose surviving writings we read: "Grafting of one on another is better in the case of trees which are similar and have the same proportions." Grafting is a useful means of accelerating growth and flowering in slow-growing species, of preserving rot-sensitive rarities and cristates, and of saving a plant that has been all but lost by rot or misadventure (6.24). It consists of bringing the cut surface of a strong root system (the *stock*) into intimate contact with the cut base of the desired plant (the *scion*) and encouraging the organic union between the two. It is much used by nurserymen, particularly on the continent of Europe and in Japan, for bringing novelties onto the market in the shortest possible time. It is mainly practised among Cactaceae, which usually unite very readily, but can also be performed with euphorbias, pachypodiums (6.25), Crassulaceae and Stapelieae. The stock and scion, as our quotation above suggests. must be more or less close relatives. For cacti, various *Echinopsis, Cereus* and *Harrisia* stocks are favourites in Europe, and the more tender *Pereskiopsis, Hylocereus* and *Myrtillocactus* in warmer countries. *Ceropegia* tubers make a good stock for delicate Stapelieae.

Even quite tiny seedlings can be grafted, and this has been the means of preserving curious mutants of cacti lacking green chlorophyll (6.27), which would normally die as soon as the food store in the seed was used up. On a green stock they can be kept going as long as green tissue is there to feed them: as soon as it begins to cork over from old age, regrafting on a new stock is necessary.

Although grafting is an immense asset

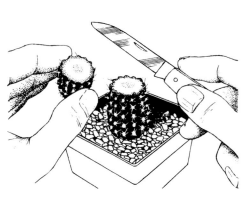

Grafting sequence (6.24): The **Echinopsis** stock has been topped with a sharp knife. It should be actively growing and pest-free; the cut should look clean and full of sap.

Bevelling the top of the stock. If this is not done, the soft centre is apt to shrink into a hollow and part company from the scion at a later stage in the grafting process.

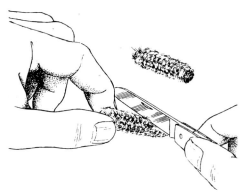

Trimming the scion. This **Wilcoxia schmollii** has a slender stem, so it is cut obliquely to expose a larger surface and to make it easier to clamp on to the stock.

Matching stock and scion surfaces. The two rings of vascular bundles are superimposed as nearly as possible and the cut surfaces brought together before they start to dry out.

An elastic band secures the scion in place. Great pressure causing distortion of the tissues is not needed. The pot now goes in a warm, moist half-shaded position for a week.

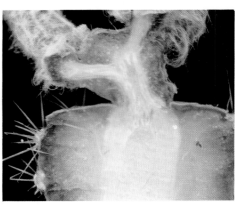

Vertical section of this graft of **Wilcoxia** on **Echinopsis** one year later. Normal vertical branches have grown up, and continuity of the vascular system across the join is complete.

to nurserymen and a means of saving the otherwise unsaveable, it can change the look of a plant if the stock is too vigorous. Botanists are therefore wary of grafted specimens, and for show purposes a plant on its own roots always has preference.

Controlling pests

A glasshouse collection of succulents is little troubled by pests since the development of "systemics". A *systemic insecticide* is one that is absorbed through the surface of the plant, above or below ground, and remains within the cells to poison any chewing or biting creatures. One or two good soakings of each plant annually should cope with such smaller pests as scale, mealy bug (6.26), root bug and aphis. *Systemic fungicides,* which deal in similar fashion with fungi, are a more recent development and offer great promise if they can lessen the incidence of rot.

It is a mistake to place all one's faith in a single product, however, because in time resistance builds up and the cure loses its effectiveness. There is thus still room for such old-fashioned contact insecticides as nicotine and derris. A few crystals of paradichlorobenzene put in the bottom of a pot when repotting is a good deterrent against soil pests. Malathion preparations have proved excellent for protecting succulents, even the Crassulaceae, despite the makers' caution against using them on this Family. Individual brands are not named here because new preparations are continually coming onto the market. Some of the best are also

Below (6.25): The fat juicy stems of Pachypodium *readily unite as grafts, as well as with the allied genus* Adenium *(centre). This has proved helpful for preserving rarities.*

6: CULTIVATION

the most poisonous, so cultivators are strongly urged to read the instructions fully, avoid direct contact with the substance, and refrain as much as possible from inhaling the fumes.

The hot, close conditions inside a propagator are favourable to the growth of rot fungi, to which some succulents (Stapelieae, for instance) are especially susceptible. Watering with mild fungicides such as Chinosol (Potassium oxyquinoline sulphate) or Cheshunt Compound (ammonium carbonate, 11 parts; copper sulphate, two parts) takes care of these. Sciara flies are especially troublesome when composts contain much humus; the currently recommended deterrent is Diazinon.

Succulents are more susceptible than most plants to rot. It seems as if, in the dry, bright conditions of their native lands, they have built up no resistance to the cosmopolitan decay bacteria and fungi that flourish in moister, cooler conditions. At the first sign of soft black or brown patches on a succulent, all infected areas should be cut away back to sound tissue, with a sharp knife, and the plant kept dry in a light, airy place until the wounds have healed. Dusting the exposed tissue with powdered charcoal, or with a powdered fungicide such as flowers of sulphur, helps. If a succulent collapses from rot at the base, the stem tips can be similarly trimmed back, and treated as cuttings or grafted. Euphorbias and caudiciform plants are more difficult to save than the average cactus once rot gets into their system. Rot is encouraged by overwatering and overfeeding, by too cold or too close an atmosphere, and by anything generally adverse to growth. Some collectors regularly spray their plants with Chinosol or Cheshunt Compound as a precaution; others place faith in systemic fungicides.

A cactophile's progress

Overall, the grower of succulents has fewer worries from pests than the cultivators of many other flowers and vegetables. It has been said with some truth that a cactophile spends the first half of his life trying to make his plants grow, and the second half trying to stop them. Overcrowding soon becomes a problem, no matter how large one's glasshouse, especially if seed is raised. Although one can go on adding shelves and hanging baskets, there comes a point when the plants are no longer accessible and begin

Below (6.26): Less of a menace now than before the introduction of improved insecticides, the mealy bug (here on **Opuntia**) *is about 2mm ($^1/_{12}$in) long and covered in protective white wax.*

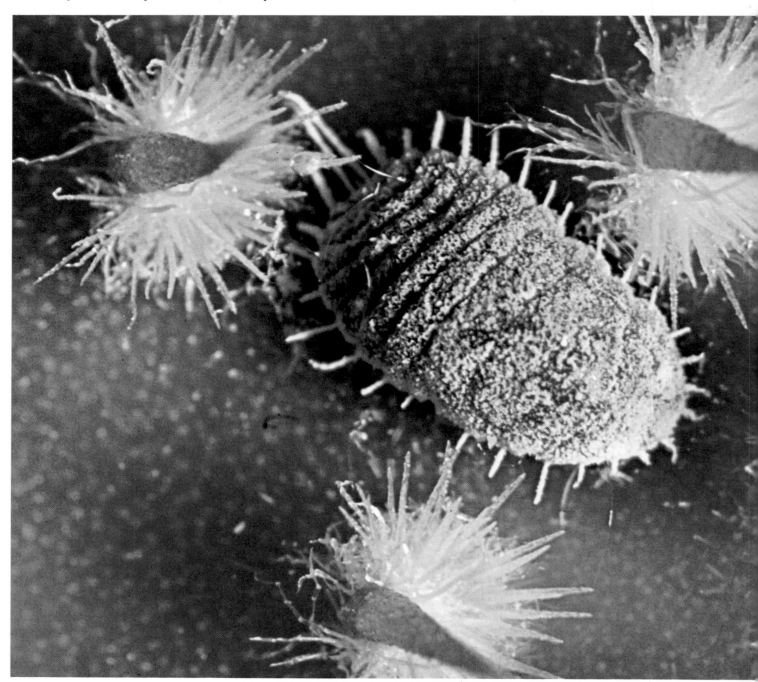

to suffer from shading and neglect. Further hazards are discovered by visitors, who are almost afraid to move for fear of being stabbed and speared. Succulents are amazingly tolerant: many not only respond to annual repotting with vigorous growth and blooms, but if left alone in the same pot for years look none the worse. However, there is little fun in nursing mummified relics, and the grower has to be strong-minded and refuse additions unless he is prepared to part with others to make room. The adding and bartering is very much a part of the hobby. Often the outcome is that the cactophile turns specialist, concentrating on a single genus or group. This is both satisfying to the grower, who becomes an expert on his own chosen favourites, and helpful to the conservationist by ensuring survival of plants endangered in habitat.

Most succulents flower annually once they are mature, although they might miss in a poor season or if badly grown. Proper observation of the resting period is important: a plant forced into continuous growth may become a huge specimen but fail to bloom (6.2). Unbalanced nutrition, such as an excess of nitrogen, can have a similar effect. On the other hand, many succulents flower on the new growth, so that a plant that has not grown cannot be expected to oblige. Lack of sunshine is one of the commonest causes of failure to bloom in a country such as England, where an exceptionally fine summer can be a great stimulus to flower production. For a beginner seeking free-flowering succulents, the best advice is to visit specialist nurseries in the early summer and pick out plants in bloom.

Photographers find succulents extraordinarily attractive. The challenge of capturing a rare bloom at its peak of perfection, which may occupy a single night only *(Discocactus)* or less than an hour *(Anacampseros* 12.3) is made doubly testing by the vagaries of the weather. A cactus flower may close up within minutes as clouds darken the sky.

The botanically minded keep records of their plants in a loose-leaf book or card index, giving each specimen an accession number—78/1, 78/2 etc—that remains permanently with the specimen even though the name on the label may change in the light of new knowledge. Facts on where the plant originated, its flowering, fruiting and seed set, and so forth can be added as desired. Records of this sort can help to fill gaps in our knowledge of many common succulents.

Below (6.27): **Gymnocalycium mihanovichii** *'Ruby Ball' ('Hibotan' in Japan) needs a green rootstock to keep it going. Japan has introduced many such coloured cultivars.*

7: CONSERVATION

A Thought for the Future

"Every plant of whatsoever kind needs four things (just as an animal needs four things), namely, a definite seed, a suitable position, and properly attempered water and air. When these four conditions are fulfilled, a plant will grow and increase: but if they do not harmonize, the plant will be correspondingly weakened."

Concern over declining populations of wild plants is no recent phenomenon. Although the animal kingdom gets the lion's—or should I say tiger's?—share of public sympathy, the fate of animals does after all, depend on the survival of plants. But whereas no one can resist the cry of a suffering animal, a plant dies quietly and unnoticed.

Flora in retreat

As early as the 1930s uneasiness was being expressed in books and journals about the fact that some species of succulents were no longer as easy to find in their native habitats as they had been, and it was pointed out that a few, illustrated in early literature, had never been reported since. The classic case concerns a wonderful folio volume of hand-coloured plates of Stapelieae painted in Africa and published in 1796. The author was Francis Masson, the first botanist sent out by the Royal Botanic Gardens, Kew, to collect specimens at the Cape. Masson did his job well. He not only introduced alive many succulents still beloved of collectors—no mean feat in those days of long, slow sea voyages and hazardous travel—but also described and illustrated 41 Stapelieae, all but five of which were new to science.

But by 1900 nearly half of Masson's plants were unknown in either cultivation or habitat, and return visits to the areas where they were first found revealed no further specimens in what had become urban or cultivated land. Unlike many stories of lost plants, however, this one has a happy ending: through the intensive field studies of Harry Hall and other great students of South African botany, "Masson's Lost Stapelieae" have been rediscovered one by one, often at some distance from their original locale. With possibly a single exception, all are known to exist alive somewhere today.

Although this testifies to the extraordinary persistence and resilience of species in nature, we must not take chances or play down the dangers to other plants. What happened in South Africa is happening now in most of the homelands of succulents. In East Africa the destruction of natural habitats by overgrazing and other factors is even more widespread and thorough. Once again the Stapelieae are among the early victims, partly because they are extremely attractive to grazing animals, partly because the seedlings are dependent on shade plants in order to become established. Of the three species shown in 7.2—part of a private collection in 1963—one is now thought to be extinct, another is possibly so, and only the third is still to be found locally in the wild. All three are difficult to cultivate and continual watchfulness from specialist growers failed to guarantee their survival.

A precarious hold on life

Although the list of extinct succulents is, mercifully, still short, there are many instances where life hangs by a thread. *Saphesia flaccida* (page 135) is a distinctive member of the Mesembryanthemaceae with a long, thick caudex and unique fruit structure. It was known in cultivation in 1804 and given its scientific name by Baron Jacquin from material studied in his famous garden at Schoenbrunn near Vienna. For a period of 130 years all that was known of it was Jacquin's very fine published colour plate[1], and one specimen in the herbarium at Kew. Then in 1934 a few plants were recognized growing in the wild at Kalabas Kraal near Cape Town. By 1950 H. Herre, curator of the Stellenbosch Botanic Garden, could find only one survivor[2] in that locale and the whole area is rapidly disappearing beneath the plough. *Xerosicyos pubescens* is a curious member of the cucumber family, very different from the other known members of its genus. It was known from a single male plant, now dead, in Tananarive Botanic Garden in Madagascar; its habitat, though not exactly located, is thought to have been in that part of the island now completely cleared of wild flora.

Some succulents are more common in cultivation than in the wild. One such is *Aloe variegata,* the 'Partridge Aloe', so familiar on cottage windowsills in the Northern Hemisphere. The reason for its decline in its native South Africa is over-collecting to meet the demand for quick sales. Field collectors are much blamed for the near-extermination of rare species, but they are only one of many adverse

Right (7.1): The Hester Malan Wild Flower Reserve near Springbok in South Africa, a fine unspoiled area of mountains and valleys covering 12,000 acres. To the rich native flora are added other plants from Namaqualand.

7: CONSERVATION

factors—a serious one, but not the worst. Even the most ruthless habitat-stripper usually leaves behind a few specimens that are too large, too old, misshapen or inaccessible, whereas grazing animals, bulldozers and weedkillers make no such distinction.

Dwarf, free-flowering succulents have suffered more than most because their rising popularity in America, Europe and Japan has increased the drain on habitats. In 1968 I visited the type locality of *Mammillaria louisae,* a most alluring miniature, near Socorro in Lower California and spent an hour searching the ground with two other lynx-eyed botanists. Although this species was once abundant in that area, we found less than a dozen, and a second visit in 1974 confirmed the scarcity. What is so frustrating is that *M.louisae* is one of the easiest cacti to raise from seed, and two-

year-old plants flower and set seed readily (7.3), so there is absolutely no justification for plundering wild populations.

The introduction of the ostrich to South Africa and the goat to almost anywhere has had a profound effect on natural vegetation. The recording angel's list of crimes committed against plant lovers by goats must run to many volumes. The unique *Talinum guadalupense* (15.4) has been eaten off Guadalupe Island, 400km (250miles) south of San Diego, and survives only on rocky islets that no goats have yet reached. Goats are not choosy about their diet, and few plants are spared. Many of the more choice succulents owe their survival to the shelter of small shrubs, and once these are removed nothing can survive, and a true desert takes over.

A long list could be made of the factors responsible for the retreat of natural

vegetation: expanding cities, agriculture, mining, the building of roads and air-strips, weedkiller spraying, polluted air, overgrazing, overcollecting and so on. We cannot demand a halt to these, any more than we can expect a "Keep out" notice on a nature reserve to deter nomadic tribes in East Africa whose survival depends upon finding new grazing grounds. It is a lot easier to catalogue the causes than to supply remedies.

Is there a remedy?

Legislation to control collecting is one obvious step to take, and it has been introduced in Africa and North America. But it has its drawbacks. One is that genuine nature lovers are made to suffer along with the commercial grabbers and grubbers. Botanists and nurserymen become involved in endless paperwork to comply with the law, and the demise of

rare plants may even be hastened by placing restrictions on their free circulation in cultivation. Meanwhile, despite the laws, digging goes on, because the areas involved are too vast for adequate policing.

Nature reserves provide an ideal answer: conserve slices of the habitat

Right (7.2): Doomed succulents: **Whitesloanea crassa** *(left), presumed extinct.* **Pseudolithos cubiformis** *(centre), possibly extinct.* **P. migiurtinus** *(remaining 3 plants) still survives in habitat and as a rarity in cultivation.*

Below right (7.3): **Mammillaria louisae** *in habitat and (inset) in cultivation, where it flowers and fruits freely. There is no possible justification for digging up plants in the wild.*

Below (7.4): A closer view of the wild plants in the Hester Malan Wild Flower Reserve. The succulent shown here is **Lampranthus,** *a member of the Mesembryanthemaceae.*

7: CONSERVATION

known to be rich in endangered species. But whereas game parks for animals are many and well-publicized, the equivalents for plants are much fewer, although some of the game parks incidentally preserve plants of the area. The Hester Malan Wild Flower Reserve near Springbok in South Africa (7.1) covers 4,860 hectares (12,000 acres) of splendid, rugged, largely unspoiled country rich in endemics, and more are added from time to time to conserve the whole of the flora of Namaqualand. We need many more flower reserves, especially in South America and East Africa. Unfortunately the problems involved in setting them up and maintaining them are daunting.

Right at the start we must face up to two difficult questions: Which plants are most endangered? And where? The areas concerned are vast, and most of the sampling is limited to roadsides. This will be apparent to anyone who has flown over the known habitats in an aeroplane and noted the long gaps between where one track ends and the next begins. The going is rough on foot, and great expanses stretch toward the horizon untracked and unsurveyed.

A code of conduct

In 1968 a project was begun to record all imperilled plants in the same way that was being done for animals. Detailed data sheets for about 120 species were published in 1970 and 1971 as volume 5 of the "Red Data Book". But the number of endangered species is in excess of 20,000 and it was soon recognized that this technique would not be rapid enough, and many species would be extinct before the list could be completed and action taken. In 1974, therefore, the International Union for the Conservation of Nature and Natural Resources (I.U.C.N.) set up the "Threatened Plants Committee" with a secretariat at Kew. Information is now being gathered by regional and specialist groups, and botanic gardens are providing support by holding and propagating threatened species. Besides the preparation of detailed records for the Red Data Book, work is going ahead on regional lists of endangered species, and these are now available for Europe and North America, with others for North Africa and Arabia approaching completion.

One of the specialist groups aiding the Threatened Plants Committee is the International Organization for Succulent Plant Study (I.O.S), which first turned its attention to problems with succulents at a congress in Reading in 1973, and has

Right (7.5): A solitary aloe lives out its lonely life in the Namib Desert where aloes have grown undisturbed for millennia. Acceptance of the Code of Conduct could make all the difference between extinction and survival.

CODE OF CONDUCT

In The Field
Aim to do as little damage to natural populations of species as possible, bearing in mind that within a species there may be local races with genetic differences—the population on one hill may not be quite the same as that on the next.

Observe national and local regulations about collecting in the spirit as well as the letter:

☐ Investigate local laws on removing and exporting plants.

☐ If a permit is necessary do not collect without one.

☐ If the permit states how many plants, or the nature of the material which may be collected, abide by what it says.

☐ Make certain the plants you wish to collect are not endangered or thought to be so.

☐ It is courteous, and in your interests, when you intend to collect in a country where there is a society for succulent enthusiasts, to make yourself known to the officials of the society.

☐ Once you have the permit, collect discreetly and do not give local inhabitants the impression that the plants have commercial value.

☐ Where possible, collect seeds, cuttings or offsets, and not the whole plant. If you must take whole plants, be content with small ones.

☐ Remember that mature plants rarely transplant well and are often damaged in transit, making them useless for show purposes. Not only this, but they are needed in habitat to produce seed for regeneration.

Make careful field notes, including so far as possible, locality, altitude, type of vegetation and soil, date of collection and your own field number. Try to assess the likely number of individuals and extent of the population; observe the amount of seed-setting and frequency of seedlings. Note any possible threats, eg through urbanization, overgrazing, or the proximity of a road, and if you believe that the population or species may be endangered make a more thorough survey and report your findings to the IOS Conservation Committee or conservation committee of any local nature or cactus and succulent society.

If practicable, take photographs and/or preserve representative material, preferably fertile, for deposition in a herbarium.

In The Nursery
Aim to develop your horticultural expertise to propagate "difficult" plants successfully: propagate, propagate, propagate!

☐ Do not advertise or sell unpropagated wild plants.

☐ To act as retailer for imported plants requires no horticultural skills whatever, and encourages despoliation of natural populations.

☐ Join the increasing number of successful growers who raise from seed or cuttings.

☐ Do not purchase stock from any supplier whom you believe to be contravening any law relating to collecting or exporting, or who does not supply data in accordance with the recommendations of this Code.

☐ Attempt to propagate rare species and distribute material to IOS-affiliated Reserve Collections.

☐ Keep more than one independent clone of rare species, even self-fertile ones, for seed-production.

☐ Keep careful records of the source of all stock, especially any of known wild origin, and be very meticulous about correct labelling.

☐ Remember that the best way to maintain a species in cultivation is to distribute it widely.

☐ If your nursery is in the native country of a species you are selling, do not sell whole plants collected in the wild and grown on in the nursery unless they have first been propagated.

At Home
Make good cultivation your criterion, not the size or rarity of the plants.

☐ Do not patronize a supplier who trades in unpropagated imported plants without regard to the recommendations of this Code.

☐ Report to IOS any cases of importation of wild plants coming to your notice which you believe may infringe national or international regulations, or may have caused appreciable damage to the wild populations of a species.

☐ Maintain good records and a high standard of labelling, particularly if you specialize in certain groups.

☐ Aim to propagate rare species and assist their survival by distributing material (with available source data) to other enthusiasts.

Showing and Judging
In show schedules, compilers should indicate that more credit will be given to plants regarded as difficult to propagate than those that are rare.

Judges should not give preference to plants which are obviously imported over well-grown seedlings.

since published, among other things, a register of specialist collections of succulents in the United Kingdom[3], and a Code of Conduct that all its members are expected to follow (7.5).

Because the Code is aimed at all persons interested in any way with succulents, be they botanists, commercial growers, managers of botanical and public gardens or private enthusiasts, it is reprinted here in full.

Many lovers of succulents are sympathetic to the cause, and ask: "How can I help?". The Code provides the answers. It is not intended as a deterrent to private collectors: indeed, well-documented collections are an essential asset to the conservation movement. But anything that can discourage bulk exporting from the habitats is good: if plants are allowed abroad at all (and several countries now have strict legislation for both exporting and importing) they should go where they are to be used as a source of study or propagation.

By way of example, I recall a memorable visit to a mountain in the Kango Valley region of South Africa in 1971, when I was privileged to see the rare and much sought after *Haworthia graminifolia* and to photograph it in habitat (7.7). The plants grow on one side of the mountain only, surrounded by tussocks of grass that they resemble so closely that, unless they are in flower, the only way to find one is to dig a sod of turf and look for the clump of fat, dahlia-like roots. A small sampling was transferred live to my glasshouse in England where they flower annually. By persevering with hand pollination of every bloom, I have had up to 100 seeds a year: enough to send out on Reading University's annual seedlist so that its survival is now assured, and my conscience is salved for having taken the liberty of collecting wild specimens.

The emphasis, then, should be on propagation: to own the only plant of a rarity and make no effort to multiply it is false economy, for one day it will die. If you had handed out offsets, someone might then be in a position to offer a replacement. "If you want to keep a plant, give it away" is a maxim that has been handed down through generations of gardeners. Even more important is the future of a whole collection—a point many a grower never thinks about. He dies, his plants are left until they become pest-ridden and unsaleable, and a life's work in building up the collection is lost in a few months. Verbal or (better) written instructions should always be left on how to dispose of your collection in the event of your death.

Greater education of the young in respect for nature, and an increased awareness among collectors of what they stand to guard, will achieve more for conservation in the long run than harsh laws that are difficult to enforce and often draw unwanted attention to the rarities they seek to protect.

Conservation—a losing battle?

Attitudes toward conservation differ widely. At one extreme we have the ultra-punctilious who would never pick a wild flower, however common. At the other extreme are those who happily leave the plants to die, because this is the pattern on which evolution has always run: extermination and replacement. Spending time and money to conserve prickly cacti may seem to them the height of folly, especially if their only knowledge of cacti is the invasive prickly pear that cost Australian farmers so much. But there are two sides to the story. There are also useful prickly pears, as we have seen. And for the few succulents whose utility is known to man, there are hundreds of others that have never been investigated. What hidden virtues might a later generation reveal in them? Already the unexpected find that the 'Elephant's Foot' plant (21.8) can help the cortisone industry is a hint of what might await discovery. Until we can create plants to order, we should think twice before allowing any species to disappear from this planet if we can avoid it.

*Right (7.6): Giant saguaros (**Carnegiea gigantea**) unmolested among spring flowers in the most famous of sanctuaries featuring succulents: the Saguaro National Monument in southern Arizona.*

*Below (7.7): **Haworthia graminifolia** in habitat in the Kango Valley, South Africa and (inset) flowering in cultivation. This rarity is being increased in cultivation by hand-pollinated seed.*

The Name Game

*"After all these considerations we ought to form some
conclusions in order that we may know trees and their
various kinds apart. similarly in the case of small herbs."*

Very few succulents have English or common names, and such as exist are often loosely applied. Thus, mother-in-law's tongue can be *Sansevieria,* or *Gasteria,* or anything with an appropriately long tongue-like leaf, and ice-plant may mean *Mesembryanthemum* or sometimes *Sedum* or other plants with glossy foliage. So there is no substitute for getting to know the latinized names, which are universal to botany throughout the world. Although Latin is, regrettably, taught less and less in schools, there is an excellent textbook by W. T. Stearn[1] that is equally useful to the veriest beginner and the advanced botanist.

How wild plants are named

Linnaeus (1707-78) standardized the use of the two-word latinized name for species that we refer to as a *binomial:* a generic name followed by a specific epithet. If accuracy requires it, this is followed by the name of the author (often abbreviated)—that is, the person who first described the species. Let us take a random example and see how much information can be extracted from such a name.

Haworthia limifolia Marl.

A botanist meeting this name for the first time is able to deduce the following:

1   It is a *taxon* of the rank of species.
2   It is a species of the genus *Haworthia.* (Named after A. H. Haworth (8.1), a renowned English plantsman-botanist, 1768-1833.) *Haworthia* is one genus of the lily Family, Liliaceae, whose general facies would be familiar to botanists.
3   The epithet *limifolia* means file-leaved (Latin: *lima* and *folium),* which aptly characterizes the leaves covered with transverse ridges.
4   The abbreviation Marl. refers to Rudolph Marloth, a celebrated South African botanist (1855-1931), whose name gives a pointer to the country and approximate date of the original publication of this name.

In common usage, the name of the author is omitted. However, it is important in critical studies, where it may be necessary to distinguish *H. limifolia* Marl. from *H. limifolia* of other botanists, or of garden origin ("hort."), where two or more taxa are confused under the one name.

The binomial system has one disadvantage: a plant cannot be named until it has been properly classified, and if the

Classification

Taxonomy (or Systematics) is the science that deals with classification.
Nomenclature is the part of that science concerned with the giving of names.
A **taxon** (pl. **taxa**) is a taxonomic group of any rank.
Species is the basic category in the classification of wild plants.
Cultivar ("Cultivated variety") is the unit in plants of garden origin and maintained in cultivation.

Words such as "family", "variety" and "form" have a special meaning in botany as categories, and are hence best avoided if all that is needed is a non-committal word such as "sort" or "kind".
Thus: "A plant of the *Sedum* Family" means any member of the Crassulaceae— not just one of the stonecrops.

---

classification changes, so must the name. More of this anon.

A nomenclature bible

The application of names to wild plants is governed by the International Code of Botanical Nomenclature[2], which lays down 75 Articles and sundry Recommendations covering naming of new taxa, name revisions and correction of past errors. It is followed voluntarily (or should be!) by all scientific workers, and names published in contravention of the Articles are outlawed.

Anyone can publish a new species: it requires only a diagnosis in Latin and the citation of a *type specimen* (holotype)— that is, one selected specimen preserved dry or bottled in a recognized herbarium. Publication must be in a printed book or

Above left (8.1): Adrian Hardy Haworth,
(1768-1833) named many new species and is
commemorated by the genus **Haworthia**.

Above (8.2): Memorial to A. H. Haworth—
although the "gravestones", necessary for
legibility in botanical gardens, are too large for
a private collection.

journal offered to the general public. It
greatly helps if the author adds illustrations, a description in a second, living
language, and indications of how his new
species differs from its allies, but none of
these is obligatory.

Nomenclature is a complicated subject
and the majority of growers will be happy
to give it a miss. But there are always a
few who, after the first flush of enthusiasm for succulents, feel inspired to
embark upon reclassifying them or describing new taxa. Before starting to do

this, it is imperative that they become
acquainted with the Code and understand
how it operates. Not a year goes by
without appalling bungles in plant
naming being perpetrated by well-
meaning amateurs, some of whom are
blissfully unaware that naming plants
follows any rules at all. What is so dis-
tressing is that other amateurs are unaware which are the good names and
which are bad, and these errors are there
for all time and must be taken into
account by future monographers. For a
simple introduction to plant naming, I
recommend the primer by C. Jeffrey[3].

Names for garden plants

The unit here is the *cultivar,* and the
gospel the International Code of Nomenclature of Cultivated Plants[4]. A cultivar is

defined as: "an assemblage of cultivated
plants which is clearly distinguished by
any characters (morphological, physio-
logical, cytological, chemical or others),
and which, when reproduced (sexually or
asexually), retains its distinguishing characters." Cultivars may have their origin
in cultivation or in the wild, as mutations
or hybrids (8.3, 4). Many are unvarying
clones (page 48), in contrast to species
having an internal range of variability
(5.1). The cristate, monstrous and variegated succulents mentioned in Chapter 2
are almost all examples of clones.

Names of cultivars are distinguished
typographically from those of species by
being enclosed in single (not double)
quotes, or preceded by "cv.". Unlike
specific epithets, they begin with a capital
initial and are not set in italic type. In the

past, cultivars were often given botanical names, although known only from gardens and never found wild. Such names, if given before 1959, can be retained, but they are written as cultivars, thus: *Echeveria* 'Hoveyi' instead of *E. hoveyi* Rose. Thus we can distinguish names of wildings from those of garden plants by their typographical presentation.

Names for hybrids

Hybrids, because they occur both in the wild and in gardens, come under both Codes. A hybrid can receive a formula name by combining those of the two parents, thus: *Echeveria derenbergii* × *setosa,* or, if considered of sufficient importance, a latinized epithet like a species—in this case: *Echeveria* × *derosa* von Roeder, which includes the author's name at the end. The "×" preceding the specific epithet is the sign of hybridity. Such a collective epithet covers all descendants from that cross, as well as backcrosses to either parent. One particular clone, picked from the first generation seedlings for its neat, compact habit, is widely distributed horticulturally under the cultivar name 'Worfield Wonder'.

Hybrids can even bridge two genera, when a new "generic" name may be coined because the product cannot be accommodated under either of the parental genera. It is compounded from the names of the two parents. Thus, × *Seleniphyllum* covers all hybrids of species of *Selenicereus* with species of *Epiphyllum;* × *Seleniphyllum cooperi* covers all crosses between *Selenicereus grandiflorus* and *Epiphyllum crenatum,* and × *S.* 'Pfersdorfii' (or × *Seleniphyllum cooperi* 'Pfersdorfii' if written out in full) is one particular clone of that descent.

"Variety" is commonly used in the sense of cultivar, but incorrectly; the term is best restricted to botanical usage as a subdivision of a species.

The classification of plants

It is basic to the human mind to classify, to break down the things we see around us and file the images for retrieval later when similar sights appear. The diversity of nature can be interpreted only by some sort of box-within-box storage system. Thus we see the logic behind the hierarchy of categories produced by the taxonomist, as set out in descending order here. This shows the classification for one of the "pebble plants", with the status and name of each category. Note that for some categories the ending (suffix) is standardized so that one can recognize the rank at a glance. Thus, anything ending in -ales is an Order, and so on.

Opinions differ as to how far these units have a real existence in nature— major or minor branchings in the evolutionary "tree", to give a visual analogy—

Categories of Classification
(With *Lithops salicola* L. Bol as an example)

		Suffix
Kingdom	Vegetable	
Division	Spermatophyta (Flowering Plants)	phyta
Order	Caryophyllales	ales
Family	Mesembryanthemaceae	aceae
Subfamily	Ruschioideae	oideae
Tribe	Ruschieae	eae
Subtribe	Lithopinae	inae
Genus	*Lithops*	
Subgenus	Leucolithops (Not cited in the full specific name)	
Species	*Lithops salicola* L. Bol (The author is Louisa Bolus)	

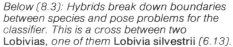

Lithops salicola L. Bol

Below (8.3): Hybrids break down boundaries between species and pose problems for the classifier. This is a cross between two Lobivias, *one of them* Lobivia silvestrii *(6.13).*

Below right (8.4): Epicacti are of mixed ancestry; even the genera may be unrecorded. For them a cultivar name is used. Top: Deutsche Kaiserin x Conways Giant; Bottom: Unnamed hybrid.

and how far they are man-made and for convenience of pigeon-holing only. For finer shades of analysis, extra categories may be interpolated. Thus a subgenus can be divided into Sections and a Section into Series. Below the species level we can have further categories also to express finer and finer shades of difference: subspecies (ssp), varieties (var) and forms (f). In *Haworthia limifolia* we find a var *stolonifera* f *major:* a large-leaved form of the variety forming stolons (long-stalked runners), for example. This is distinguished from the type form, which is *H. limifolia* var *limifolia* f *limifolia.*

Because of the impossibility of exactly defining the units of our classification, botanists gravitate into one of two camps: the "splitters" who favour many, small, finely separated units, and the "lumpers" who prefer fewer, broadly circumscribed units. If either policy were pursued uni-formly and in moderation throughout the plant kingdom, there would be nothing to choose between them on logical grounds. Unhappily, we have great inconsistencies, and succulents are among the groups where extreme splitting has been pursued. Whereas a conservative taxonomist accepts *Notocactus* in a broad sense, radicals split off *Brasilicactus, Eriocactus* and *Wigginsia (Malacocarpus)* on minor differences of flower, fruit and seed. In professional circles the trend is now towards moderation and amalgamation, but undoing past wrongs often involves further changes of names, as in the case outlined below.

In the present book I have tried to adopt conservative treatments wherever they are available, giving the alternative name or names in brackets where felt necessary. It is peculiarly irritating to a grower to be confronted by such ambig-uities: he orders several different names from seedlists and ends up with indistinguishable seedlings, or alternatively meets with the same plant under several different names. Books also are a source of confusion, according to which authority they follow. It is natural to ask: Why are there so many names? And which among them is correct? A full answer would fill many pages: only the principles involved can be summarized here.

A Borzicactus by any other name

Changes of name may be taxonomic or nomenclatural: two quite different causes. The former is personal and subjective; the latter is a matter of applying the Code. Taxonomic changes are the outcome of renewed study and, sometimes, extra information: what was once regarded as

one unit is now seen to be two or three; what once looked like three separate entities are now seen to be linked by so many intermediates that a merger is called for. Such changes are marked (T) in the example cited below.

Nomenclatural changes result from strict application of the articles of the Codes, for a number of reasons. For instance, the same binomial may have been given twice over to different species. Or one species may have been independently named twice. Either situation would lead to chaos and must be corrected. For instance, in 1973 Lavranos named a new aloe *Aloe pulchra* Lavr., overlooking an early use of the same binomial. Although the latter is now universally accepted as a species of *Gasteria,* it invalidates the later use of the same binomial, under the rule of priority. So Lavranos's aloe had to have a new name. *A bella* was chosen because it preserved the same meaning: "beautiful aloe". Nomenclatural changes are marked (N) in the following example, which includes both types of situation.

An attractive new golden-spined cactus (8.5) was described by Ritter in 1962 as *Winteria aureispina,* the only species of a new genus christened in honour of Mrs. Hildegard Winter, wife of a German nurseryman. Unfortunately Ritter failed to notice that the name *Wintera* was already in general usage for an unrelated shrub, and the difference in spelling of only one letter would undoubtedly lead to confusion. Hence under the Code the early name *Wintera* (1784) stands and *Winteria* Ritt. needed a new name. Two people independently supplied one: Backeberg, putting the finishing touches to his Lexikon, called it *Winterocereus,* and Ritter himself amended it to *Hildewintera,* both in 1966. Ritter's article appeared in print four months in advance of Backeberg's book, and therefore his name has priority. In 1974 Buxbaum decided that *Hildewintera* was indistinguishable from *Loxanthocereus,* and in 1975, taking a still broader concept of genera, I included both in *Borzicactus*[5]. We can summarize this chronology so far thus:

1 *Winteria aureispina* Ritter, Jan 1962.
2 *Hildewintera aureispina* (Ritter) Ritter, Jan 1966 (N)
3 *Winterocereus aureispinus* (Ritter) Backeberg, May 1966 (N)
4 *Loxanthocereus aureispinus* (Ritter) Buxbaum, Apr 1974 (T)
5 *Borzicactus aureispinus* (Ritter) Rowley, May 1975 (T)

The double author citation is an optional refinement in which the first name in brackets refers to the original publisher of the species, that following to the publisher of the revised binomial.

Reviewing the above names, 1 and 3 are out, as contrary to the Code, but 2, 4 and 5 are valid and all may be used: they reflect respectively the narrow, middle and broad concept of genera.. The grower must make his own choice, depending on his general attitude and the sources of literature he follows. It will be evident, then, that to answer fully the question: "Which is the right name?" one has to study the evidence and the reason for changes. A taxonomic change is a matter of opinion; a nomenclatural change, if properly handled, will be accepted by future writers of books and monographs, so it is best to swallow the pill even if it means loss of a familiar binomial.

Right (8.5): **Borzicactus aureispinus,** *a handsome cactus of many names, as is explained in the text. The novel container simulates its natural habitat on rock faces.*

Below (8.6): **Dudleya brittonii** *from Baja California commemorates two famous American botanists: W. R. Dudley of Stanford University and N. L. Britton of New York Botanical Gardens.*

PART TWO

The Families of Succulents

As pointed out in the Foreword, no attempt is made here to describe and key down all 10,000 or so recognized species of succulents. Rather, the interest is confined to higher levels in the classification—the genera and Families—and their positioning in relation to each other and to non-succulent relatives. Ten Families, five of leaf succulents and five of stem succulents, are singled out for separate treatment in Part 2. These contain the bulk of succulents most familiar in

cultivation today, although size ranges from about 2,000 species in the three largest down to a mere handful where only a small fraction of the Family is succulent. The remaining, still smaller units, are summarized in Chapters 9, 15 and 21.

With some misgivings I have adopted an artificial breakdown on life form into Leaf, Stem and Caudiciform Succulents, knowing that some Families and genera qualify for inclusion in more than one

group. Similarly, the two keys will incur the wrath of the pure in heart because I have omitted certain border-line or rarely encountered succulents whose inclusion would merely complicate the scheme and give maximum prominence to minor elements. The presentation is intended for non-technically minded plantsmen; not for the advanced botanist who will prefer his monographs and floras anyway. It must be emphasized that the only real way of distinguishing plant Families is

by flower and fruit characters; any attempt to do without is a poor compromise. Unfortunately, certain groups of succulents are hardly ever seen in flower in cultivation (Didiereaceae, for instance)—hence the impasse. But do not despair if initial attempts to name unlabelled succulents get nowhere. Familiarity with plants lends a wonderful perceptiveness to the trained eye. Just as we recognize our nearest and dearest among a crowd of thousands, regardless of dress and hair-

style, so the persevering cactophile learns to tell a haworthia from an aloe or agave just by the look and feel of the leaf, although a description would be long and complicated. If Part 2 does no more than excite the urge to look closer and inquire further, it will have served some purpose.

Left: **Echinocactus grusonii** *(rear)* and **Ferocactus acanthodes** *(front) in a nursery.*

Below: **Euphorbia caput-medusae,** *the 'Medusa's Head Spurge', shows by its curious flowers that it is no relative of the cactus.*

Leaf Succulents

"Some have leaves and not others; some plants shed their leaves, others do not."

Leaf succulents, in which the main water storage tissue is concentrated in the foliage (1.3), make a natural starting point for a survey of all succulents, because in their less extreme forms they are closest in appearance and functioning to their mesophyte ancestors. In the two largest Families, however—the Crassulaceae and Mesembryanthemaceae—one encounters the full range of degrees of specialization from relatively thin-leaved "conventional" shrublets (species of *Kalanchoe, Aptenia* and *Mesembryanthe-*

mum) to extreme xerophytes where it is not at first obvious that the plant body is made up of leaves at all *(Crassula columnaris* (2.7) and *Conophytum* (11.26), for example.

In addition to the five Families singled out for special treatment, representatives of many others have evolved fleshiness in a greater or lesser degree, and seven of the most interesting to collectors are summarized below. As pointed out in the Introduction, certain Families are omitted: Bromeliaceae because they are more

the realm of specialist growers of epiphytes, halophytes because nobody wants to grow them, and Zygophyllaceae because nobody can.

Readers are referred to the diagram on pages 16-17 in which the Families including succulents are set out in context of a scheme covering all flowering plants.

Commelinaceae

This is a moderate-sized Family of the Monocotyledons comprising about 38 genera and 500 species. It includes *Tradescantia,* the spiderworts of our gardens, and a number of tender pot plants with foliage decorative for our homes, such as *Rhoeo* and *Zebrina.* Succulence is most developed in *Tradescantia navicularis* from northern Peru, an attractive miniature in which each keel-shaped leaf has the upper surface distended by development of a massive translucent water-storing tissue beneath the epidermis. This can best be seen by snapping a leaf in two and viewing against the light. It is an easy plant to grow on a sunny windowsill or in a frost-free glasshouse. Well fed and watered, it puts out long, zigzag, creeping stems. At the onset of drought, these die back but leave compact buds at the nodes, which root readily and can be used for propagation. Other species of *Tradescantia* are also sometimes included in succulent collections, as is *Cyanotis somaliensis,* with white furry fleshy leaves and blue flowers.

Compositae

This, arguably the largest of all plant Families with an estimated 900 genera and over 13,000 species, owes its success to the highly efficient pollination and dispersal mechanisms described and figured in Chapters 4 and 15. Although the standardized head of small flowers surrounded by bracts is more or less constant and at once recognizable

Left (9.1): A succulent-leaved relative of the popular house-plant, Coleus pentheri *tolerates much drier conditions and is at home in a 9cm (3½in) pot. Note the zygomorphic blue flowers—rare in succulents.*

Above right (9.2): Peperomias, left to right: P. nivalis, P. dolabriformis *(at rear),* P. galioides *(front),* P. columella *and an unidentified species from Honolulu.*

Overleaf (9.3): Leaf succulents in a park in Barcelona: Crassula arborescens *(foreground centre) and* Agave americana *'Medio-picta'.*

throughout, the vegetative habit ranges from tiny annuals to trees, and includes leaf, stem and caudiciform succulents. Distribution is worldwide, although the leaf succulents are confined to South Africa in the genera *Senecio* (including *Kleinia* and *Notonia)* and *Othonna*. Jacobsen (1975) lists over 60 leaf-succulent species of *Senecio,* relatives of the weedy ragworts and groundsel of temperate gardens. They are cherished for their extraordinary variety of leaf and habit patterns rather than the flower heads, which suffer from over-familiarity in many showier garden plants. *Senecio medley-woodii* is one of the more attractive in bloom, and a few have a sweet fragrance. *Othonna* is less common in cultivation, except for the ubiquitous *O. capensis (crassifolia),* a rank grower when watered but better if starved in full sun, when the yellow "daisies" contrast with the soft, juicy, glaucous green club-shaped leaves.

Cucurbitaceae

The cucumber Family (110 genera, 640 species) qualifies on several counts for inclusion among caudiciform plants (Chapter 21), but also includes one bizarre genus of four species of climbing leaf succulents endemic to Madagascar: *Xerosicyos.* The leaves are elliptical to circular; the flowers small and unisexual as in cucumbers and marrows. Cuttings can be rooted, and a winter minimum temperature of 10°C (50°F) is needed.

Gesneriaceae

Streptocarpus is a glasshouse ornamental that needs no introduction to gardeners, and *S. rexii* and hybrids contribute much to beautify our homes. Less known is *S. saxorum* from Tanzania, which has a modest claim to be succulent although it thrives in warmth and a fairly moist atmosphere. It bears long-stalked showy pale mauve flowers from compact rosettes of fleshy, somewhat crystalline leaves. The Gesneriaceae embrace about 120 genera and 2,000 species, mainly from the tropics and subtropics.

Labiatae

This large Family, which covers some 180 genera and 3,500 species, includes mint and many popular aromatic herbs as well as garden ornamentals. It has advanced into the desert regions of southern and tropical Africa with fleshy-leaved representatives of the related genera *Coleus* and *Plectranthus,* which can stand extreme drought. *Coleus pentheri* (9.1) is very unlike the gaudy-leaved pot plants beloved of florists *(C. scutellarioides* cultivars), but it is a neat and welcome addition to succulent collections —doubly so for the blue of its flowers, a colour rare in succulents. Of several fleshy and very xerophytic species of *Plectranthus,* the gem is *P. prostratus,* with violet blooms, but be warned! It seeds itself readily and can invade the whole glasshouse. Propagation of all these labiates is easy from cuttings.

Peperomiaceae

As set out by Willis (1973) this Family runs to four genera only, of which *Peperomia,* with around 1,000 species, is by far the largest (9.2). A relative of pepper, it is centred in tropical South America but extends widely, and many species grow as epiphytes. To our window-sills it contributes some tough, long-lived, leathery-leaved foliage plants, at home in full sun or shade so long as they are kept warm. There is no sharp division between the non-succulent and succulent species; all have a tendency to fleshiness. *P. dolabriformis* has curious hatchet-shaped leaves with a translucent strip or "window" along the narrow upper margins; in *P. asperula* leaves of similar shape are rough from surface papillae. Very attractive miniatures are *P. galioides* and *P. columella.* The flowers are minute and borne on terminal, tail-like spikes.

Urticaceae

Pilea serpyllacea from Peru is not unlike a *Peperomia* in habit, but is a member of the unrelated nettle family. Its most noteworthy feature is the pellucid "window" on the underside of each tiny leaf. It is a delicate plant and likes adequate warmth. *Pilea* is credited with 400 species, and is the largest genus of the Urticaceae (45 genera, 550 species). Several species of *Pilea* are in cultivation under the name 'Artillery Plant', from the explosive ejection of the anther contents as a cloud of pollen.

9: LEAF SUCCULENTS

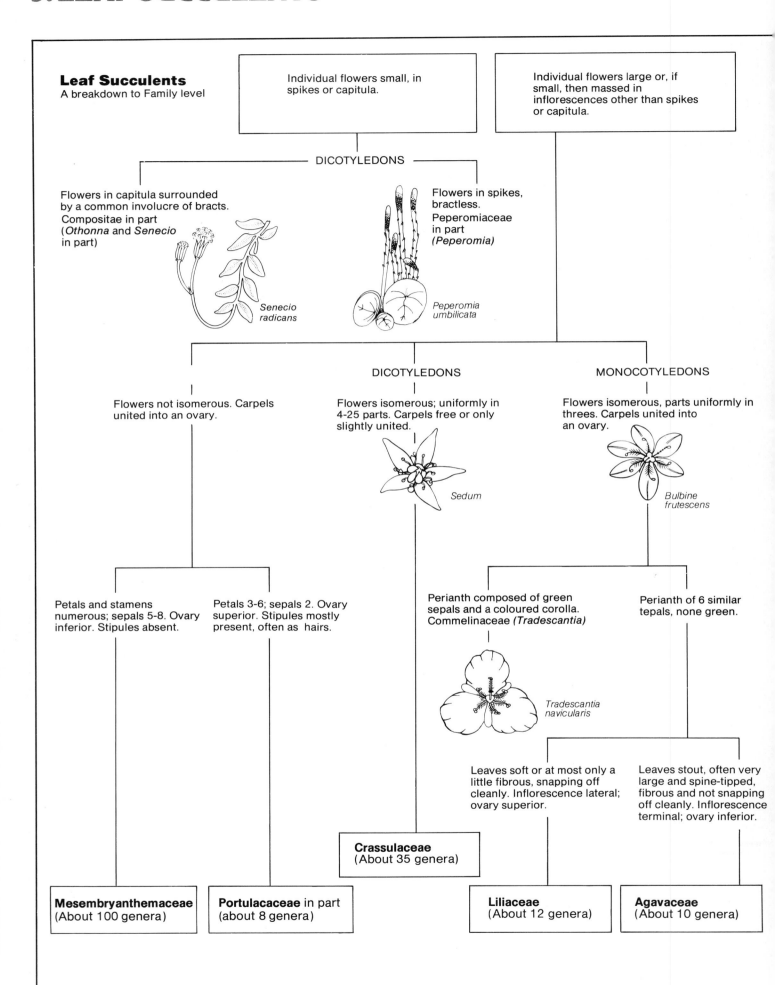

Leaf Succulents
A breakdown to Family level

Individual flowers small, in spikes or capitula.

Individual flowers large or, if small, then massed in inflorescences other than spikes or capitula.

DICOTYLEDONS

Flowers in capitula surrounded by a common involucre of bracts. Compositae in part (*Othonna* and *Senecio* in part)

Senecio radicans

Flowers in spikes, bractless. Peperomiaceae in part (*Peperomia*)

Peperomia umbilicata

DICOTYLEDONS

MONOCOTYLEDONS

Flowers not isomerous. Carpels united into an ovary.

Flowers isomerous; uniformly in 4-25 parts. Carpels free or only slightly united.

Sedum

Flowers isomerous, parts uniformly in threes. Carpels united into an ovary.

Bulbine frutescens

Petals and stamens numerous; sepals 5-8. Ovary inferior. Stipules absent.

Petals 3-6; sepals 2. Ovary superior. Stipules mostly present, often as hairs.

Perianth composed of green sepals and a coloured corolla. Commelinaceae (*Tradescantia*)

Tradescantia navicularis

Perianth of 6 similar tepals, none green.

Leaves soft or at most only a little fibrous, snapping off cleanly. Inflorescence lateral; ovary superior.

Leaves stout, often very large and spine-tipped, fibrous and not snapping off cleanly. Inflorescence terminal; ovary inferior.

Crassulaceae
(About 35 genera)

Mesembryanthemaceae
(About 100 genera)

Portulacaceae in part
(about 8 genera)

Liliaceae
(About 12 genera)

Agavaceae
(About 10 genera)

The Stonecrop and Houseleek Family

Crassulaceae are the third largest Family of succulents, and form a good starting point for a survey of the group as a whole. Botanically, the flowers are the simplest structurally, and *isomerous*— that is, having the same basic numbers of sepals, petals, stamens (one or two whorls) and carpels. They have the widest range of habitats from marsh to desert, and the widest temperature tolerance, from the maximum borne by flowering plants down to sub-zero winter temperatures. They also have a wide distribution, and not many countries are without at least a few of the weedy annuals in their flora. They have the broadest appeal, not only to specialist growers of succulents, but also to lovers of alpines, screes and rock gardens, and a few aspire to be florists' flowers and delight those who find prickly cacti abhorrent. Finally, some are so unkillable that they bring solace to failed gardeners who never made good with any other plant.

Form and variety

Most of the Crassulaceae are herbaceous perennials, but a few are annual *(Sedum coeruleum)* or biennial *(S. pilosum, sempervivoides* 10.13). The largest, *Crassula arborescens* (9.3) and *argentea,* form small trees with fat, fleshy trunks 2m (6½ft) or more in height. Almost caudiciform is *Cotyledon paniculata* the "botterboom" of southern Africa, with a massive gnarled trunk and more or less deciduous leaves. It has a close parallel in the giant Mexican stonecrops *Sedum frutescens* and *S. oxypetalum.* Stem succulence takes on a different guise in *Cotyledon wallichiana,* which has a rather cactiform look from the thick branches covered with persistent leaf bases forming long slender tubercles. One or two other peculiarities of habit are to be found described in the chapter on caudiciform plants (Chapter 21).

The leaves of all the Crassulaceae are xeromorphic, although in *Crassula coccinea,* some kalanchoes and sedums only slight succulence develops. Drought resistance is not, however, proportional to the bulk of water-storing tissue. The ability of stems of the native European roseroot *(Sedum rosea* 10.1) and orpine or livelong *(S. telephium)* to stay fresh and green and even to flower long after cutting was noticed early and led to the first recognition of succulents as a group (page 12), as well as to superstitious beliefs similar to those mentioned under the account of *Sempervivum* (page 127).

Flowers of Crassulaceae are generally on the small side (2.19), but are usually massed in flat or domed heads which make them conspicuous to insects. Some are sweetly perfumed, others musky or foetid. Especially welcome are those African species that flower in the autumn and winter in cultivation: species of *Crassula,* for instance, that brighten the glasshouse when much else is dormant. The colour range is from white to pink, red, orange and yellow, with one solitary species of a beautiful pale sky blue, the annual *Sedum coeruleum.* The fruit is a follicle: that is, like a tiny pea pod, splitting along the inner margin to release quantities of fine, dust-like seed. The best way to collect the seeds of Crassulaceae is to cut off the inflorescences after flowering and invert them in a paper bag (not polythene, which holds the moisture too much), leaving this undisturbed on a dry, light top shelf until ready to packet or sow the seeds. It is a mistake to sow too thickly: one way to avoid this is to mix the seed with fine sifted sand or peat.

A natural Family

The Crassulaceae are a natural Family, which is to say that it is easy to recognize plants that belong to it by vegetative appearance and the regular, isomerous flowers with free carpels. The closest ally is the saxifrage Family, Saxifragaceae, but this is never truly succulent and has united carpels and other more advanced features. But, as with many natural Families, the internal classification into subfamilies and genera is unmanageable, as will be apparent even from the oversimplified synopsis given here.

A few subfamilies, such as Kalanchoideae and Sempervivoideae, are sharply defined and readily recognized. But Sedoideae is the 'dump' into which every genus that does not fit comfortably elsewhere is thrown. Uhl (1963) has done good work in attempting to clarify the position, adding data from chromosome numbers, which segregate some groups and not others. As for the genera, although they appeared distinct when first defined on a limited number of known species, many are now linked by intermediates. Consequently, some species have been shuffled

Right (10.1): Predominantly leaf-succulent, the Crassulaceae also exhibit stem-succulence and, in **Sedum rosea,** *development of a caudex (Chapter 21) with annual branches.*

10: CRASSULACEAE

THE STONECROP AND HOUSELEEK FAMILY (CRASSULACEAE) — A breakdown to genus level

Stamens as many as petals	Stamens twice as many as petals	
		Flower parts in fives
Inflorescence terminal or lateral	Flower parts in fours; petals united above halfway into a tube; inflorescence terminal	Petals united above halfway into a tube; inflorescence terminal
Subfamily 1 **CRASSULOIDEAE**	Subfamily 2 **KALANCHOIDEAE**	Subfamily 3 **COTYLEDONOIDEAE**

Subfamily 1
Vauanthes dichotoma

Subfamily 3
Cotyledon orbiculata dinteri

Subfamily 2
Kalanchoe pumila

Subfamily 1
CRASSULOIDEAE
Crassula
Dinacria
Vauanthes

Subfamily 2
KALANCHOIDEAE
Kalanchoe

Subfamily 3
COTYLEDONOIDEAE
Adromischus
Chiastophyllum
Cotyledon
Mucizonia
Pistorinia
Umbilicus

Petals united for less than halfway into a tube; inflorescence lateral, axillary

Subfamily 4
ECHEVERIOIDEAE

Flower parts usually in fives— can be 3 to 12; inflorescence usually terminal

Subfamily 5
SEDOIDEAE

Flower parts in sixes or more; petals free; inflorescence terminal

Subfamily 6
SEMPERVIVOIDEAE

Subfamily 4
Echeveria pulvinata

Subfamily 5
Sedum cauticola

Subfamily 6
Sempervivum grandiflorum

Subfamily 5
SEDOIDEAE
Afrovivella
Cremnophila
Diamorpha
Hypagophytum
Lenophyllum
Meterostachys
Orostachys
Parvisedum
Pseudosedum
Rosularia
Sedum
Sempervivella
Sinocrassula
Tacitus
Villadia

Subfamily 4
ECHEVERIOIDEAE
Dudleya
Echeveria
Graptopetalum
Pachyphytum
Thompsonella

Subfamily 6
SEMPERVIVOIDEAE
Aeonium
Aichryson
Greenovia
Jovibarba
Monanthes
Sempervivum

from one genus to another and may end up as sole representatives (monotypes) of a new genus to themselves. For instance, the lengthy synonymy of the plant now known as *Graptopetalum paraguayense* results from its classification, at one time or another, in five different genera. Thus there are exceptions to all characters used to define the higher categories in Crassulaceae, and it is clear that convergent evolution has taken place many times over. The six subfamilies are retained in absence of better, and at least they have a geographical foundation and occupy separate, although overlapping, areas.

Intergeneric hybrids are known between species of related genera in subfamily Echeverioideae (× *Graptoveria* (10.2) = *Graptopetalum* × *Echeveria*, etc) and subfamily Sempervivoideae (× *Greenonium* = *Greenovia* × *Aeonium*, etc) as well as between subfamilies Echeverioideae and Sedoideae (× *Pachysedum* = *Pachyphytum* × *Sedum* and × *Sedeveria* = *Sedum* × *Echeveria*). This suggests close affinity between the genera and adds to the suspicion that they are artificially segregated.

Crassuloideae

Subfamily I is set apart from the remainder by the single whorl of stamens, equal in number to the sepals, petals and carpels. It is not a primitive character, because it results from suppression of a second whorl, and a reduced pollen output is characteristic of more specialized flowers that can afford to be less wasteful of pollen. A phylogenetic classification of

Above (10.2): An attractive intergeneric hybrid between Graptopetalum paraguayense *and* Echeveria setosa, *called* x Graptoveria, *combines features of both parents.*

Below (10.3): Crassula dejecta *from the southern Cape area of South Africa. Many* Crassulas *flower in winter in northern Europe which makes them welcome in glasshouses.*

the Crassulaceae, according to Uhl, would look to *Sedum* as a more likely starting point.

The 250 to 300 species of *Crassula* run from tiny, cosmopolitan annuals ignored by collectors to the tallest members of the Family, and cover the broadest ecological tolerance of any genus of flowering plants, from the deserts of South West Africa, where the leaf rosette is condensed to a sphere giving minimal surface for evaporation, to marshy and even aquatic habitats. South Africa is the centre of greatest diversity, with outliers extending far and wide. Nearly all perennial species have collector appeal, and the genus as a whole can be recommended to anyone in search of a group of succulents ideal for specializing upon, and not already wedded to the more popular genera of cacti. Xeromorphic features are much in evidence and provide the principal attraction, as in the white glaucous "bloom" of *C. cornuta* and *deltoidea,* the hairs of *C. barbata, lanuginosa* and *tomentosa,* the incrustations of papillae in *C. falcata, hystrix* and *tecta,* and the packing of leaves into columns, square in *C. arta* (10.5), *barklyi* and *pyramidalis,* almost spherical in *C. columnaris* (2.7) and *hemispherica* (10.4).

Crassula falcata and *C. (Rochea) coccinea* are raised as florists' flowers and widely valued as pot plants for their long-lasting showy heads of crimson blooms. *Crassula sarcocaulis* (6.12) and *C. milfordiae* are sufficiently hardy to overwinter in the open in frosty areas. A useful introductory book is *Crassulas in*

Above (10.4): **Crassula hemispherica,** *showing the leaves overlapped like tiles, giving mutual protection and reducing water loss. The rosette usually dies after flowering.*

Below (10.5): **Crassula arta** *also shows extreme surface reduction, with only the leaf edges exposed and the whole plant having a wax-like coating which diminishes water loss.*

10: CRASSULACEAE

Cultivation by Vera Higgins, 1964.

The other genera of Crassuloideae, *Dinacria* and *Vauanthes* (page 118), are short-lived annuals and rarely cultivated.

Kalanchoideae

In contrast to the hardy members of other subfamilies, the large genus *Kalanchoe* (130 species approximately) comes mainly from Madagascar and tropical Africa and appreciates more warmth in cultivation—a winter minimum of at least 10°C (50°F) for best results, and a correspondingly richer soil and ample watering. The subfamily is sharply distinguished from all others by the flower parts in fours, but species of *Cotyledon* run very close and can be separated only by this feature, so they are, I suspect, blood relatives. Most kalanchoes are rather large-growing and hence shunned by collectors, although, given space, the flowers can put up quite a show. The smaller species, such as *K. pumila* (page 118) and *K. manginii,* are justly popular and make good basket plants. The former has grey leaves with a waxy bloom that act as a foil to the beautiful mauve flowers; the latter has vivid red tubular blooms against soft green foliage. *K. marmorata* has agreeably dappled leaves, and *K. tomentosa* (10.7), which has an overall covering of white felt with dark tips to the leaves, is called the 'Panda Plant' and rarely blooms. A delightful miniature is *K. rhombopilosa,* similar in habit to *Adromischus,* but less robust. *K. tubiflora,* with cylindrical leaves, and *K. daigremontiana* (6.23), with triangular ones—both sometimes classified as a separate genus, *Bryophyllum*—are among the most ubiquitous of succulents from

Right (10.6): **Kalanchoe thyrsiflora** *in habitat on a wooded slope in Makowe, Natal. Flowering stems go up to 60cm (2ft) in height.*

Below (10.7): Downy and furry-leaved succulents are forever popular. Compare this **Kalanchoe tomentosa** *from Madagascar with the Mexican* **Echeveria leucotricha** *(10.10).*

the ease with which they drop adventitious buds from the leaf margins and spawn large numbers of offspring.

Cotyledonoideae

The Cotyledonoideae are centred in South Africa but extend northward and, in the genus *Umbilicus* (3.1), through Ethiopia to Europe and Western Asia. The single species of *Chiastophyllum, C. oppositifolium,* a popular hardy rock plant with nodding sprays of pale yellow blooms, comes from the Western Caucasus.

Cotyledon (10.8) is really two genera in one, half its 50 species having opposite, persistent leaves and a shrubby habit like *Kalanchoe,* the other half having spirally arranged deciduous leaves and a more or less caudiciform appearance. Both have relatively large, showy, tubular flowers with parts in fives. There are many hybrids recorded, but none between species of the two different groups. The flowers of *Cotyledon* hang down in the manner of bells; those of the closely related *Adromischus* are held stiffly erect. *Adromischus* (10.9) is a justly popular genus of dwarf, trouble-free plants that are at home in 7-9cm (3-3½in) pots and propagate freely from single leaves. They are esteemed for the great variety of leaf forms and markings, some mottled with purple, some silvery and glaucous, and differing in shape often on one branch. *A. herrei* is a miniature oddity whose leaves are shaped like small lemons, rough and pustulate and deep purplish — something like currants to look at. Although there

Above (10.8): **Cotyledon orbiculata** var. dinteri, *an attractive small variety of a variable species, with squat, almost white waxy leaves. This plant is 14cm (5½in) high.*

Below (10.9): **Adromischus maculatus** *with age develops quite a massive caudex. Propagation is easy from single leaves. All species of this genus are happy in small pots.*

10: CRASSULACEAE

are a great many described species in *Adromischus,* in habitat in South and South West Africa they intergrade, and a future monographer may well prefer to reduce the number drastically.

Echeverioideae

The Echeverioideae are exclusively American, centred in Mexico, and are especially attractive to collectors (2.2). A glasshouse filled with echeverias is uniquely attractive, the banks of rosettes of all colours and sizes looking like a huge floral display. Many border on frost hardiness and are quite well-known outside the ranks of the cactophiles for their use in summer bedding. Floral clocks and similar massed bedding displays at seaside resorts make much use of echeverias. The elegant inflorescences of red to yellow flowers (page 119) last a long time and are popular with flower arrangers. Propagation is easy, by division, from single leaves or even from old flower stalks, which can be rooted and eventually grow. A standard monograph of *Echeveria* by E. Walther was published posthumously in 1972. It is difficult to make a choice of names from among the 150 species, because all are worth growing, and there are in addition many hybrids, some fantastically ornate.

Dudleya, with 43 species, is a close ally

Above (10.10): **Echeveria leucotricha** *has flower-like rosettes of leaves covered in silky hairs— an effective means of reflecting the light and conserving water.*

Below (10.11): **Pachyphytum oviferum:** *"oviferum" means "egg-bearing", a reference to the leaves which recall a plover's egg. A beautiful plant in flower or without flowers.*

Above (10.12): **Sedum hintonii,** *a collector's piece from Mexico, is not easy to adapt to cultivation for long. Starvation intensifies the compactness of habit and whiteness of leaves.*

Below (10.13): **Sedum sempervivoides** *mimics a houseleek rosette the first year, but bears a fine corymb of red flowers the second. It is a hardy biennial, raised only from seed.*

and has beautiful white-powdered foliage (8.6). *Graptopetalum,* with 11 species, is notable for the dappling of dark spots on the corolla (10.18). In *Pachyphytum* the leaves are usually thick, smooth and glaucous; *P. oviferum* (10.11) is so named from the egg-shaped leaves. There are about a dozen species, all from Mexico.

Sedoideae

Sedum, with 600 species, is the largest genus of the Family and the least well-defined, most of the other Sedoideae being "splits" or at one time or another included within it. It covers the North Temperate regions, with outliers extending south to Peru, Central Africa and Madagascar, and occupies an equally wide range of habitats including a few species in marshes *(S. villosum)* and some epiphytes *(S. epidendrum).* Some of the hardy species are herbaceous perennials, with leafy shoots that die down to an underground rootstock in winter. *Sedum sieboldii* from Japan does this, and its fine hybrid with *S. telephium,* 'Autumn Joy', is a well-known border plant for hot, dry places. The roseroot, *S. rosea* (10.1), is dioecious and sometimes classified in a separate genus *Rhodiola.* The creeping and prostrate perennials are legion and widely grown, but a few, such as *S. album* and *S. reflexum* (3.1), are difficult to stop from taking over the whole rock garden. A special word of praise should go to the biennials, *S. pilosum* and *sempervivoides* (10.13), well worth the trouble of raising from seed for their neat compact rosettes, which open out during the second year into broad

10: CRASSULACEAE

heads of deep pink and crimson flowers respectively.

More to the tastes of the average cactophile are the tender species of Mexico and North America, which are also the most succulent of the genus. *Sedum* flowers are small and star-like and arranged in mostly large and showy corymbs. They come in all shades including pale blue in *S. coeruleum*.

Rosularia, with *Sempervivum*-like rosettes but axillary inflorescences, extends from Asia Minor to the Himalayas, and *Meterostachys* and *Orostachys* from Korea to Japan. Although nominally hardy, these are best covered against excessive moisture in winter or removed to the unheated alpine house.

Tacitus (10.20) is the latest discovery, from Mexico, just making its way into collections. The large, vivid red flower has a corolla tube with the mouth almost closed by an overhang at the top.

Sempervivoideae

The humble houseleek, *Sempervivum tectorum* (10.14), has had a place in history from very early times, having been credited with numerous virtues

Above (10.14): **Sempervivum tectorum,** *the common houseleek of Europe, was long planted on cottage roofs as a supposed protection from lightning.*

Below (10.15): **Aeonium arboreum** *'Zwartkop' earns a place in every bedding display for the fine dark colour and texture of its foliage. Another cultivar has yellow-edged leaves.*

deriving from its abundant, cool juice and long survival of desiccation. Its country names reflect some of the supposed uses: healing blade, thunder plant, sengreen [= evergreen] and welcome-home-husband-drunk-though-you-be. Planted on cottage roofs it is held to protect against lightning. The leaves were used, much as were those of *Aloe*, as poultices and cures for warts and corns, and from Columella in the first century BC we learn that soaking seeds in the expressed juice will deter pests when they are sown. A more picturesque use is in helping a country maid to select her future husband. If she picks a houseleek flower for each of her lovers, that which opens best and lasts the longest will be the one for her.

Of the 50 or more rather ill-defined species of *Sempervivum*, those with bell-shaped flowers with parts in sixes or sevens have by some been split off as the separate genus *Jovibarba (Diopogon)* (10.16). All are more or less hardy and native to Europe and Western Asia. Their tender relatives are to be found on the Canary Islands, the "tree houseleeks" belonging to the genus *Aenium* (5.8), which has over 30 species and numerous interspecific hybrids. *Aeonium arboreum* has been in cultivation since 1727 and has produced attractive mutants with leaves variegated ('Variegatum') and very deep purple ('Zwartkop' 10.15). The flower axis in *Aeonium*, as in *Sempervivum*, is terminal (10.17) and the rosette that bears it dies. For species that do not normally offset, such as *A. tabuliforme*, this means starting again from seed, although leaf cuttings can be rooted if taken in time. Another solitary species is the giant *A. nobile*, justly named for its fine large rosette up to 50cm (20in) across of thick, green, slightly viscid leaves and broad corymb of many small purplish red blooms (the other species have yellow flowers). Although no aeoniums will survive a Northern Temperate winter unprotected, they are excellent plants for summer bedding in the open.

Monanthes, with 18 species and nine hybrids, includes small *Sedum*-like plants with usually rough, somewhat crystalline leaves and a ring of conspicuous nectar glands in each flower (4.3).

Cultivation

Having more frost-hardy species than all the other Families of succulents put together, the Crassulaceae are as much the

Top left (10.16): **Jovibarba hirtus** *ssp* **allionii** *from the south western Alps is hardy and a favourite for the rock garden.*

Left (10.17): **Aeonium** *is the "tree houseleek" from the Canary Islands, and requires frost protection. As in* **Sempervivum,** *the rosette bearing the flowers dies.*

concern of alpine and rock garden addicts as of succulent collectors. The genera *Sedum* and *Sempervivum,* in particular, can occupy niches unsuitable to most other plants and beautify the bare corners and rough patches: chinks in rocks, walls and paths that are too dry for other plants to survive. The popularity of the latter genus led to the formation of a Sempervivum Society in 1970, responsible for testing and certifying newly introduced cultivars.

Turning now to collections under glass, one devoted wholly to Crassulaceae can be of no little appeal and interest. The rosettes, in many pastel shades from white and powdery through shades of green, tan, yellow and pink to almost black, give the appearance of large flowers and are much longer lasting. It must be confessed, however, that to maintain such a collection in perfect trim takes more work than the equivalent collection of cacti. Once potted, a cactus can look after itself for a year, provided it is given water, without coming to harm as a rule. Many Crassulaceae quickly outgrow their space if watered, and drop their leaves if kept too dry. One must first position them carefully so that choice miniatures do not get crowded out of view by rampant

growers that throw out aerial roots and trespass across other pots. In the wild many rosette plants are protected during the dry season by their old dead leaves. Sempervivoideae, in particular, can survive the most extreme droughts: even if the roots are killed off, the last part to die is the growing apex, protected as it is by a sheath of outer leaves like a bulb. In *Greenovia* the rosettes annually close up tight during the rest period and open out again when amply watered. In the milder conditions of cultivation, however, it is usual to remove the dead leaves, which look untidy and harbour pests. A pair of blunt-ended forceps is useful here: grasp each leaf near the base and give an outward rolling motion to twist it down the axis if it shows any resistance to part company.

Shrubby Crassulaceae quickly become leggy in pots, and benefit from repropagation. The tips can be rooted as cuttings and the base kept under the staging for further propagation or planted outdoors to take its chance. Some tall-growing species are shy to branch, and it is best to pinch back the tips repeatedly when they are young to encourage formation of a neat shrublet. Clustering types such as *Crassula schmidtii* are apt to die out in

the centre with age, and likewise benefit from repropagation.

Pest control can be a slight problem if one believes the manufacturers who warn that sprays containing malathion may be harmful to Crassulaceae. I have not found this to be so myself, but be warned! Contact insecticides such as Volck will wash off the delicate powdery bloom that is the chief attraction of many species, and it takes a long time to regenerate. However, watering the roots with systemic insecticide seems to do no harm and is the most efficient control I know.

Right (10.18): **Graptopetalum filiferum** *shows the characteristic mottled petals which make the flowers of this small genus extra appealing. It comes from Chihuahua in Mexico.*

Lower right (10.19): **Sempervivum giuseppii** *from Spain forms dense cushions of small furry rosettes, and is quite hardy to frost. No rock garden is complete without its full quota of houseleeks.*

Below (10.20): An exciting novelty from Mexico, **Tacitus bellus** *was discovered as recently as 1972. Happy in a 6cm (2½in) pot, it has a big flower of 2.5-3.5cm (1-1½in). It offsets sparingly, but propagation is possible from single leaves.*

The Ice-plant Family

The Mesembryanthemaceae, as reference to the chart on pages 16-17 will show, introduce us to the Order Caryophyllales, which includes a concentration of Families of succulents, large and small. Although there would seem at first sight to be little in common between a cactus and an ice-plant, or a *Didierea* and an *Anacampseros,* they are linked by embryological, anatomical and biochemical as well as morphological characters to form one of the most natural of plant Orders. Reference has already been made (page 31) to the common possession of betacyanin in place of anthocyanin (2.5); the different type of red pigment in the flowers perhaps contributes to the distinctive look of the blooms throughout the Order.

Family background

The Mesembryanthemaceae have had a checkered career at the hands of classifiers. In Linnaeus's day, everything we now include here was placed under a single genus *Mesembryanthemum* ("midday flower"), which aptly describes the majority. *Mesembryanthemum* was later put in the Family Aizoaceae, along with a number of only very slightly fleshy pantropical weedy annuals. As the number of species introduced from South Africa increased, so the genus became more and more unwieldy, and efforts were made at the start of the nineteenth century by Haworth and Salm-Dyck to divide it up. However, no satisfactory subdivision was possible until N. E. Brown at Kew revealed the secrets of the fruit structure in 1921, and began a systematic breakdown into separate genera. Thus to identify any member of the Family to genus, one must have the fruit to examine, although fortunately many of the popular genera can be approximately separated by eye on habit: *Faucaria, Glottiphyllum, Drosanthemum, Lithops,* etc.

Conservative botanists still include the *Mesembryanthemum* complex within the Aizoaceae, lowering the hierarchic rank to that of subfamily and the other divisions accordingly. As a supporter of conservative taxonomy, I agree with this. But the narrower concept is adopted here because it makes presentation simpler by splitting off the succulents of interest to collectors and omitting their weedy relatives. We still have a sizeable Family, which rivals the Cactaceae at an estimated number of species of around 2,000, although such figures may well be reduced after more field study. Already 22 proposed species of *Aridaria* have been reduced to one by examining the pattern of variation of each.

Although the splitting up of Linnaeus's

Below (11.1): **Conophytum bilobum** *showing two leaf lobes fused at the base into a spherical body, from which the flower emerges in the centre. A new leaf pair is produced each year.*

Right (11.2): **Lampranthus roseus,** *valued for bedding displays in frost-free areas where there is unobstructed sunlight.* **Lampranthus** *flowers come in all colours except blue.*

one genus *Mesembryanthemum* into over 100 may seem excessive, the genera are on the whole better defined than those in other large Families of succulents, and the almost total absence of intergeneric hybrids, in the wild or made by man, suggests strong genetical isolation between the genera.

Range and variety

As understood here, the Mesembryanthemaceae are annual or perennial herbs or small shrubs with simple leaves (lobed in one species) and no stipules. Beyond that, there is enormous variation in general habit, exploiting the gamut 'of xeromorphic features associated with surface reduction and water retention. Long leafy stems become telescoped into compact shoots with few leaves; flat expanded leaves into hemispheres or finger- or half-egg-shaped bodies; or two of a pair fuse to form a conical body *(Dinteranthus, Lithops)* or a close approximation to a sphere *(Conophytum)*. Heterophylly (the production of two or more types of leaves on one shoot in succession) occurs in *Vanzijlia, Mitrophyllum, Cheiridopsis* and others; and leaf windows are found in *Fenestraria, Frithia, Conophytum* subgenus Ophthal-

mophyllum and some *Lithops,* associated with a semi-subterranean habit so that only the window is exposed to the light. Mimicry, discussed more fully in Chapter 5, is found in all species of *Lithops,* and to a lesser degree in several other genera. A caudiciform habit, with an amorphous underground tuber and deciduous aerial shoots, is developed in several species of *Sphalmanthus (Phyllobolus).* Crystalline papillae cover the leaves of *Mesembryanthemum* and *Drosanthemum* ("ice-plants") and some others, and *Psammophora* has sticky leaves that become clothed in a protective sheath of the dust and sand of the habitat.

The flowers are usually showy and many-petalled, which gives them a superficial resemblance to daisies and other members of the Compositae. They tend to have set hours of opening and closing; a few open at dusk, and these are sweetly scented. Few expand in the sun's absence.

The typical fruit is a dehiscent capsule: that is, a seed pod that opens mechanically to allow escape of the seeds. Both structurally and biologically the functioning is very complex, and it is discussed more fully at the end of Chapter 4, on Dispersal. In most cases water is the agency causing opening and, to some

extent, washing out of the seeds. Variations in fruit structure are the basis of the division of the Family into subfamilies, Tribes and genera, of which the briefest summary is given in the chart on pages 134-5.

The seeds of Mesembryanthemaceae can be 2mm (1/12th in) or more across or fine and dust-like *(Dinteranthus).* In tests on 253 samples in 1951 I found that germination took anything from three days to a number of weeks, but annuals germinated more slowly and erratically than perennials, some coming up better the second year after sowing. This is understandable because an annual is more vulnerable to adversities of climate than a perennial: a reserve of seed allows

Right (11.3): **Cheiridopsis candidissima.** *Abundant in the Van Rhynsdorp district of South Africa, a collector's piece elsewhere, this is fascinating even without the flowers.*

Below right (11.4): **Pleiospilos bolusii.** *The dark spotted leaves resemble the granite forming the background to this species in nature. The large bloom has a fragrance of coconut.*

Below (11.5): **Dinteranthus wilmotianus** *comes near to* Lithops *in appearance, but not in ease of cultivation. Since it never branches, propagation is from seed only.*

11: MESEMBRYANTHEMACEAE

THE ICE-PLANT FAMILY (MESEMBRYANTHEMACEAE) — A breakdown to genus level

Placentation axile				Placentation parietal to bas
Fruit a hygroscopic capsule (opening when moistened)		Fruit a schizocarp (splitting up into separate sections)		Fruit a dehiscent capsule
				Fruit opening when wetted
Subfamily 1 **MESEMBRYANTHEMOIDEAE**				Fruit without seed pockets, usually closing again when dry
Petals soft Tribe 1 **MESEMBRY- ANTHEMEAE**	Petals stiff Tribe 2 **DACTYLOPS- IDEAE**	Annual Subfamily 2 **HYMENO- GYNOIDEAE**	Perennial Subfamily 3 **CARYOTO- PHOROIDEAE**	Tribe 3 **RUSCHIEAE**

Tribe 1
Prenia pallens

Tribe 3
Conophytum elishae

Subfamily 2
Hymenogyne glabra

Tribe 2
Dactylopsis digitata

Subfamily 3
Caryotophora skiatophytoides

Tribe 1
MESEMBRY- ANTHEMEAE
Amoebophyllum
Aptenia
Aridaria
Eurystigma
Mesembryanthemum
Opophytum
Platythyra
Prenia
Psilocaulon
Sceletium
Sphalmanthus
Synaptophyllum

Tribe 2
DACTYLOPS- IDEAE
Aspazoma
Dactylopsis

Subfamily 2
HYMENO- GYNOIDEAE
Hymenogyne

Subfamily 3
CARYOTO- PHOROIDEAE
Caryotophora

Tribe 3
RUSCHIEAE

Acrodon	Cerochlamys
Argyroderma	Chasmatophyllum
Astridia	Cheiridopsis
Bergeranthus	Conophytum
Bijlia	Cylindrophyllum
Braunsia	Delosperma
Calamophyllum	Dicrocaulon
Carpanthea	Didymaotus
Carruanthus	Dinteranthus
Cephalophyllum	Diplosoma

family 4 **RUSCHIOIDEAE**

Fruit a fleshy berry

Fruit opening without wetting; cells 5

Fruit with seed pockets, opening once only (transitional from hygroscopic capsule to schizocarp)

Fruit cells 10-24
Tribe 4
APATESIEAE

Fruit cells 4-7
Tribe 5
SKIATOPHYTEAE

Tribe 6
SAPHESIEAE

Tribe 7
CARPOBROTEAE

Tribe 6
Saphesia flaccida

Tribe 7
Carpobrotus deliciosus

Tribe 4
Conicosia pugioniformis

Tribe 5
Skiatophytum tripolium

Tribe 4
APATESIEAE
Apatesia
Conicosia
Herrea

Tribe 5
SKIATOPHYTEAE
Skiatophytum

Tribe 6
SAPHESIEAE
Saphesia

Tribe 7
CARPOBROTEAE
Carpobrotus

Disphyma	Frithia	Lapidaria	Monilaria	Pherolobus	Semnanthe
Dorotheanthus	Gibbaeum	Leipoldtia	Muiria	Pleiospilos	Stoeberia
Dracophilus	Glottiphyllum	Lithops	Namibia	Psammophora	Stomatium
Drosanthemum	Hereroa	Machairo-	Nananthus	Rhinephyllum	Titanopsis
Eberlanzia	Herreanthus	phyllum	Nelia	Rhombo-	Trichodiadema
Ebracteola	Jensenobotrya	Malephora	Neohenricia	phyllum	Vanheerdia
Ectotropis	Juttadinteria	Mestoklema	Neorhine	Ruschia	Vanzijlia
Erepsia	Kensitia	Meyerophytum	Odontophorus	Ruschianthemum	
Faucaria	Khadia	Micropterum	Orthopterum	Schlechteranthus	
Fenestraria	Lampranthus	Mitrophyllum	Oscularia	Schwantesia	

11: MESEMBRYANTHEMACEAE

it to perpetuate after the current season's seedlings have been destroyed.

Seedlings develop in different ways: in some the cotyledons (seed leaves) elongate and are like adult foliage *(Conicosia* 6.19); in others they remain more compressed and succulent, so that in *Herreanthus* the juvenile plant looks like a *Conophytum* for two to four years before the expanded adult leaves grow out.

The Mesembryanthemaceae are centred in South Africa, with isolated, mostly annual species to be found in St Helena, Madagascar, North Africa and Arabia. *Carpobrotus* and *Disphyma* are perhaps native in Australia and New Zealand; the occurrence of *Mesembryanthemum* in the New World seems to be the result of an introduction at an early date by man.

Right (11.6): **Mesembryanthemum barklyi** *is an annual or biennial "ice-plant" notable more for colourful, papillate foliage than flowers.*

Below (11.7): **Cephalophyllums** *are low-growing, carpeting plants with showy flowers in a wide range of colours. They flourish in full sun and a dry rather poor soil.*

Minor subfamilies and Tribes

All but one of the subdivisions within the Family can be dealt with briefly: few of the plants concerned are of interest outside botanical circles. Taking them in the order shown in the table on pages 134-5, *Mesembryanthemum* in its present, narrow sense includes 40-50 species of annual or biennial, very soft, sappy, brittle herbs with mostly flat expanded leaves and insignificant pallid flowers (11.6). I have seen one species growing near Springbok with leaves 40-50cm (16-20in) long—the largest in the Family—and sparkling like diamonds in the sun from the papillae that cover the whole surface of the plant. So soft were the leaves that it was impossible to pick one without reducing it to a pile of mush. *M. crystallinum* is the original ice-plant, now widespread and naturalized in the Mediterranean area, the Canary Isles and California. Each papilla is an enlarged surface cell of the epidermis that acts like a flask for water storage. *Sceletium* is a flat-leaved perennial shrublet in which the old leaves persist as skeletons at the base of the plant.

Tribe 2 features the extraordinary *Dactylopsis*, which would be in every collection if it were more adaptable to cultivation. It has very long, thick anchoring roots and fleshy finger-like growths made up of alternate united leaves from which the flower extrudes like a small white shaving brush. This is strictly for the connoisseur.

Hymenogyne (Subfamily 2) and *Caryotophora* (Subfamily 3) are flat-leaved weeds notable only for their unique fruits, which split up into large, winged part-fruits, each with a seed that is distributed by the wind. The same applies to Tribes 4-6, whose distinctive features are summarized in the table. *Conicosia* has a place in collections as a robust grower with thick roots, a rosette of long, three-edged, spirally arranged green leaves and profuse yellow blooms. It does poorly in a pot but thrives with a free root run, although, being self-fertile, it is apt to seed all over the place. It has massive fleshy roots and is almost hardy. Its extraordinary fruits with three different means of seed dispersal are dealt with on page 59. *Saphesia* is all but extinct (pages 96 and 135).

Finally, the Carpobroteae (Tribe 7) are set apart from all the others by the fleshy, indehiscent fruit, which ripens like a fig, whence the common names fig marigold and Hottentot's fig. *Carpobrotus* (3.11, 12) includes vigorous, prostrate growers that cover many square metres with their rooting stems; some, which are nearly hardy and flourish on sea coasts, have been found useful for consolidating dunes. *Carpobrotus* (11.8) is one of the few genera of the Family to occur outside South Africa, although the extent to which it has been artificially introduced is uncertain. According to S. T. Blake, four species are recorded from Australia, one from Norfolk Island and one from Chile; the remaining twenty or so are South African. Among its species are the largest of all blooms in the Mesembryanthemaceae. Jacobsen records that the fruits of *C. muirii* are dried and sold locally in South Africa, and those of *C. deliciosus* and *C. dulcis* are eaten raw.

Below (11.8): Most vigorous of the prostrate growing Mesembryanthemaceae, **Carpobrotus** *also has the largest flowers. Those in* **C. deliciosus**, *seen here, are 7 to 8cm (2¾-3¼in) across.*

11: MESEMBRYANTHEMACEAE

Ruschieae—the annuals and shrublets

Three quarters of all the genera come within the one Tribe Ruschieae, and almost all are plants with collector appeal. They share the common character of a fruit that opens by hygroscopic valves when wetted, releases the seeds, and closes again when dry. Schwantes divided this Tribe into 22 subtribes, partly on habit and partly on minute characters of the fruits. The best botanical treatment of the Family is *The Genera of Mesembryanthemaceae* by H. Herre, 1971. Here it is more convenient to adopt the gardener's breakdown into annual bedders, shrubby mesems, stemless mesems and mimicry plants, allowing that there is overlap.

Right (11.9): **Ruschia uncinata,** *hardiest of Mesembryanthemaceae, flowering in the author's garden in the London area. Propagation is from softwood cuttings.*

Below (11.10): **Dorotheanthus** *hybrids, along with* **Portulaca grandiflora,** *are the most popular and colourful of annual succulents.*

Above (11.11): **Mitrophyllum compactum** *showing a good example of heterophylly: a pair of widely expanded leaves followed by a pair united almost to the tip, forming the resting body.*

Below: (11.12): **Delosperma pruinosum,** *better known as* D. **echinatum,** *is immediately recognizable from the covering of bristles on the leaves. It is native to Little Namaqualand, South Africa.*

The group for annuals is dominated by those splendid embellishers of the flower border, the 'Livingstone Daisies', commonly marketed as seed of "Mesembryanthemum criniflorum", but correctly assigned to hybrids descended from *Dorotheanthus bellidiformis* crossed with *D. gramineus* and perhaps other species. Whatever the name, they are most lovely carpeters (11.10) and ideally suited for hot dry sites on a poor soil, where *Portulaca grandiflora* is their only rival.

In the second group we find the large genera *Lampranthus* (11.2), *Ruschia, Delosperma* (11.12), *Cephalophyllum* (11.7) and *Drosanthemum* with several hundred species between them, as well as other lesser stars. These are seen at their best bedded in the open in full sunshine — the more sun, the more profuse will be the floral display, and under such ideal conditions as in California or southern Europe nothing can surpass the sheets of dazzling colours in early summer. *Lampranthus,* the favourite genus, has a flower colour range covering most of the spectrum except blue. It is best to treat these as annuals, taking cuttings in the autumn and rooting them in trays of sand and peat under the glasshouse staging ready for planting out the following spring. Attractive smaller genera are *Oscularia* and *Malephora* with grey or pruinose leaves, *Eberlanzia* with thorns and *Trichodiadema* with a cluster of bristles at the tip of each leaf giving a quaint reminder of the cactus areole. *Ruschia uncinata* (11.9) is the hardiest of all, in my experience, and has survived outdoors unprotected in London and Reading for many years now.

Very different from the foregoing are the *Mitrophyllums* (11.11), considered by Jacobsen in 1960 as "among the rarest and most interesting of the Family". The interest remains, but, thanks to supplies of seed from South Africa, they are not as rare as they were. This genus introduces us to heterophylly: the leaf pair produced during the growing season is much more open and expanded than the conical, united pair that follows and remains during the rest period. Comparing a dormant plant with one in full growth, one would never think them the same species. The 29 species, which include some originally described as *Conophyllum,* form small, sparingly branched shrublets rarely more than 10–50cm (4–20in) high. Cuttings do not root readily and flowers are hardly ever seen in Europe. As suggested on page 74, this may be a day-length phenomenon that a little experimenting with shades and extra lights might overcome. The growing season is late summer and autumn. *Monilaria* is a related genus in which the nodes (stem joints) are swollen and look like a string of large beads.

11: MESEMBRYANTHEMACEAE

Ruschieae — the stemless types

The plants included here have the leaf pairs so tightly packed together that there are no visible internodes between. *Faucaria* is a good plant for beginners, being comparatively easy to grow if it has sharp drainage and is not overwatered. It has a few pairs of opposite decussate leaves with the upper margins usually more or less toothed or bristly. In *F. tuberculosa* (11.15) these cartilaginous teeth extend also to the leaf surface. *Carruanthus* has similar toothed foliage. The fancied resemblance of the top pair of leaves to the gaping jaws of an animal led Bradley to christen the last-mentioned 'Dog's Chaps', and the Latin epithets of *Faucaria felina* (of cats), *F. lupina* (wolves) and *F. tigrina* (tigers) perpetuate similar analogies. Both genera should be watered in summer and rested dry in winter. They flower freely, and the bloom is large, yellow, and sits tightly in the centre of the rosette. In full sunshine, the leaves take on an attractive purplish colour. *F. candida* has white petals. There are reputedly 33 species of *Faucaria*.

Somewhat similar are the *Stomatiums* (11.14) (40 species), which are usually smaller in all parts, but the flower colour range extends to pink *(S. alboroseum)*. Some open their blooms at dusk and are fragrant. *S. agninum* I have found to survive outdoors in England in mild winters.

Glottiphyllum is one of the most immediately recognizable genera (11.13), the leaves being extremely soft and juicy, typically bright green and arranged in pairs in two series obliquely on short branches that hug the soil. This is true of *G. linguiforme*, Bradley's 'Smaller Dwarf Tongue-leav'd Fig Marygold', the type species and longest known. Many of the 57 species resemble *G. linguiforme* and are a little rampant in collections, but there are some fine compact species such as *G. herrei* with glaucous pinkish leaves, *G. pygmaeum* with very squat rounded leaves and *G. semicylindricum (bidentatum)* with lax shoots bearing small, pustulate leaves each with two prominences set obliquely, one on either margin. *Glottiphyllums* have splendid large yellow flowers (scented in *G. fragrans*) and deserve to be better known, at least in the distinctive dwarf representatives. The reason for their neglect is the surfeit of sprawling, badly grown, nondescript plants of the *G. linguiforme* type that give the genus a bad name. The secret is to keep the plants in small pots in full sun and to be utterly hard-hearted about watering: they thrive on starvation and quickly spoil if overfed.

Cylindrophyllum is another easily grown genus comprising *C. calamiforme* and five doubtfully distinct segregates. The long, cylindrical, finger-like leaves make it easy to recognize. Bradley called it the 'Onion or Quill-leaved Fig-Marigold'.

Bergeranthus is credited with 11 species, although only *B. multiceps, B. scapiger* and *B. vespertinus* are common. Here the leaves are densely crowded in basal rosettes, semicylindrical, long-tapered, smooth and green, and the habit is clustering. They grow in summer, flower freely and keep out of trouble in my experience.

Right (11.13): Glottiphyllum praepingue *is best kept in full sun and starved of water to avoid too lush, pallid growth.*

Below right (11.14): Stomatium jamesii *has teeth on the leaf margins and is covered in conspicuous papillae.*

Below (11.15): Faucaria tuberculosa, *characterized by the marginal teeth, which in this particular species are supplemented by further teeth on the leaf tip.*

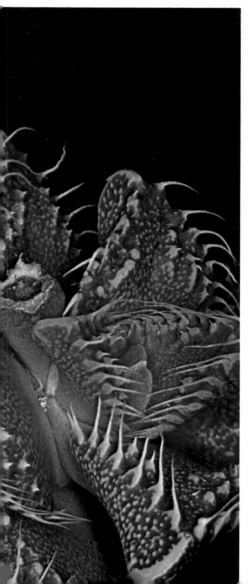

11: MESEMBRYANTHEMACEAE

Machairophyllum has a similar but more compact look and forms large clumps. There are ten described species, of which the best known is Bradley's 'Dwarf Triangular White-leaf'd Fig-Marygold', *M. albidum.* As he correctly tells us, "it loves a dry warm air and little water."

With *Nananthus* (syn. *Aloinopsis*) (11.16) we come to the midget species forming a natural link to the mimicry genera. Often the most voluminous part of the plant is the rootstock, which bears short branches at soil level with only one or two leaf pairs at the tip of each. Pot-grown, young plants look best; with age the centre becomes bare and unsightly. This is a cue to cut off the tips at the start of the growing season and propagate new plants from them. *Nananthus schoonesii* forms a carpet of tiny, closely packed, flat-topped leaves that look as if sheared off level with a knife. At the Worcester Gardens in the Cape, where my specimen came from, it is an abundant weed in

Right (11.16): Nananthus transvaalensis—
Nananthus means "midget flower"—is one of many miniatures approaching in habit and markings the mimicry Mesembryanthemaceae.

Below (11.17): To encourage flowering, as in this Cheiridopsis, *stemless members of the Mesembryanthemaceae need full sun and an annual rest period when they are kept quite dry.*

chinks between the paving stones.

Cheiridopsis is a genus of great appeal to collectors, no species being unworthy of attention (11.3, 17), even if it is hard to believe that over 100 merit recognition as separate species. All are highly succulent and dwarf species and, like *Mitrophyllum*, show a degree of heterophylly, the resting plant looking very unlike a growing one. *C. peculiaris* shows this in a marked degree. This is a true mimicry species, found only against purplish brown rocks, which its bronzed foliage matches perfectly. When in the dormant condition the expanded leaves die back and are replaced by an erect cone that protects the growing centre from desiccation. *C. candidissima,* looked upon as rather a choice and costly rarity in cultivation, is extremely common in parts of South Africa; uncountable clumps, 30–50cm (12–20in) across, dominate the flat open landscape with their trim, glaucous, pointed leaves and white to pale pink blossoms—a magnificent sight.

Left (11.18): Didymaotus lapidiformis, *an excellent example of natural camouflage, amid granite rocks in habitat at Beukesfontein, S. Africa. This endangered species was growing within feet of an expanding quarry.*

Below (11.19): Pleiospilos *species in the famous outdoor garden of Pinya de Rosa on the Costa Brava, Spain. An overhead frame screens them from excess wetness in winter.*

Ruschieae—the mimicry types

We now come to genera where mimicry, as defined on page 71, is the rule rather than the exception (5.10). The preceding genera are not particularly difficult to keep, once one has mastered the essentials of porous soil, light and observation of the resting period. Since they adapt to summer growth in the Northern Hemisphere this is no problem. Now we turn to plants that are not only among the great prizes of collectors, but they include a few that tax the patience in efforts to preserve them alive. *Didymaotus* is one example. Not many growers manage to keep it for more than a few years, and if they do it looks nothing like the "split rock" it is in its habitat (11.18). Jacobsen recommends full sun, little water and a resting period in early summer.

Pleiospilos, no less attractive in its dwarf species *P. bolusii* (11.4) and *P. nelii,* is fortunately much easier to grow. These two species, each with one or two pairs of almost hemispherical leaves of greyish colour with darker spots, look like granite pebbles. Others of the 33 species have more elongated leaves (11.19) and some form large clumps. The showy yellow flowers come late in the season and sometimes smell strongly of coconut.

A different type of "mimicry" is shown by *Titanopsis* (11.20), which grows

among quartz rocks and has a white crystalline appearance from large papillae covering the leaf tips. A much-quoted story tells how Professor Marloth, a leading authority on the African flora, discovered *T. calcarea* by accident when he rested against it under the impression that it was a rock. All five species are distinctive in leaf patterning and immediately attractive to the collector, but it is best to raise seedlings every few years because they tend to be short-lived and die without warning, so can hardly be recommended to beginners.

Neohenricia is like an even smaller version of *Titanopsis* but its tiny flowers open at dusk and exhale a powerful fragrance that would justify the inclusion of *N. sibbettii,* the only species, in a collection even if the plant were less demure and charming. Fortunately it is easy to grow and propagates readily from short runners.

Fenestraria and *Frithia* are taken together because both have "window leaves" (page 24), the rosette being buried in the soil with only the translucent tips

Above (11.20): The white, incrusted leaves of **Titanopsis** *match the quartz chips among which the species grow in South and South West Africa: a fine example of camouflage.*

Below (11.21): The white-flowered form of **Fenestraria aurantiaca** *popularly referred to as 'Baby's Toes'. It can be multiplied by dividing the clumps. Note the window leaf tips.*

Above (11.22): **Frithia pulchra** *is superficially like* **Fenestraria,** *but not closely related. It is a short-lived perennial, propagated only from seed, and comes from the Transvaal, S. Africa.*

Below (11.23): *Most species of* **Gibbaeum** *have the leaves of the pair unequal in size. This is* **G. dispar** *in a 7cm (2¾ in) pot. The leaf surface is velvety and the flower purplish pink.*

of each curved, club-shaped leaf exposed to the sun. In cultivation they are grown above soil. But the two genera, both of one species each, are not closely related. *Fenestraria aurantiaca,* 'Baby's Toes' (11.21), is the easier to keep; it has flowers of various shades from buff to pinkish yellow, and its form *rhopalophylla* is white. Dividing a clump is the easiest means of multiplication. *Frithia* has vivid crimson blooms (11.22) and forms no offsets. It is short-lived and can only be raised from seed. It rests in summer and needs watering in early spring.

Gibbaeum introduces us to another popular genus including 21 species of compact but diverse form whose linking character is the lopsided leaf pair. Occasionally the two leaves are only slightly unequal in size *(G. esterhuyseniae* with expanded leaves; *G. cryptopodium* with leaves fused into an egg-shaped body). In *G. pubescens* the leaves are very unequal, one being represented only as a small lobe at the side of the other. Nel, whose unfinished monograph of the genus was published posthumously in 1953, records that all species of *Gibbaeum* occur in an area of the Little Karroo 135km (85mi) by 40km (25mi) with two outliers to the northwest, *G. gibbosum* and *G. heathii.* Within the main area some species are widespread, others local. *G. schwantesii* is limited to a patch about 90m² (100yd²), so is of concern to the conservationist. Up to six species grow sympatrically (that is, side by side in the same area) and there is a fascinating field for study here on the nature of the barriers that prevent hybridization in the wild. In cultivation, flowering is at the start of the growing season; this differs from species to species, and may contribute to keeping the species apart in nature. Authorities differ with their watering recommendations for *Gibbaeum*: it seems safest to play it by eye, watching each plant for signs of awakening, and easing off watering after it has flowered. *G. album, dispar* (11.23) and *velutinum* seem to prefer to grow in winter.

Close to *Gibbaeum,* and one of the most specialized of all succulents, is the extraordinary monotypic genus *Muiria.* Its anatomical peculiarities are mentioned on page 12. At the classic habitat I visited in the Little Karroo in 1971, *Muiria hortenseae* was confined to one of many quartz patches a few metres across. Outside the patch, none was to be seen. Inside, they were so thick on the ground that one could not step without treading on them. Each plant looks like a circle of ripe, downy greengages: the two leaves of a pair are so completely fused that only a tiny slit on one side shows where they join, and through this the brush-like flower emerges. Unfortunately this wonder of the vegetable kingdom resists

11: MESEMBRYANTHEMACEAE

the advances of cultivators, although large numbers have been imported in vain.

Argyroderma, the 'Silverskin' (11.24), has been the subject of a recent monograph by Heidrun Hartmann, who recognizes ten variable species. The growths are solitary or form a clump, each made up of two opposite leaves shaped like a halved egg or a short finger and characteristically quite smooth and silvery grey. The flower colours are white, yellow or purple, but can vary within one species. The growing period is in middle to late summer when minimal watering should be given, just to prevent shrivelling. *Argyroderma* is prone to develop brown disfigurements or split if overwatered. Full sun is essential.

Of rather similar form, but closer to *Lithops* in body markings, is *Dinteranthus* (11.5), with six species, all collec-

tors' pieces and reputedly ephemeral in cultivation. *D. vanzijlii* has been mistaken for a *Lithops,* from which it can be distinguished by the ten-celled capsule and the smaller seeds, perhaps the most minute in the Family.

Conophytum (11.25, 26), with 315 species described by Jacobsen, only awaits a modern monograph to launch it into the popularity it deserves. An evolutionary climax group within the Mesembryanthemaceae, it shows maximum surface reduction in relation to bulk, and a most efficient and economical life form, in which a single body composed of two united leaves withers to protect the next season's bud and transfers its stored food to nourish it. During half the year a *Conophytum* looks dead: but do not despair! Life goes on beneath the brown leathery sheaths. Keep it dry and at most just moisten the topsoil until the plant

itself gives the cue to begin watering by starting to split open the sheaths. Some *Conophytums* have almost spherical bodies; others, the bilobes, have the two leaves free at the tip (11.1). For both sorts the growing season is late summer, but the bilobes make an earlier start, so watering for them should begin around June; for the others, a month later, stopping at the end of the year. *Conophytums* in nature are lithophytes: plants growing in rock chinks and cliffs with a minimum of soil and water. I have seen bare rock faces clothed in mats of *Conophytum* that could be stripped off like lichen; indeed, one marvels how any plant can survive in such spartan conditions. Yet they adapt well to pot culture if the correct watering ritual is observed, and a collection of specimen plants is indeed a sight (11.29), especially when covered in yellow, white, orange and red

Above (11.24): **Argyroderma pearsonii,** *one of the 'Silverskins'. Caution with watering is advisable; too much makes the leaves split. All* **Argyrodermas** *come from the Van Rhynsdorp District of the Cape, South Africa.*

Above left (11.25): Hugging the bare rocks, **Conophytum ectypum** *in habitat in Little Namaqualand. Each 4-6mm (¼ in) head of two leaves is renewed each growing season.*

Right (11.26): **Conophytum saxetanum** *from Namibia. Each tiny growth is only 2-4mm (¹/₁₂-¹/₆in) across. The plants grow on rock like lichens, which they superficially resemble.*

blooms. The white flowers are mostly nocturnal and fragrant. It takes many years to build up a large clump from a single head, but they are remarkably long-lived and tolerant of neglect, seeming none the worse for standing on a top shelf for years without repotting. *Ophthalmophyllum,* sometimes treated as a separate

11: MESEMBRYANTHEMACEAE

genus, is a subgenus of *Conophytum* with windowed leaves.

Finally we come to *Lithops* (5.10), at once the most popular and most distinctive of all genera of Mesembryanthemaceae: the renowned "pebble plants" or "living stones". The body here is reduced to a single pair of opposite leaves united into a cone (2.11), with a fissure across the centre through which the flower emerges and then the next leaf pair, at right angles to the old. Some remain solitary; others branch to produce small clumps by developing two leaf pairs from a single head. As in *Conophytum*, the old leaf pair nourishes the new and the delicate growing apex is safely hidden below soil near the base of the cone. Unlike that of *Conophytum*, however, its growing season readily adapts to the

Unique in the Plant Kingdom, the 'pebble plants' resemble the mineral background of their natural environment. Each top-shaped growth of two leaves is renewed annually. They are all sun-lovers but not difficult to manage and easy to raise from seed. Flowers are yellow or white. There are 37 species, some of them with several varieties. Right (11.27): **Lithops bromfieldii** *and below (11.28)* **Lithops hallii.**

Northern Hemisphere cycle, so if plants are kept quite dry in winter, and watered only after the skin has started to split to reveal the new body, all should be well. Overwatering produces a grotesque, untypical appearance (6.2).

Lithops grows buried in the soil, only the flattened leaf tips being exposed. These are never plain green but usually elaborately mottled and spotted, and harmonize with the colours of the surrounding soil. This "mimicry" is further discussed on page 71. The colours and patterning are the chief characters whereby the 37 species are identified, together with the flower colour, which is either yellow or white. The recent conservative classification by Desmond Cole (1973) is the best so far. *Lithops* is a perfect subject for a specialist collector with ample sunshine but little space. As in *Conophytum*, all the species can be accommodated in small pots, and maintenance is minimal. They are among the easiest Mesembryanthemaceae to raise from seed, and singularly free from pests and diseases. No collection should be without at least a few species of *Lithops*: they are among the marvels of the vegetable kingdom and never fail to excite great interest and comment from visitors.

Cultivation

Mesembryanthemaceae are creatures of the sun, and resent shading more than most succulents. The stems elongate, the lovely glaucous bloom and coloured markings become a pallid green, and flowering is suppressed. Therefore in any mixed collection of succulents they should head the queue for sites in the sun, preferably close to the glass. The shrubby kinds do well outdoors in summer, and because winter temperatures do not need to be high and aeration is important, a frost-proof frame can be put to good use for the less delicate sorts. Good air circulation is important at all times, even in winter on milder, brighter days. Where smog and other adversities afflict the local flora, plants that change their skins once a year are at an advantage. One of the most celebrated collections of dwarf Mesembryanthemaceae long throve in Hounslow in the suburbs of London, which is not renowned for either pure air or high light intensity.

The importance of a restraining hand on the watering can has already been stressed: watch the plants and they will tell you when growth is commencing or when, after flowering, a rest is needed. Those that insist upon growing in winter —*Conophytum, Dactylopsis, Frithia*, some *Gibbaeums*, etc — must be watered cautiously and supplied with extra warmth and all the light possible. Nothing rots a succulent quicker than standing in cold damp soil. Hence it may be necessary to shift the pots around in autumn to obtain the favoured places for winter growers.

Propagation by both seed (6.19) and vegetative means is possible for most species. A few, such as *Mitrophyllum*, root with difficulty, and for single-headed plants such as *Frithia*, and some *Lithops* and *Argyrodermas*, seed is the only way. Single leaves, even if you can root them, do not regenerate plants. When taking cuttings of a dwarf *Lithops* or *Conophytum*, be sure to cut as low as possible, at the narrowest point. If you miss the growing apex near the base of the cone, the attempt will be in vain.

Below (11.29): Part of a collection of **Conophytums**, *small plants ideal for the specialist with little space. Large clumps like this take many years to develop.*

The Purslane Family

This is another Family of the Order Caryophyllales, and all its members are more or less succulent. However, many are small-flowered annuals and of interest only to the botanist. Of the 19 genera, about seven are represented in succulent collections. All are leaf succulents, although with a frequent tendency to the caudiciform in *Anacampseros* (*A. alstonii*, 21.22), *Talinum* (*T. caffrum*, *T. guadalupense*, 15.4) and some *Portulacas*. The leaves are always entire and often bear at the base long white hairs that are interpreted as modified stipules. An extreme development of the stipules is noted under *Anacampseros* below. Among the generally small flowers are a few more showy ones, and it is these that have caught the eye of the horticulturist and earned the bearers a place in our gardens. Typically there are two fleshy green sepals, five (sometimes four or six) free petals and one, two or more whorls of stamens, the largest flowers (*Portulaca, Lewisia*) having most stamens. The ovary has three (or up to five) united carpels.

Below (12.1): Portulaca grandiflora *rivals* Dorotheanthus *(11.10) as the most colourful and popular annual succulent. Note the equally wide range of flower colours.

Portulaca is a widespread and prolific genus, although the present tendency is to reduce its 125 described species to about 15. Some are annual, some perennial. One scarcely succulent species, the common purslane, *P. oleracea,* has a long history as a potherb, and has been carried from country to country. It was probably native to India but is now a cosmopolitan weed. Gerard (1598) says of it: "It cooleth an hot stomack". *P. grandiflora* (5.3, 12.1) is an admirable half-hardy annual that brings colour to the drier, poorer parts of a garden. It has been subject to intensive selection for colour variants and double flowers, and its genetical background has been worked out in detail (see page 65).

Ceraria (12.2) and *Portulacaria* are closely related genera of tender, perennial species that grow into large shrubs in nature, although in cultivation they are more familiar as tiny plants, their thick, rather fleshy stems giving them, when young, an attractive bonsai appearance. The leaves are small, simple, fleshy and flat to nearly cylindrical. The flowers are minute and hardly ever seen in cultivation. The variegated form of *Portulacaria afra,* with yellow patches on the foliage, is justly popular.

Lewisia is most in favour among rock and alpine gardeners, but no true lover of succulents should overlook it. It comprises about 16 species from the western USA through Mexico to Bolivia. Typically there is a stout perennial rootstock that can endure long desiccation and bears a rosette of flattened or cylindrical fleshy leaves that are evergreen in some species, deciduous in others. Most of the kinds offered by florists are of hybrid origin, and the pedigrees are largely conjectural. The flowers, mostly in shades of pink and apricot, are quite showy (12.4, 7). Despite their hardiness, *Lewisias* are sensitive to waterlogging, and the protection of a frame or alpine house is recommended. Propagation is by dividing up clumps or

Right (12.2): Ceraria namaquensis, *perfect as a bonsai plant, but a tall scarcely succulent shrub in old age. Judicious pruning each autumn will keep the plant bushy.*

Below right (12.3): Anacampseros papyracea. *The white scales are stipules enveloping minute green leaves beneath. The flowers expand for an hour or two only. The pot is 7cm (2¾in) wide.*

Overleaf (12.4): Although Lewisias are hardy, they mostly do better with the protection of a frame or unheated alpine house in winter. These are hybrids of L. cotyledon.

THE PURSLANE FAMILY (PORTULACACEAE)—A breakdown to genus level (succulent members)

Ovary inferior or half-superior; ovules numerous	Ovary superior		
	Capsule indehiscent; ovule solitary	Capsule dehiscing by a lid or valves splitting from the base upwards; ovules more than 6	Capsule dehiscing by valves splitting from the top downwards; ovules more than 6
Tribe 1 **PORTULACEAE**	Tribe 2 **PORTULACARIEAE**	Tribe 3 **LEWISIEAE**	Tribe 4 **TALINEAE**

Tribe 2
Ceraria namaquensis

Tribe 3
Lewisia cotyledon hybrid

Tribe 4
Anacampseros papyracea

Tribe 1
Portulaca grandiflora

Tribe 1 **PORTULACEAE** Portulaca	Tribe 2 **PORTULACARIEAE** Ceraria Portulacaria	Tribe 3 **LEWISIEAE** Lewisia	Tribe 4 **TALINEAE** Anacampseros Calandrinia Talinum

raising seed. *Lewisia rediviva* is the State flower of Montana, called bitter-root by allusion to the bitter taste of the bark, which is stripped off by the Indians before they boil the root as food. It first came to the notice of botanists when a herbarium specimen came to life after some years and, on being potted and watered, flowered and revealed itself as a new species.

Calandrinia and *Talinum* are among the genera of which isolated species occasionally find their way into the glass-houses of succulent enthusiasts, but are usually soon ushered out again because the flowers are so inconspicuous or the seed comes up everywhere. *C. grandiflora* and some allied species are grown as border annuals: the blue-grey glaucous foliage is somewhat fleshy and pleasantly sets off the purple-magenta flowers.

This leaves *Anacampseros*, a fascinating and highly evolved genus of succulent xerophytes offering much to the seeker after the unusual. About half of the 50 or so described species are very easy to grow; they thrive in full sun and a porous soil, with ample water in summer and frost exclusion in winter, and they show their appreciation by seeding themselves everywhere. They are all small enough to accommodate in 7–9cm (3–3½in) pots. The leaves are more or less flattened, very fleshy, simple and rosetted, usually with

silky hairs at the base clothing the stems. The pink (or rarely white) flowers are held high in inflorescences. *A. rufescens* is a common example of this kind; *A. telephiastrum* is larger in all its parts. Very different are those species in which the leaves are minute and completely enveloped by large, white, papery stipules (12.3). Here, presumably, we have another device associated with water conservation and reducing the light intensity reaching the chlorophyll: the plant grows its own sunshades. Certainly the plants are intense xerophytes, occurring in full sunshine on exposed flat places in South Africa as well as in rock crevices, usually associated with the quartz rock with which their white shoots blend and are difficult to see.

Contrary to what one might expect, the small-leaved species of *Anacampseros* seem to like as much water as those with large leaves in cultivation: it is a mistake to keep them too dry. The soil should be very porous and a winter minimum of 7°C (45°F) is advisable. The flowers are solitary at the stem tips and it is quite an occasion to see one open at all (12.5). Mostly they ripen capsules of seed without opening (4.17)—an example of cleistogamy.

The stem-succulent Portulacaceae are dealt with in Chapter 15, and the caudiciform species in Chapter 21.

Above (12.5): Flower of **Anacampseros bremekampii** *showing the six red petals, eight stamens and three styles, readily distinguishable from the isomerous flower of Crassulaceae (page 31).*

Right (12.6): **Anacampseros albissima** *from Namaqualand and South West Africa, in a 6cm (2½in) pot. Each papery white scale on the stem conceals a tiny green leaf.*

Below (12.7): Lewisia hybrids in the author's garden. The natural clay soil has been lightened with grit and peat, and the plants are set among light-reflecting rocks.

The Lily Family

With the lily Family we come to the first of the Orders of Monocotyledons. It is regarded as a key Order, the structurally simple flowers and fruits standing near the start of the ancestral line from which evolved more specialized groups: the grasses, bromeliads and orchids. The Liliaceae cover an estimated 250 genera and 3,700 species. The distribution is cosmopolitan, although it is usual to find each of the 28 Tribes into which it is divided confined more or less to one area or continent. Distinguishing features are a radially symmetrical flower with a perianth composed of six similar members without a distinction into green calyx and coloured corolla. Stamens also number six and carpels three; the ovary is never inferior.

Minor tribes

The Liliaceae provide our gardens with many fine flowers besides lilies, particularly in spring and early summer, including tulips and hyacinths and many bulbous genera; the Family also includes such vegetables as onions and asparagus. Some species of *Asparagus* are extreme xerophytes and grow alongside euphorbias and the Stapelieae in South Africa. One species I collected in the Lebombo Mountains, in pachypodium territory, has fat watery underground tubers and is as good an example of root succulence as I know. Bulbs are also well adapted to store food underground and endure long seasons unfavourable for growth. Whether or not some desert bulbs qualify as succulents is long disputed. It is very much a matter of taste whether or not you extend your collection to include *Scilla violacea, Ornithogalum caudatum, Drimia, Buphane, Haèmanthus* and many more. *Bowiea volubilis* (page 158) has long been accepted by succulent growers: if planted above ground the large spherical bulb turns green and never produces anything nearer a leaf than a few "blades of grass". Instead it sprouts a long twining annual shoot with finely divided side branches and small greenish flowers that set abundant seed—altogether an oddity, of novelty value in a mixed collection. A recently described curiosity from near Steinkopf is *Albuca unifoliata* (page 158), in which we have the ultimate economy: a single, club-shaped, very fleshy leaf one year, and a flower stalk and three to five small starry blooms the next, but never

Right (13.1): **Bulbine succulenta** *produces very soft pale green foliage annually from perennial fleshy roots. The yellow flowers are noteworthy for the bearded filaments to the stamens. Pot size 7 cm (2¾ in).*

both together. I have had bulbs rest for two years, and in habitat they may well remain dormant for even longer, awaiting sufficient rain to stir them into activity. *Lachenalia patula* is rather similar, and no more amenable to cultivation.

Another manifestation of succulence in Liliaceae is in the genus *Bulbine*, most of whose many species have pale green, somewhat fleshy leaves. It is widely spread over South and East Africa, but only a few species are at all common in cultivation. The starry flowers borne in long racemes are mostly yellow, but in *B. frutescens* there is an orange cultivar, 'Hallmark', and a white one, 'Virgo'. The spot character for recognizing *Bulbine* is the presence of shaggy hair on the filaments of the stamens. *B. latifolia* has rosettes of soft, aloe-like leaves borne on a short thick stem, and flowers over a

long season. More for connoisseurs are the dwarf tuberous species that die down for a part of the year; these need strict observation of the resting period or they will quickly fade away. *B. succulenta* (13.1) is one such, with a subterranean caudex crowned by bristles and producing two to four erect, very soft and watery grooved leaves. In habitat these remain short, but in cultivation all the dwarf species lose character completely and the leaves become much longer and thinner. Highly prized is *B. mesembryanthoides*, with one or two squat watery leaves with truncated translucent tips—a true "window plant". Strangest of all is *B. haworthioides*, which looks like a miniature *Haworthia tessellata*. It was found as recently as 1962 and at that time was considered rare, but on a search in 1971 populations came to light so dense that

the plants almost touched one another.

Aloineae

The fourth Tribe to be considered is Aloineae, composed wholly of succulents. It is allied to the Kniphofieae, which include *Kniphofia*, the redhot poker of our gardens, hardier and non-succulent. Aloineae are perennial rosette plants, solitary in some species, suckering in others to form clumps, and occasionally tree-like with a thick but curiously spongy

Overleaf (13.2): Aloe shrubs and trees are a memorable feature of the African landscape. Here the widespread **Aloe arborescens** *is seen at the mouth of Storms River, South Cape.*

Below (13.3): **Aloe thompsoniae** *represents a small but interesting group of "grass aloes", seen here in habitat in North East Transvaal. It is a parent of the hybrid 'Bountiful'.*

13: LILIACEAE

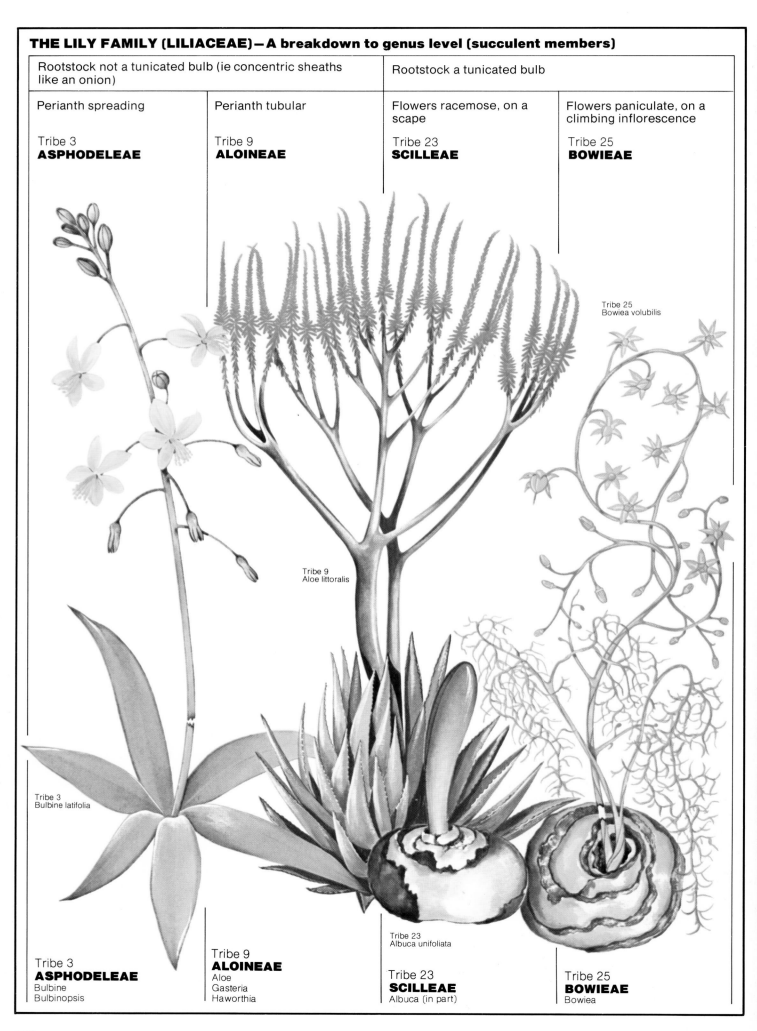

THE LILY FAMILY (LILIACEAE)—A breakdown to genus level (succulent members)

Rootstock not a tunicated bulb (ie concentric sheaths like an onion)		Rootstock a tunicated bulb	
Perianth spreading	Perianth tubular	Flowers racemose, on a scape	Flowers paniculate, on a climbing inflorescence
Tribe 3 **ASPHODELEAE**	Tribe 9 **ALOINEAE**	Tribe 23 **SCILLEAE**	Tribe 25 **BOWIEAE**

Tribe 25
Bowiea volubilis

Tribe 9
Aloe littoralis

Tribe 3
Bulbine latifolia

Tribe 23
Albuca unifoliata

Tribe 3
ASPHODELEAE
Bulbine
Bulbinopsis

Tribe 9
ALOINEAE
Aloe
Gasteria
Haworthia

Tribe 23
SCILLEAE
Albuca (in part)

Tribe 25
BOWIEAE
Bowiea

13: LILIACEAE

trunk. The inflorescence arises laterally, so that the rosette bearing it does not die after flowering, as it does in agave, and the flowers are borne in racemes or panicles. The fruit is a dry, three-celled capsule, except in one Madagascan section of the genus *Aloe (Lomatophyllum)*, where it is a fleshy berry. All are predominantly South African, *Aloe* alone extending the range to Madagascar, Arabia and some Atlantic islands.

Aloe is the largest and earliest described genus, which at one time included all the species. As monographed by Reynolds (1950, 1966) it now includes 359 species—or more, if the small segregate genera are also included. The smallest, *A. (Leptaloe) saundersiae*, has a rosette of grass-like leaves lying flat on the soil and barely 10cm (4in) across; the largest is probably *A. bainesii*, a tree of massive bulk and singular appearance up to 20m(67ft) tall—among the largest of Monocotyledons. *A. dichotoma* (3.3, 13.4) is almost as large. They do not form solid wood like Dicotyledons: a cross-section of the stem is like a dense aggregation of fibres with barely a hint of annual rings, so that the age of large specimens can only be guessed. Although very light, the wood must be extremely strong to support the crown of water-filled branches. The bark is smooth and leathery and flakes off in plates. A few aloes such as *A. ciliaris* have long, weak, scrambling stems.

Aloe leaves are arranged spirally in terminal rosettes (13.7), or rarely distichous (in two series), an example being *A. plicatilis*. In species where the stems elongate there are sometimes scattered leaves along the axis too (13.2). Leaves may be triangular or parallel-sided, plain or variously striped and spotted, flat or channelled and entire or prickly along the margins. When cut they exude a sticky, bitter sap containing aloin, the source of medicinal aloes. The flowers are tubular and pendant, and come in shades of red, orange and yellow or rarely white (13.6, 10). Sunbirds and bees are the principal pollinators, and copious nectar is offered to them (4.4). The inflorescence is a simple raceme, a spike or a panicle.

The genus has much to offer collectors, although many of the species eventually outgrow the space available in an amateur glasshouse. However, even these are worth having for the beauty of the seedlings. In frost-free countries where aloes can be grown in the open, a collection of species is a noble sight, and in South Africa they are popular garden subjects, being largely trouble-free, floriferous and tolerant of drought. New hybrids are continually being named and introduced, with even greater vigour and profusion of flowers. In Europe hybridization is also popular, but it is the dwarf species that are most in demand. A few of these have long been popular as house plants— *A. variegata*, the 'Partridge Aloe', for instance. *A. aristata* (13.9) resembles a *Haworthia* in leaf form and is the hardiest of the genus. Collectors' pieces are the Madagascan miniatures *A. haworthioides* and *A. descoingsii* (13.5). *A. (Guillauminia) albiflora*, with bell-shaped white flowers, is also appealing. Needing special

Right (13.4): **Aloe dichotoma**, *the kokerboom, one of the larger true aloes, is the involuntary host here for nests of the sociable weaver bird.*

Below (13.5): **Aloe descoingsii** *is a native of Madagascar and recalls* **Haworthia** *in habit. It is one of the smallest aloes (this particular clump is about 8cm (3¼ in) across) and requires warmth and cautious watering.*

care are the so-called "grass aloes" with long, narrow deciduous grassy leaves (13.3). Some even form a bulb at the base: *A. kniphofioides,* for example. Water must be withheld after flowering, and the plant allowed to die down; it will usually give the first sign itself when water is again needed, by sending up new green leaves.

No succulents are easier to cross than aloes. They tend to be self-incompatible, and hybrids can be made not only within the genus but with other Aloineae, for example *Aloe* × *Gasteria* (= × *Gastrolea).* Some of the progeny can be real improvements, such as the free-flowering 'Bountiful' *(A. albiflora* × *thompsoniae* 13.3) and 'Sabra' *(A. albiflora* × *bellatula).*

'American Aloe', it should be noted, is a misnomer for agave.

Gasteria consists of dwarf, almost or quite stemless succulents with rosettes similar to *Aloe* but showing more tendency for the leaves to remain in two series (13.8). They all start that way: in some species they become spiral with age, in others they do not. Unlike those of *Aloe,* the leaves are never prickly, although they may be covered in white papillae *(G. verrucosa),* or rough with small green and white pustules *(G. batesiana).* The shape is parallel-sided and rounded at the tip with a small, sharp, white point; some are flat, others grooved or V-shaped in cross-section. The racemes are usually unbranched, and the most noticeable feature of the flowers is the swollen base of the perianth tube, which gives the genus its name *(gaster* = a belly). The colour is pink, with the lobes lighter or greenish at the tip. The genus is confined to South and South West Africa.

Jacobsen (1975) lists 76 species, but they are mostly ill-defined and the number will certainly be reduced when we know more about their variability in the field. Different names have been applied to young and mature shoots of the same species! Horticulturally, they are all attractive, unassuming, undemanding plants with great variety in the shapes and markings of the leaves, which are often splashed or spotted with paler patches. In addition to those mentioned above, *G. pulchra* and *G. liliputana* form clusters of neat rosettes and flower freely in summer. But the gem among the miniatures is *G. armstrongii,* with usually a single, slow-growing rosette of fat, blackish green tongue-like leaves in two series like the pages of a book. By way of colour contrast, there are some fine variegated gasterias.

Right (13.6): The smaller aloes are dependable for flowers, undemanding and generally long lived in collections. This one is **Aloe inyangensis** *from Rhodesia.*

The genus exhibits in varying degrees the phenomenon of juvenile and adult phases, the habit of the plant changing as it matures. The most dramatic example is *G. beckeri,* in which the young rosette looks much like *G. armstrongii* but abruptly goes over to the adult phase of spirally arranged, smooth, obliquely V-shaped foliage with yellow spots. So different are the two phases that one would never associate them as the same species if seen separately. *G. beckeri* flowers only from the adult growths. In *G. armstrongii* the juvenile phase is retained and flowers without changing to adult leaves. We call this type of arrested juvenility *neoteny,* a term borrowed from zoology.

Gasteria forms interesting hybrids with both *Aloe* and *Haworthia.*

Haworthia enjoys great popularity among collectors of succulents, some of whom specialize in the genus and bring together all the myriad variations of leaf shape and form, colour and texture, of which 13.11, 12 give but a small idea. There are 68 species recognized in the latest monograph by Bayer (1976), with 41 subspecies, varieties or forms.

Haworthias are compact-growing solitary or clumping plants with tight rosettes close to the soil level. A few form a very short stem with age, covered in spirally arranged leaves sometimes set in three rows. In some species the leaves are very firm and tough, usually dark green in colour and commonly set with white pustules, tubercles or ridges; in others they are soft and pale green, often with translucent lines or patches at the tip ("windows" 2.6), which sometimes bears a white bristle. In nature, haworthias seek out the shade of rocks and shrubs, often hiding completely from view, and to photograph some species it is necessary to clear away the undergrowth in order to reveal the plant at all. The fleshy, long roots have a fibrous core that, by shrinkage, draws the rosette down into the soil, especially during drought, when it may become partly covered in windblown sand. We call such roots *contractile.*

The flowers of *Haworthia* are borne in rather slender, rarely branched, racemes and there is little variation throughout the genus. The perianth members are off-white with darker veins. The distinction from all the other Aloineae lies in the mouth of the perianth, which is obliquely flared—a rare example of zygomorphy in

Top left (13.7): A rare endemic from the mountains of western Lesotho, **Aloe polyphylla,** *the "spiral aloe" is much in demand by collectors. The spiralling shows up with age.*

Left (13.8): A typical **Gasteria (G. maculata)** *showing the alternate, entire, spotted leaves arranged in two series.* **Gasterias** *tolerate shade better than most succulents.*

13: LILIACEAE

the Liliaceae. One section of the genus has a regular (rather than zygomorphic) perianth, and for that reason is sometimes segregated as a separate genus, *Astroloba*. Even more distinctive is the species *H. (Poellnitzia) rubriflora,* with erect, tubular, red flowers adapted to bird pollination.

The range of the genus is over the drier parts of South and South West Africa. As with many genera beloved of collectors, all the species are deemed worthy of growing and each addict has his own favourites. Here I shall merely mention some of the extremes of evolutionary development. In one direction we have the formation of an underground bulb with grass-like leaves: *H. graminifolia* (7.7) is the halfway stage and *H. (Chortolirion) angolensis* has a fully formed bulb. A parallel development was noted in *Aloe*. Even more bizarre are *H. maughanii* and *H. truncata* (13.12), whose windowed leaves in flat spirals or two rows look exactly as if freshly cut level with the soil with a knife. They are difficult to find and fascinating to study in habitat, and are always a magnet to lovers of unusual plants.

Cultivation

Of all succulents, Aloineae tolerate shade best, and as a result are usually consigned to the darker corners of a glasshouse — under the staging, for instance, where little else can flourish except spiders and woodlice. This is a pity, because, although they tolerate the indignity, a little sun colours up the leaves beautifully, and haworthias, in particular, need to be viewed at eye level for the full beauty of their leaf rosettes to be appreciated (6.16). Also, like all leaf succulents, they need regular attention to keep them tidy by removal of withered and discoloured leaves. High temperatures are not needed; indeed, even the tropical African aloes seem none the worse for a winter minimum of 5°C (40°F). Most are adaptable to a routine of summer watering, with the exception of the "grass aloes", where one lets the plant indicate when it wants to grow. A few aloes with very thick stems, such as *A. longistyla,* I find extra susceptible to black rot if overwatered.

Outside the Aloineae, *Bowiea* is no trouble, nor are the larger growing bulbines, but the dwarf deciduous sorts are not recommended to beginners. Again strict observance of the dry season is the key to success.

Top right (13.9): **Aloe aristata,** *the only hardy aloe, has enjoyed long popularity since its introduction into cultivation in 1700. The rosette rarely needs a large pot and blooms readily.*

Right (13.10): Superficially all alike, aloe flowers bear closer study and show much variation in form and colour. These are the 3.5cm (1½in) blooms of **Aloe compressa.**

All succulent Liliaceae can be raised from seed, some very readily, although it must be remembered that seed from one's own plants may well be hybrid if no precautions were taken to isolate the plant from other species at the time of flowering. The larger aloes make especially attractive seedlings even if one has to dispose of them when they get too big. Vegetative propagation by suckers and cuttings is practicable for most. Gasterias and the soft-leaved haworthias mostly root from single leaves and eventually regenerate new plants, and *Bowiea* can be raised from single bulb scales if they are removed and stuck in sand and peat like normal cuttings.

Left (13.11): **Haworthia fasciata,** *with white incrusted bands.* **Haworthias** *owe their popularity to their compact growth, shade tolerance, and diversity of leaf form and marking. The flowers are all rather similar to one another.*

Below (13.12): **Haworthia maughanii** *(left) with spiralled leaves,* **H. truncata** *(right) with leaves in two-series, and the hybrids (foreground) with attempts at both: In nature the species grow buried in the soil, with only the leaf tips exposed to the sun. Each contains a translucent window.*

The Century Plant Family

Up to 1934, *Agave,* the 'Century Plant', was classified in the *Amaryllis* Family and *Yucca,* the 'Adam's Needle', in the Liliaceae. In that year John Hutchinson of Kew realized that there was a strong affinity between the two genera (14.1) and placed them together in a new Family by themselves, the Agavaceae. His decision has been amply supported by later work, notably on the chromosomes and embryology. *Yucca* includes a number of hardy species and has fibrous, non-succulent leaves; it will not be considered further here.

No tabulation of the genera of the Agavaceae is given here because the limits of the Family are still being worked out, and a full discussion of the different viewpoints would be out of place. It will suffice to mention by name a few obviously related plants, mostly from the New World semi-deserts, that border on being succulents and certainly consort well with them in mixed plantings.

The agaves

Agave has more or less succulent leaves, but they are also rich in fibre, making it one of the few succulents of economic value—the source of sisal hemp. Agaves are plants of such striking appearance that they are hardly likely to be mistaken for anything but a few of their close allies. The leaves are always arranged in a basal, stemless rosette, which may remain solitary or form clusters by suckering. The size ranges from *A. pumila* (14.2), at home in an 8cm (3in) pot, up to the largest of all leaves in succulents, 2m (6½ft) or more long, 0.5m (20in) thick at the base and proportionately wide. The leaves are long and tapered, stiff and outstretched, with a needle-like tip that may be several centimetres long, and sometimes fearsome curved prickles along the margins (2.16, 14.4). Truly they are plants to command respect, and, as with opuntias, one handles them with care. The larger species make an excellent impenetrable boundary fence. An attraction of many is the back of the leaf, which bears the imprint of adjacent leaves from the bud.

A legend dispelled. *Agave* is responsible for the original legend that cacti flower once in 100 years. Not only is agave totally unrelated to the Cactaceae, but the interval from germination to blooming is on average much less than a century. Some have been recorded as living for 70 years before blooming, but others perform in seven years. Flowering terminates the life of the plant, which pours all its accumulated energies into a spectacular display: a central panicle that grows 15–30cm (6–12in) a day, and becomes covered with many thousands of blooms. The flowers have six similar perianth members and secrete copious nectar, which attracts hummingbirds. The fruit is a stout three-chambered capsule packed with flat black seeds (2.20). As the fruits ripen, the leaf rosette withers and dies, but some species throw up suckers that grow into new plants. Others produce adventitious buds on the inflorescence that drop off and similarly

Right (14.1) **Agave** *(left) and* **Yucca** *(right) in a Spanish garden. The agave produces flowers terminally and the rosette will die after flowering; the yucca produces flowers laterally and repeatedly. Further agave leaves can be seen in the right foreground.*

Below (14.2): Smallest of all agaves, **Agave pumila** *is at home in an 8cm (3¼in) pot.*

14: AGAVACEAE

give rise to daughter plants.

Agave is an exclusively New World genus, being centred in Mexico and extending into the southern USA, the West Indies and northern South America. *A. americana* was introduced to Europe in 1561, or perhaps even earlier, and created a sensation when it first flowered in 1586. Thereafter we have a series of reports of this event, which never fails to arouse wonder even today: in the largest growing species the axis may exceed 11m (37ft) in height. An early rumour arose that the emergence of the flower stem was accompanied by a great explosion, apparently because of a mistranslation of a French writer who said that flowering caused "un grand eclat"! More recently an enterprising practical joker took serial photographs of a flower stem over a period of weeks and hoaxed a newspaper into publishing them with a sensational story that it all happened in a matter of minutes! A flowering agave may be a source of embarrassment in a small glasshouse. If it happens in the summer, the usual procedure is to remove glass from the roof and allow the inflorescence to soar skywards.

Some larger agaves have become semi-naturalized following their introduction to countries bordering the Mediterranean, and contribute much to the exotic look of holiday resorts. Especially fine are the variegated cultivars. In *A. americana* alone there are at least seven different striped variants, surely not only the finest in succulents but among the most spectacular of all variegated plants.

Agaves in cultivation. In countries where succulents must be grown under glass, agaves would surely be more popular if they took up less space. Although their tough foliage allows them to stand outdoors during the summer, they must be carefully positioned in winter to avoid contact with passers-by (14.3), and a specimen that has to have its leaf tips trimmed off is worse than no specimen at all. There are, however, many smaller, solitary species, of which the best known is *A. victoria-reginae* (14.5), with hemispherical rosettes of 12-15cm (5-6in) stiff, blackish green leaves with black spiny tips and attractive white longitudinal markings. It is exceedingly slow growing, and large specimens are always treasured showpieces. In a related group the species have the leaf margins split off into curling white fibres. *A. schidigera* is the finest of these, and *A. parviflora* a perfect miniature. *A. utahensis* in some of its forms wins the prize for the most bizarre corkscrew leaf tips of all. A rather distinct subgenus, sometimes recognized as a separate genus *Manfreda*, has softer, only slightly fleshy leaves, usually dappled with brownish pink. *A. maculosa* is an example that will flower within a few years in a 12cm (5in) pot.

Agaves thrive in a rich soil, if it is porous, and need plenty of water in summer. If kept dry in winter they need no more heat than suffices to keep out the frost—indeed, many need no heat at all (6.12). In humid climates such as that of northern Europe the greatest danger outdoors is water collecting in the centre of the crown, which causes rot (6.14). It can be prevented by a glass or plastic canopy overhead, or by planting the rosette more-or-less vertically on rock-

Right (14.3): **Agave stricta** *in a Barcelona park. Agaves are tough, trouble-free and need little attention, but must be carefully sited because of their fierce armature.*

Below left (14.4): **Agave shawii** *in the Arroyo Seco, Baja California. After flowering, the rosette will die. It rarely offsets, and propagates itself almost entirely by seed.*

Below (14.5): **Agave victoria-reginae,** *one of the slowest growing of succulents. It is among the most highly prized agaves for exhibition.*

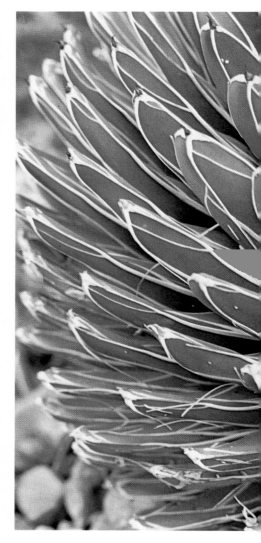

work. The tough leaves are resistant to all common pests except the worst of all, *Homo sapiens,* who feels impelled to carve his initials and leave a scar on the leaf for life. Suitable chemical deterrents exist, but the law prevents their use!

Other important genera. *Dracaena draco* is the 'Dragon Tree' of the Canary Islands, capable of reaching an enormous height and bulk in old age. *Nolina recurvata* and *Calibanus hookeri* produce a massive more-or-less spherical caudex from which arise fountain-like rosettes of long, narrow, fibrous recurving leaves.

Finally, from Africa there is the large genus *Sansevieria,* whose species typically spread by means of massive underground stems. The few leaves are cylindrical, channelled or flat, very tough and long-lived, and so fibrous that they provide the bowstring hemp of commerce — a parallel development to agave. *Sansevieria* provides us with some of the most adaptable and long-suffering of all house plants, ideally suited to windowsills in centrally heated rooms where little else will survive. The species with blotched or variegated leaves are the most favoured, notably cultivars of *S. trifasciata.* In addition to standing full sun, they can survive in deep shade, although they then grow very slowly and must be watered cautiously or they rot off. About the only thing that deters *Sansevieria* is frost: a winter minimum of 10°C (50°F) should be the aim.

Stem Succulents

"Some plants have joints, reeds, for example; some have thorns, like the bramble. Some have no branches, others have a great number, like the sycamore."

Stem succulence implies a greater modification of the plant body than leaf succulence, where the leaves are still the main centres of photosynthesis and the habit may differ little from that of "normal" plants. In stem succulence the green tissue, and in consequence the vital centre for food-making, is more and more shifted to the stems (2.8) — completely so in those plants, such as columnar cacti, where leaves are undeveloped. There are many plants in which the transfer of leaf functions to stems is unaccompanied by succulence. We call them "switch plants" and familiar examples are the broom (*Sarothamnus*) and butcher's broom (*Ruscus*). They are xerophytes, surviving drought by means other than water storage. The leaf-like organs in *Ruscus* are actually stems. But such plants are not our concern here.

As with leaf succulents, five Families are singled out here for separate treatment, leaving a small residue of others that can be dealt with first in summary. All are examples of widespread, adaptable Families rich in different life forms among which are a few succulents.

Compositae

This ubiquitous and bewilderingly large Family has already been mentioned under leaf succulents and makes an appearance a third time in the chapter on caudiciform plants. Although it shows extraordinary diversity in the vegetative characters, the flower heads are standard throughout and are the unifying principle whereby botanists recognize the Family. They repay a closer look, not only because of the beauty of their design and functional efficiency, but because an understanding of their structure enables one to recognize the Family at a glance and avoid referring to a head of chrysanthemum or dahlia as "a flower".

What appears at first sight to be a single bloom is seen to be made up of a number of small, separate, tubular flowers *(florets)* packed tightly together in a level or domed head at the end of the axis, and surrounded by a protective cup made up of many leafy bracts — an

Right (15.1). The capitulum of **Senecio stapeliiformis** *(left) showing the many tubular disc florets surrounded by a sleeve-like protective involucre of bracts. The calyx is represented by a ring of hairs (below left) that persists as a parachute on the fruit. Structure of a single floret is shown at right. For a capitulum showing both disc and ray florets see illustration 4.12.*

Below (15.2): **Senecio articulatus,** *the tough, easily multiplied and long-popular 'Candle Plant'. Shape of joint and colour of markings vary according to the method of cultivation.*

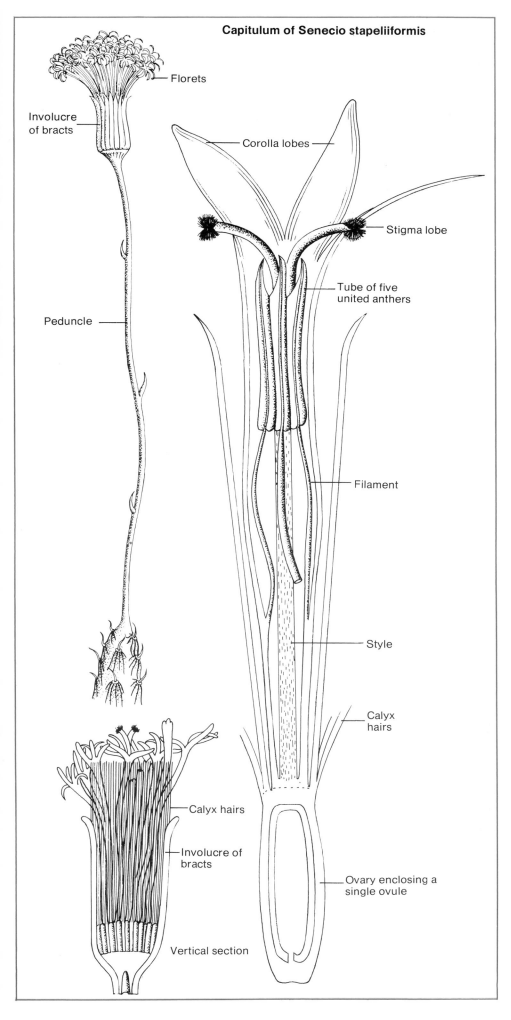

Capitulum of Senecio stapeliiformis

Florets

Involucre of bracts

Corolla lobes

Stigma lobe

Tube of five united anthers

Peduncle

Filament

Style

Calyx hairs

Calyx hairs

Involucre of bracts

Ovary enclosing a single ovule

Vertical section

involucre. It is thus a very condensed form of inflorescence: a *capitulum* ("little head", literally), to use the official term. In *Senecio stapeliiformis* (15.1), all the florets are alike: tubular, with a regular five-parted corolla. We call them *disc florets.* In *S. crassissimus* (4.12) two sorts of florets are present in the one head: disc florets at the centre and, surrounding them, *ray florets* in which the corolla of each is pulled out on one side into a long, strap-shaped, coloured ray. Thus the resemblance to a single large flower is even more striking, each ray floret being a single "petal". Often the ray florets are unisexual or sterile.

Looking now at a typical disc floret (15.1) we see that the five stamens are united by their anthers, which form a long sleeve surrounding the central style. Initially the style is short, with closed inactive stigma lobes, and by its elongation as the flower opens it pushes out pollen from the centre of the anther tube like a piston. Look at any freshly opened flower head of the Compositae and you will see golden blobs of pollen freshly extruded from the centres of the youngest florets near the middle. After most of the pollen has been taken by insects feeding or crawling over the capitulum, the two stigma lobes spread outward and the tips become receptive. As in the cactus flower described on page 48, there is in many Compositae a further device that allows selfing if the flower head is unvisited: the wilting stigmas contact the anthers.

After detailing the niceties of a mechanism ideally suited to guarantee fertilization and seed set, preferably by outcrossing, it is unfortunate to have to admit that, although it works perfectly in habitat, seed is hardly ever set on the succulent representatives in cultivation, even when hand pollination is used. Presumably the delicate mechanism is upset by a more humid atmosphere, lower light or some other little-understood factor. Propagation therefore has to be by vegetative means alone, except when imported seed is offered.

The fruit, when set, is crowned by a brush of fine silky hairs (all that remains of a calyx), which cluster around the top of each ovary. They form a parachute that aids dispersal, as in the dandelion, a common weed of the same Family.

Of stem-succulent Compositae, an old favourite is the 'Candle Plant', *Senecio articulatus* (15.2), introduced from South Africa in 1775. It is almost hardy and very easy to propagate, because the sausage-shaped joints drop off at a touch and readily strike root. The plant puts out lobed flat leaves when watered, and drops them when kept dry. It looks best in full sun; in the shade the joints elongate and lose their bright colours. A variegated cultivar is also in cultivation.

Senecio anteuphorbium occurs in

171

South Africa and Morocco; *S. kleinia* in the Canary Islands. The variegated cultivar of the latter, called 'Candystick' (15.3), is the one to choose. *S. deflersii* has stems like cucumbers, and *S. stapeliiformis* lives up to its name and looks much like a *Stapelia* with an angled stem and scale leaves from low tubercles. These species grow upright, but *S. pendulus* curls over and burrows in the soil, producing a series of arching low stems—the 'Inchworm'. The last two have showy flower heads in crimson and orange-red respectively. The above species may also be met with under the generic names *Kleinia* and *Notonia*.

Portulacaceae

This Family, which is predominantly leaf-succulent, has been introduced in Chapter 12. One of its most isolated and curious members is endemic to the island of Guadalupe off the coast of Mexico: *Talinum guadalupense* (15.4). Caudiciform in nature, it produces long, sausage-shaped stems and becomes shrubby in captivity. The rosettes of grey, semi-persistent leaves recall *Echeveria,* and the delicate, purplish pink flowers are showy. It is a rare and difficult plant to keep in Europe, but seems to thrive in California.

Also worth mentioning is the genus *Ceraria,* curious small-leaved shrubs of South and South West Africa, with thickened stems. Young specimens have an attractive bonsai look (12.2) that is worth trying to preserve by keeping them underpotted and underwatered and trimming off any long shoots they produce. I have failed to propagate them by cuttings.

Vitidaceae

The Vitidaceae take their name from the most important genus, *Vitis,* the vine. Among their dozen genera and 700 species, stem succulence has evolved in a few species of *Cissus,* and a caudiciform habit in *Cyphostemma* (2.21, Chapter 21). *Cissus quadrangularis* (15.5) is a wide-ranging and variable species from southern and tropical Africa and India; it produces long climbing stems that support themselves by means of tendrils. The stems are short-jointed, square in cross-section with thin, slightly wavy angles, and produce a lobed leaf at each node. The tiny flowers are followed by black "grapes", but these are not edible. The plant is worth growing as a novelty, but relishes heat: a minimum of 10°C (50°F) in winter, and more if possible.

Right (15.3): **Senecio kleinia,** *endemic to the Canary Isles, forms a stem-succulent shrub up to 3m (10ft) tall. This is the variegated cultivar, called 'Candystick', introduced by the author in 1973. Propagation is by cuttings, which are rather temperamental about rooting.*

Above (15.4): **Talinum guadalupense** is an endangered and extraordinary endemic of Guadalupe Island off the coast of Mexico. It is rare in European collections but thrives in California.

Above (15.5): **Cissus quadrangularis,** showing the square, jointed, fleshy stems and bunches of red "grapes" which are decorative but hardly to be considered palatable.

Below (15.6): **Senecio,** perhaps the largest of all genera, has some species with fleshy leaves and others with fleshy stems, and some with both, like this **S. corymbiferus** from S. Africa.

Stem Succulents
A breakdown to Family level

Stems without felted areoles, although spines may be present and even clustered on horny shields. *(Didierea, Euphorbia)*

Stems with felted areoles often bearing clusters of spines or bristles.

Sap milky.

Sap not milky.

Plants never with both spines or prickles and leaves.

Plants bearing both spines or prickles and leaves (at least during the growing season).

Individual flowers minute, assembled in capitula with a common involucre. Compositae in part *(Senecio* in part).

Flowers not in capitula with a common involucre.

Senecio stapeliiformis

Didierea madagascariensis

Spines in threes *(Pachypodium* in part).

Spines, four or more together. *(Didierea)*

Spines or prickles, one or two together.

Leafless with stems conspicuously or inconspicuously angled or tubercled *(Caralluma frerei* has leaves) or leafy climbers without tendrils.

Shrub with branches circular in cross section and flat, varyingly persistent laurel-like leaves. *(Adenium)*

Branch system not zigzag.

Branch system zigzag. *(Decaryia).*

Tendril climber with jointed square stems and deciduous lobed leaves. Vitidaceae *(Cissus)*

Midrib conspicuous. *(Pachypodium* in part)

Midrib inconspicuous. *(Alluaudia, Alluaudiopsis)*

Cissus quadrangularis

Asclepiadaceae in part (About 27 genera)

Didiereaceae (four genera)

Euphorbiaceae in part *(Euphorbia* plus five genera)

Apocynaceae in part (two genera)

Cactaceae (80 or more genera)

Right (15.7): Globular cacti in a private collection in England. They are much more popular than the columnar species, which take up too much space and flower less freely.

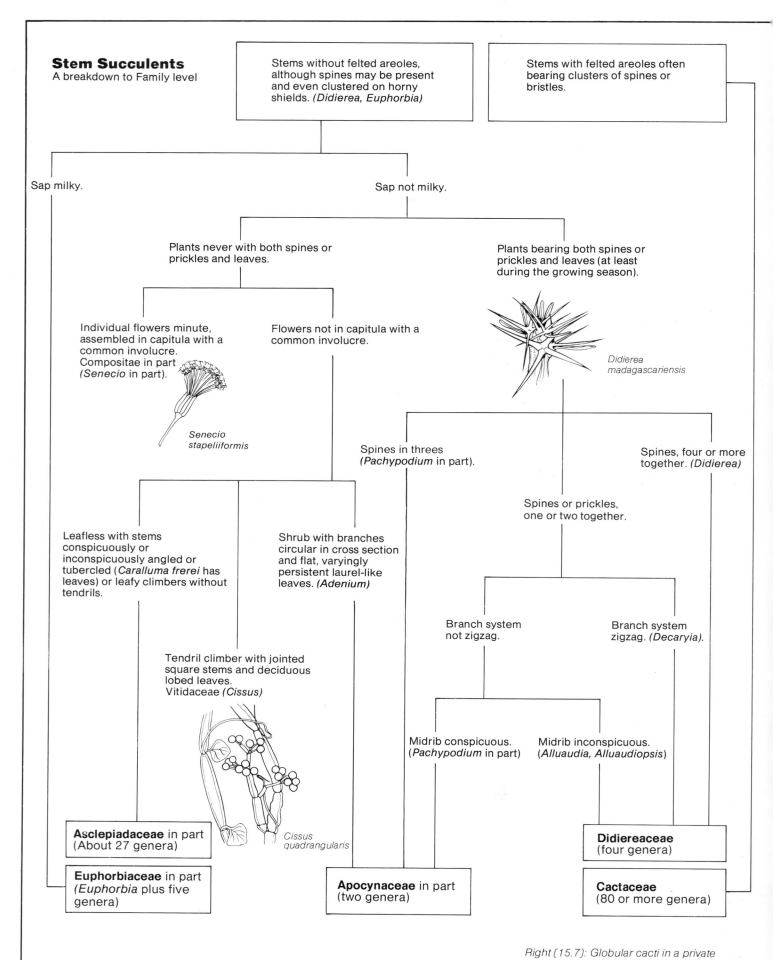

The Cactus Family

More books are written about cacti than all the other succulents put together, and some add a final injustice by including a chapter on "other succulents" rather as an afterthought. Indeed, the very word "cactus" has been taken over by the general public for any fleshy, prickly, bizarre-looking plant: a sad distortion of its botanical meaning as a member of the Family Cactaceae.

The most popular succulents

The reasons for the popularity of cacti are not hard to find. First, they all look so different from other plants: the general lack of leaves, the spikiness, the geometric patterns of spines, tubercles and ribs— these, although matched by isolated African euphorbias, pachypodiums and didiereas, set them in a Family by themselves. Second, they are ideal collectors' pieces: a majority not too difficult to obtain and keep, a minority offering just that challenge that inspires the perfectionist and connoisseur. On this balance of factors collectormania thrives.

Then again, cacti have a remarkable tolerance of neglect, looking after themselves while the owner goes on holiday or recovers from influenza, yet they respond wonderfully to good management and hence are well fitted for the exhibition table at flower shows. Flowering is always something of an event: although not half as rare as some believe, it usually covers only a small part of the whole season, and when the subject is as spectacular as the "seven hours' wonder" of the night-blooming cerei, it is an occasion for calling in the neighbours and uncorking the champagne. Yet the plants are attractive all the year round, even if they never flower, which cannot be said for roses and many other garden favourites.

Classification of cacti

The name *Kaktos* occurs in classical literature, being used by Theophrastus for the prickly cardoon *(Cynara)*. However, it was taken up in 1753 by Linnaeus as a genus, *Cactus L.,* in which he placed all the then known 22 species of cacti. Linnaeus was ultra-conservative, and his 22 species are today referred to 12 separate genera. But the generic name *Cactus* is no longer used, because it invites confusion with the cactus of common parlance, which is any member of the whole Family. The dictionary, by the way, allows both plurals: cacti and cactuses, but only the former has come into common use.

Nineteenth-century studies of cacti culminated in a monograph by Karl Schumann, who in 1903 recognized 21 genera and 760 species. This is still a classic work, and a model of thoroughness and moderation in a Family that has proved exceptionally difficult to classify. The twentieth century saw many new systems, mostly radical, from that of Britton & Rose in 1919–23 to that of Backeberg in 1958–62 with over 300 genera and over 2,000 species. In absence of a more conservative treatment, Backeberg is followed by many, but for the synopsis of genera here the basis is a review by D. R. Hunt in Hutchinson's *Genera of Flowering Plants* Vol. II, 1967, where the total of genera is reduced to 84.

A cactus chronology

The garden history of cacti is no less topsy-turvy than their taxonomic history. The first specimens to reach Europe in the sixteenth century came from the West Indies, and it so happens that no cactus is more difficult to establish after uprooting than a mature *Melocactus*. The impression arose that all cacti needed great heat, and later arrivals from less tropical regions were assigned to the stove house and given next to no water, a soil devoid of all nutrients and inadequate lighting.

The most widely publicized of cacti are those of the southwestern United States. Everyone is familiar with the giant saguaro *(Carnegiea* 5.7) and prickly pears *(Opuntia* 1.7) of Arizona through Hollywood westerns, Disney epics, schoolboy penny dreadfuls and literature from tourist brochures to highly respected picture magazines such as *Arizona Highways*. Mention a cactus to many folk and this is the image that at once springs to mind. Yet, surprisingly, these are the cacti least seen in European collections. *Carnegiea* is so subtly adjusted to life in the southwestern drylands that it languishes away from them, and in any

Right [16.1]: **Echinopsis (Trichocereus) spachiana** *is one of the most vigorous and easy growing columnar cacti, but needs to be a metre or so tall before blooming. It also makes one of the best grafting stocks.*

Below [16.2]: Life forms in Cactaceae: flat— and cylindrical— jointed **Opuntias** *(right and centre) and columnar, ribbed* **Cereus** *(left).*

THE CACTUS FAMILY (CACTACEAE)—A breakdown to genus level

Leaves present		Leaves absent or microscopic

Leaves present

Glochids absent; seeds black, without an aril	Glochids present; seeds covered by a pale bony aril or winged
Subfamily 1 **PERESKIOIDEAE**	Subfamily 2 **OPUNTIOIDEAE**

Leaves absent or microscopic

Glochids absent; seeds black or brown, not covered by a bony a

Habit more or less columnar (cereoid) with usually few-ribbed, jointed stems or, if dwarf, then flowering from the old areoles

Tribe 1
CEREEAE

Terrestial plants without aerial roots; spines usually conspicuous

Receptacle tube naked or armed, sometimes scaly	Receptacle tube thinly hairy or rarely naked, narrow-scaled
Subtribe 1 **CEREINAE**	Subtribe 2 **ECHINOPSIDINAE**

Subfamily 1
Pereskia aculeata

Subtribe 1
Carnegiea gigantea

Subfamily 2
Opuntia vulgaris

Subtribe 1
CEREINAE

Acanthocereus	Jasminocereus
Armatocereus	Lemaireocereus
Brachycereus	Leptocereus
Browningia	Lophocereus
Calymmanthium	Monvillea
Carnegiea	Myrtillocactus
Cephalocereus	Neoabbottia
Cereus	Neoraimondia
Corryocactus	Nyctocereus
Dendrocereus	Pachycereus
Echinocereus	Peniocereus
Escontria	Rathbunia
Eulychnia	Stetsonia
Harrisia	

Subtribe 2
Rebutia muscula

Subtribe 2
ECHINOPSIDINAE

Arthrocereus	Leocereus
Borzicactus	Lobivia
Cleistocactus	Mila
Denmoza	Oroya
Echinopsis	Rebutia
Espostoa	Zehntnerella
Haageocereus	

Subfamily 1
PERESKIOIDEAE

Maihuenia
Pereskia

Subfamily 1
OPUNTIOIDEAE

Opuntia	Quiabentia
Pereskiopsis	Tacinga
Pterocactus	

Subfamily 3
CACTOIDEAE

Habit more or less dwarf (cactoid) with usually many-ribbed, non-jointed stems, flowering from the new areoles

Tribe 2
CACTEAE

Epiphytic plants with aerial roots; spines weak or absent	Receptacle tube woolly, with spines developed on the upper areoles	Receptacle tube naked or woolly, without spines	
		Flowers borne on a terminal cephalium	No cephalium developed
Subtribe 3 **HYLOCEREINAE**	Subtribe 4 **NEOPORTERIINAE**	Subtribe 5 **CACTINAE**	Subtribe 6 **ECHINOCACTINAE**

Subtribe 3
Rhipsalis gaertneri

Subtribe 4
Notocactus
tabulari

Subtribe 5
Melocactus maxonii

Subtribe 6
Astrophytum myriostigma

Subtribe 3
HYLOCEREINAE

Aporocactus	Nopalxochia
Disocactus	Rhipsalis
Epiphyllum	Schlumbergera
Heliocereus	Selenicereus
Hylocereus	Weberocereus
Morangaya	

Subtribe 4
NEOPORTERIINAE

Austrocactus	Neoporteria
Blossfeldia	Notocactus
Eriosyce	Parodia
Frailea	Uebelmannia

Subtribe 5
CACTINAE

Discocactus
Melocactus

Subtribe 6
ECHINOCACTINAE

Ariocarpus	Gymnocalycium
Astrophytum	Leuchtenbergia
Aztekium	Lophophora
Copiapoa	Mammillaria
Coryphantha	Neolloydia
Echinocactus	Pediocactus
Echinofossulocactus	Pelecyphora
Epithelantha	Strombocactus
Escobaria	Thelocactus
Ferocactus	

16: CACTACEAE

case flowers only when some metres tall. Many dwarf United States cacti, although attractive to collectors, do not adapt well to countries with moist summers and less intense sunshine. It is from Mexico and South America that most of the collectors' cacti come, and these did not reach Europe in any quantity until well into the nineteenth century.

In the past two or three decades there has been a veritable flood of novelties as new roads push ever deeper into Brazil, Peru and Chile: *Notocactus, Neoporteria, Parodia* and *Gymnocalycium* by the dozen, and new genera such as *Uebelmannia* and *Buiningia*. Although many of these occur south of the Equator, they acclimatize better to the reversed seasons of the Northern Hemisphere than do the desert species of the U.S.A. (see page 74). Today they are firm favourites, but the old myths of starvation diet, small pots and intense heat linger on and are slow to disappear.

What makes a cactus?

The Cactaceae are perennials ranging in stature from tiny button-sized *Blossfeldias* to candelabra *Pachycereus* (16.3) and *Carnegiea* up to about 10m (33ft) tall and weighing many tons. *Pereskia* is tallest of all, forming forest trees up to 24m (80ft), and is considered the least specialized, being sparingly succulent and bearing large, expanded, semipersistent leaves. In the remainder, the functions of leaves are transferred to the thick fleshy stems, which are green when young although they become woody with age. Leaves are absent or, in the Opuntioideae, reduced and more or less scale-like. The stems are typically ribbed and star-like in cross-section, or covered in tubercles in straight or spiral rows. Most cacti have spines, and these arise, as do the branches and flowers, from special felted cushions called *areoles* (2.14, 15), which may be regarded as telescoped lateral branches (spur shoots) in which spines represent all that remains of undeveloped leaves.

The flowers are solitary (rarely two or more from an areole) and sessile (that is, without a stalk), *Pereskia* again being exceptional. The numerous bracts, sepals and petals are spirally arranged and typically show a transition from one to the other (16.4)—a very primitive feature. They are more or less united to form a tube, which may reach 30cm (12in) in length in the Hylocereinae (2.17). The stamens are also numerous and spiralled, arising from the inner wall of the tube, and surround a single style with branching stigma lobes at its tip. Flower colours run from white through yellow to pink, orange, red and purple; blue is absent. The inferior ovary often bears areoles on its outside with spines, bristles and wool, and ripens to a juicy "berry", although there are transitions to a dry, dehiscent capsule. The seeds are usually black and have a curved embryo within.

The Cactaceae have no close relatives and for a long time defied efforts to fit them neatly into systems of classification. Now they are well sited in Caryophyllales alongside Phytolaccaceae, Portulacaceae and Mesembryanthemaceae, with which they share many less obvious features including the pigment betacyanin. They are exclusively New World plants, most highly concentrated in the dry mountainous regions on either side of the Equator, but extending north as far as Canada and south to the tip of South America. Elsewhere they have been introduced and naturalized.

Right (16.3): **Pachycereus pringlei** *in habitat in Baja California, where it is the counterpart of the giant saguaro* (**Carnegiea**) *in Arizona.*

Below (16.4): **Pereskia grandifolia** *flowers freely on a small plant in a 12.5cm (5in) pot, given rich soil, water and heat at all times.* **Pereskia,** *with its large leaves, is regarded in Cactaceae as a link with the past.*

16: CACTACEAE

Pereskioideae

If *Pereskia* did not exist, it would have had to be invented to explain the missing link between cacti and their mesophytic ancestors. This is not to assert that it is in the direct line of descent of the other, more advanced genera. Rather it is a survivor, an early offshoot of the family tree, which by remaining within the moist tropics has evolved fewer specializations for desert survival. Not all *Pereskia* characters are unspecialized: the advanced areole and spines are already present in all species. As tall shrubs and trees the species are usually seen away from habitat only in botanical gardens, but the best-suited to pot culture is *P. grandifolia* (16.4), which produces its showy pink flowers, like single dog roses, in a 12cm (5in) pot. *P. aculeata* (page 178) is the commonest species and its long branches climb by means of stipular prickles: a hooked pair at the base of each leaf. Pereskias require a rich soil and much warmth — a winter minimum of

10°C (50°F) at least — and will take plenty of water in summer, less in winter.

Opuntioideae

The pictures of *Opuntia* (16.7) give a good idea of the general look of this subfamily, where the stems are characteristically long- or short-jointed and sometimes tuberculate but hardly ever ribbed. Leaves are rarely flat *(Pereskiopsis*, 16.5), more often cylindrical. In *Opuntia subulata* they can be up to 12cm (5in) long and fairly persistent, but that is exceptional. Mostly they are tiny scales that quickly wither and fall, and perform no useful function in photosynthesis. Seedlings have two conspicuous flat cotyledons.

Spines are present, and also *glochids:* smaller, bristle-like spines with recurved

barbs like a bee-sting that detach readily and make these the most unpleasant of all succulents to handle.

Pterocactus has a large winged seed; in others the seeds are also quite big and covered in a bony shield called an *aril,* which makes them slow to germinate.

Of the four small genera, the only one that need be mentioned here is *Pereskiopsis,* which is an excellent grafting stock for tiny seedling cacti, although too tender to recommend for a permanent union.

By contrast, *Opuntia* is the largest and most widespread genus of the Cactaceae, extending from Canada to Patagonia — the limits of the Family. It thus includes the hardiest of cacti, a few of which can be successfully grown outdoors in northern Europe. Three subgenera are recognized

Right (16.5): **Pereskiopsis** *has the flat leaves and shrubby habit of* **Pereskia** *but a flower and fruit that have more in common with* **Opuntia**. *In collections it is most valued as a grafting stock for accelerating tiny seedlings.*

Below (16.6): **Opuntia acanthocarpa,** *one of the cylindrical opuntias or chollas from the southwest U.S.A. Several variant flower colours occur. Some of the spines have a detachable sheath.*

on the shape of the joints: Cylindropuntia (16.6) with cylindrical stems and branches, Tephrocactus (5.5) with globular or ellipsoidal joints, and Opuntia (16.7) with flat, disc-like pads. These are treated by some as separate genera.

Most opuntias are too rank-growing for a small glasshouse. A single pad of *O. vulgaris (monacantha)* stuck in a bed of the cold section of my glasshouse grew to eight pads the first year and 64 the second, when it had to be taken out for fear it would break the glass. Also they mostly need to be large before flowers can be expected—a pity, because the blooms are extremely beautiful (4.1) and have sensitive stamens (page 54).

Subgenus Cylindropuntia occurs both north and south of the Equator. The North American species have sheathed spines (16.6): when a spine is touched, the barbed sheath sticks in the skin and slides off like a glove finger, leaving the spine itself on the plant. For those with space problems, I recommend the slowest growing species, *O. pachypus,* of which there is also an attractive cristate form. *O. invicta* has short joints and huge dagger-like spines.

Subgenus Tephrocactus includes mostly smaller plants of great diversity in shape and spination of the joints: their principal attraction in cultivation as flowers are sparse. Despite the existence of a good handbook by Leighton-Boyce and Iliff, the plants are not as widely grown as they deserve.

Subgenus Opuntia introduces that Jekyll-and-Hyde plant, the prickly pear, hated as a weed in Australia where it has infested large areas of farmland, but cultivated in other countries for its fruit or as cattle fodder. *O.(Nopalea) coccinellifera* is the principal host plant for rearing a scale insect that is the source of the red dye cochineal, although nowadays a synthetic dye is cheaper substitute. *Opuntia* finds a further use as hedges: woe betide anyone who tries to get through one!

Those accustomed to see opuntias as tiny specimens cramped in pots have no idea what a splendid effect they make when well grown in the open. In Europe the best display I have seen is near Blanes in Spain. But no collection, however

*Below (16.7): **Opuntia vulgaris,** the prickly pear, in flower and with unripe fruits. **Opuntia** is naturalized in many places outside the Americas; this was photographed in Kenya.*

16: CACTACEAE

cramped, should be without one or two. If the glochids are a deterrent, there is even one—*Opuntia microdasys* 'Albatus'—where the bristles are so soft that it can be handled with impunity.

Cactoideae—Cereinae

Cereinae, like Opuntioideae, include some largish plants that look their best and flower only when given space and room for their roots. In a glasshouse collection they can stand at the back of the staging, or larger ones can go at floor level, making a foil for the globular types. If planted out in a bed their sturdy growth and improved spination will be a surprise to those used only to pot culture.

Cereus, with a massive candelabra of few-angled stems and large, white, nocturnal flowers with only a few scales on the tube, is a genus of great adaptability. It tolerates temperatures from tropical heat to near freezing, and seems equally indifferent to excess or deficiency of water. Although native to South America, some of the species (there are several, all very much alike) grow successfully outdoors in many warmer countries (6.9), and often reach a large size. *Monvillea* is smaller in all parts and better tailored for the amateur's glasshouse. *Cephalocereus* is one of a number of genera in which the onset of flowering leads to a great development of hairs or bristles at or near the stem apices: a *cephalium,* as it is called (16.10). We shall encounter many variants of cephalia: terminal, lateral, or in between the two. In *C. chrysacanthus* the flowering stems develop extra wool all round; in *C. brevicylindricus* the golden cephalium is lopsided, suggesting the mane of a lion. This species has short stems, usually broader than tall, and has been put in a separate genus, *Buiningia.* Even more startling is *C. (Backebergia) militaris,* where the small flowers push out from a dense, golden brown, terminal cephalium. From time to time these tops of flowering stems have been cut off in habitat, imported and offered at high prices. Technically, they are inflorescences, not plants, and although they can be rooted, casualties are high, and subsequent growth either spoils the cephalium or consists of normal, barren shoots from beneath it. *C. senilis,* the 'Old Man Cactus', has for long been a favourite for its overall covering of shaggy white hairs (16.8). It is a slow-growing and sensitive to overwatering, so a well-grown sizeable plant will always be a treasure.

Pachycereus includes the giants of the candelabra cacti (16.3), a dominating

Above right (16.8): **Cephalocereus senilis,** *the 'Old Man Cactus', is prized because of its slow growth. It needs careful management, however, to avoid rotting and loss of roots.*

Right (16.9): **Pachycereus pecten-aboriginum** *gets its name from the very prickly, dry fruit, which is fancifully called "aborigine's comb".*

feature of any Mexican landscape where they occur. The fruits of *P. pecten-aboriginum* (16.9), are more bristly than chestnuts and, as the name implies, are supposed to be used as combs by the natives. I was not tempted to try them. This dry spiny fruit distinguishes *Pachycereus* in Mexico from its counterpart *Carnegiea* in Arizona. *C.gigantea,* the saguaro and sole species, is the State flower of Arizona and one of the most photographed and familiar of all cacti (16.12), although one of the least interesting as small pot specimens, which grow very slowly and never flower.

Carnegiea has a fleshy berry that is harvested by the Indians by means of long strips of wood obtained from the skeleton of the plant itself: the flesh is edible, and the seeds can be ground up for meal. Large areas where saguaros used to grow have now been urbanized, and the species is susceptible to various diseases and hazards, mostly attributable to man's activities. Because of its low regeneration, it has been much studied by ecologists and conservationists, and surviving populations are now protected or set aside as national parks (7.6).

Lophocereus is a cactus of many faces.

The barren shoots are like those of *Cereus,* but when sufficiently mature they form copious bristles at the apex and a terminal cephalium (16.11). But there is also a very different monstrous form beloved of collectors because of its scarcity and novel appearance, like a sculpture in jade, lacking spines and regular ribs.

Myrtillocactus seedlings are handsome pot plants on account of the bluish

Below (16.10): **Cephalocereus (Neobuxbaumia) polylophus,** *the flowering top of a 3m (10ft) specimen in a Californian garden. The solitary stem is about 23cm (9in) thick.*

pruinose stems. They need to be large before they bloom. Seedlings can be used as grafting stocks, but are noticeably more tender than *Echinopsis*.

Lemaireocereus is a mixed-up genus taxonomically, but this is no place to elaborate the problems. The many species are noble columnar cacti characteristic of the drier areas of Mexico, where they add a distinctive look to the skyline. For the glasshouse grower some are attractive as seedlings, especially the choice and delicate *L. beneckei* covered in a powdery white "bloom".

With *Echinocereus* we come to plants of dwarf stature, with solitary or clump-forming columnar or globose stems, and mostly at home in medium-sized pots. The 70 species extend from Mexico up to the northern USA, where it is represented by the frost-hardy *E. triglochidiatus (coccineus)*, the 'Claret Cup', with brilliant red funnel-shaped blooms on five- to eight-angled stems, and *E. viridiflorus,* a dwarf solitary or few-headed species with flowers of varying yellowish shades, sometimes, as the name implies, distinctly green. Something of an oddity is the unarmed variety, *inermis,* of *E. triglochidiatus* (16.14) that occurs very locally in Colorado: it is exactly similar to the species except for the almost complete lack of spines, yet holds its own in nature. Echinocerei are noted for the soft-fleshed stems, green and usually somewhat ribbed. The flowers range from small (*E. davisii*) to 10–12cm (4–5in) across, and can be yellow (*E. papillosus*) orange (*E. salmdyckianus*), pink (*E. amoenus*),

Right (16.11): The barren stems of Lophocereus schottii *have distant areoles with tiny spines. Only the flowering tops develop these bristles. Two or more flowers may appear at one areole.*

Below (16.12): Flowers of the giant saguaro (Carnegia gigantea) *crown the tall stems in May and are succeeded by fleshy fruits. Notice the very large number of stamens.*

purple *(E. caespitosus)* or brownish *(E. chloranthus)* as well as green. The effect is made more dramatic by the contrast with yellow anthers and green stigma lobes. In cultivation I find that light is a more important factor in success than high temperatures—indeed, the mixed collection I keep in the south-facing end of my glasshouse seem none the worse for drops below freezing point in winter, provided I keep them quite dry. In summer they are watered freely as long as the weather is mild. Very little attention is needed.

E. pectinatus var. *rigidissimus* is the 'Rainbow Cactus' of Arizona, a beauty at all seasons from the consecutive bands of pink, white and straw-coloured spines up the stem. *E. knippelianus* (16.13) is a miniature, with a soft, solitary, flattened, almost unarmed stem the size of a golfball. Some echinocerei produce large flowers when no more than 3cm (1⅙in) high, whereas *E. delaetii* is one of the shy-flowering species, but much prized because its white shaggy hairs make it a miniature 'Old Man Cactus'.

Echinopsidinae

Hunt's classification lays stress on the presence of hairs and narrow scales on the outside of the flower tube as distinguishing this subtribe from the preceding, with habit taking second place, so we again have a mixture of columnar and dwarf species, sometimes within one genus. Starting with the tall-growing types, *Espostoa, Haageocereus, Cleistocactus* and *Borzicactus* (16.15) are worth considering even for a small collection because of the beauty of their stems, with

Left (16.13): **Echinocereus knippelianus** *is one of the smaller growing species, and rarely offsets. This one comfortably fills an 8cm (3¼in) pot. Notice the small, weak spines.*

Below (16.14): **Echinocereus triglochidiatus inermis** *in habitat in Colorado, a rare unarmed mutant of the species which is normally heavily spined. It is a collector's curio.*

16: CACTACEAE

spines in various colours and designs. Most of them grow stiffly erect, but *Haageocereus decumbens* is best suspended so that its curling stems can hang over the pot. Espostoas are superb as seedlings: *E. lanata, E. melanostele* and *E. senilis* have the green stem concealed beneath snow-white bristles and hair. *Cleistocactus strausii* is another justly popular all-white plant; the tubular red flowers are unremarkable and borne on tall stems. Several *Haageocerei* and *Borzicacti* have golden yellow spines, as for instance *B. aureispinus* (8.5). Most need to be 50cm (20in) or more tall before they begin to bloom, but *B. sextonianus* is a delightful miniature with chains of stem joints only 3cm (1⅙in) long but flowers as large as those of the columnar species. Generally these plants do better if kept on the warm side in winter. *Borzicactus* includes a number of globular cacti formerly segregated as *Matucana*. These are doubly welcome in collections, their showy, oblique flowers appearing in

Right (16.15): **Borzicactus samaipatanus:** *beautiful stems and beautiful flowers of an unusual shape, with an oblique spread of the perianth. This species comes from Bolivia.*

Below (16.16): **Echinopsis rowleyi** **(Trichocereus grandiflorus).** *Plants in the large genus* **Echinopsis** *range from tall trees to dwarf clustering types, with flowers of most shades excepting blue.*

188

summer and early autumn. *B. madison-iorum* loses its few, weak spines at maturity and looks more like *Lophophora* (16.34).

Oroya includes neat, depressed globose cacti from high in the Andes, which form rings of small, usually yellowish orange flowers around the stem apex (16.17). *O. borchersii,* with sturdy, golden brown spines, is the showiest.

In *Echinopsis* we have a large genus of both dwarf (16.16) and tall columnar species with funnel-shaped, often very large blooms (4.11), which are frequently white, nocturnal and scented, but occasionally coloured. The genus now includes species formerly classified as *Tricho-cereus* (tall columnar), *Helianthocereus* (short columnar), *Acanthocalycium* (glob-ular) and others. The nearly spherical species include many veteran favourites of European glasshouses: *E. eyriesii, E. tubiflora, E. oxygona* and others, all long-suffering, long-lived, and rewarding the grower annually with superb large trumpet-shaped blooms. They have been

Left (16.17): **Oroya peruviana depressa.** *Oroya is one of several South American genera enjoying popularity and easily adapting to cultivation. The stem is typically unbranched.*

Below (16.18): **Rebutia neosteinmannii.** *Rebutias are the ideal miniature cacti for the beginner with limited space and a thirst for dazzling flowers every year.*

unfairly overlooked in the rush for the latest novelties. Together with the equally tough and columnar *E. spachiana* (16.1) and *E. lamprochlora,* they provide some of the best grafting stocks. No cacti are easier to raise from cuttings or offsets, which in the dwarf species often root while still attached to the parent plant. *E. pachanoi* contains hallucinogenic alkaloids and has long been used in religious ceremonies in Peru, as has *Lophophora* in parts of Mexico (page 18).

With *Lobivia* and *Rebutia* we come to two of the most popular of all genera of cacti, and it is hard to imagine a collection without them. Both are small to very small, compact and neat in habit but sufficiently varied to be interesting all the year round. *Lobivia* has the larger flowers, in dazzling reds and yellow (16.19). *Rebutia* produces greater profusion in rings from around the base of each head, and the colour range includes white, pink, orange and magenta (16.18, 20, 21).

Some flower in two years from seed, which is easy to raise. These are the perfect cacti to offer a beginner who insists upon flowers and is limited to a small space on a sunny windowsill. I purposely forgo listing species names: all are desirable, and it is merely a matter of personal choice.

Hylocereinae
Here we come upon plants more typical of tropical forest regions than semi-deserts, and adapted for life as epiphytes or lithophytes. The stems are typically long and flexible—many metres in some —and, except in *Aporocactus,* have few

Right (16.19): **Lobivia densispina** *flowering in a 6 cm (2½in) pot. Like* **Rebutia,** **Lobivia** *is a good genus for beginners and flowers freely on small specimens.*

Below (16.20): *Rebutias set seed readily in captivity but the seed is often hybrid. For pure seed, hand-pollination of two plants of the same species is needed.*

ribs. They put out adventitious roots into the air, which assist in water absorption and, when they contact suitable surfaces, take hold and support the plant. The spines are mostly minute or hardly developed at all. The flowers range from the smallest to the largest in the Family.

Some root in the soil *(Hylocereus, Selenicereus)* and ascend high up tree trunks or rock faces much like ivy clinging to a wall. Eventually, contact with the ground may be lost by the death and decay of the primary root. Others grow naturally hanging from steep rock faces *(Aporocactus, Morangaya)* or from the boughs of forest trees *(Epiphyllum, Nopalxochia, Rhipsalis* 4.18) in the same way as do orchids and bromeliads, with which they often keep company. Nourishment comes from windblown humus that falls amid the stems and decomposes.

Aporocactus, with about five similar species, includes *A. flagelliformis,* the celebrated 'Rat's Tail Cactus' that has long adorned cottage windows and is one of the hardiest and most tolerant of all cacti. Although introduced to Europe as early as 1690 its native habitat remained unknown until a few plants were located in the wild in Mexico within the past 20 years. The flowers of this genus are oblique, being slightly S-shaped in profile.

Heliocereus is a small genus of more erect growth in cultivation, although scrambling or climbing in the wild. The elongated stems have from two to seven wings, and the flowers are large, regular, and mostly red, and open by day. The best-known is *H. speciosus* (16.22), parent of the hybrid epicacti (page 72), to which it contributes the brilliant vermilion of the petals with a steely blue flush along the inner margins. There is a pure white form, and *H. cinnabarinus* is the colour of cinnabar.

Hylocereus consists entirely of epiphytes, which usually start at ground level and form great canopies hanging from trees, climbing to a height of up to 10m (33ft) by means of their sturdy, three-winged, long-jointed stems with copious aerial roots. They are essentially plants of the tropics, needing ample root room, water and warmth. In a suitably large glasshouse a *Hylocereus* can be trained on wires to hang from the roof, where it will reward the grower by its marvellous large white flowers, which open at night and are powerfully scented. They are followed by large fleshy fruits.

Top left (16.21): **Rebutia marsoneri** *from northern Argentina. Flower colour in* **Rebutia** *is red or yellow, sometimes orange, pink, purple or intermediate shades and, rarely, almost white.*

Left (16.22): **Heliocereus speciosus,** *one of the parents of the epicacti, to which it transmits day-opening along with the vivid red and steely blue flush of the flowers.*

Selenicereus differs in having slender cylindrical stems with from three to ten low ribs, and a more slender flower tube covered with tiny scales and felt instead of the large scales of *Hylocereus*. It now includes plants formerly segregated as *Mediocactus* and *Deamia*. The largest and most gorgeous of all cactus flowers are found here in *S. megalanthus* and *S. macdonaldiae,* up to 38cm (15in) long and 30cm (12in) in spread. The best-known is the original 'Queen of the Night', *S. grandiflorus,* from Jamaica, cultivated since 1700. Although nothing to get excited about when not in flower, a *Selenicereus* takes up little space if positioned at the back of the staging and trained to fill in corners. The floral display is all the more breath-taking for appearing on such unpretentious stems.

Epiphyllum species are epiphytes, rarely growing at soil level and more at home in crotches of the branches of trees, often many metres above the ground. The flattened green branches with tiny areoles and few or no bristles are often mistaken for leaves. The margins are variously notched or lobed *(E. anguliger)* or, in one species *(E. chrysocardium),* so deeply incised as to look like the frond of a cycad. The flowers are white and nocturnal, with a long narrow tube. *E. crenatum* is one parent of the epicacti (5.11, 12) *Nopalxochia* (16.23) is a related genus, whose flowers are pink *(N. phyllanthoides)* or red *(N. ackermannii).*

Schlumbergera includes another great favourite of cottage windows, the 'Christmas Cactus', variously labelled *Zygocactus truncatus* and other names, but correctly *Schlumbergera × buckleyi,* a hybrid descended from *S. truncata × S. russelliana.* The plant consists of chains of short, flat, green, leaf-like, unarmed stem joints with rounded notches and bears terminal almost regular flowers about 7cm (2¾in) long. The true *S. truncata* is less common, and has more pointed teeth on the stem segments and a very oblique corolla.

Rhipsalis is one of the largest genera in the Cactaceae, and perhaps the most varied in general habit, showing remarkable diversity in the lengths and geometrical arrangements of the jointed stems. These may be flat, cylindrical, angled or ribbed, often assembled in whorls and of different shapes on the one plant. Spines are absent or fine bristles on young growth only. The flowers are very tiny and white, pinkish or yellow, but make up in number and, in some species, by appearing in winter—a welcome novelty. They occur all along the hanging stems and are followed by small juicy berries: "mistletoe cactus" is the

*Right (16.23): Flowers of 'Deutsche Kaiserin', a cultivar of **Nopalxochia,** which has flat, leaflike stems and no spines. **Nopalxochia** species grow naturally as epiphytes in Mexico.*

common name of species with white fruits (4.18). *Rhipsalis* species make excellent basket plants and their neglect by collectors is hard to understand. Two species are, however, well-known and exceptional for producing larger, colourful blooms: *R. gaertneri,* the 'Easter Cactus' (page 179), with vivid vermilion flowers, and *R. rosea* with pink ones.

Neoporteriinae

Some of the most popular of the dwarf globular cacti from South America are to be found within this subtribe, distinguished from others by flowering toward the centre of the crown rather than near the stem base, and by the presence of wool and small spines on the outside of the flowers and fruits.

Neoporteria encompasses perhaps as many as 66 variable species from Chile and southern Peru (16.24, 25). Spination is diverse and body colours also vary, from green to blackish purple. These are justly in demand among collectors and easy to manage. Immediately appealing

Left (16.24): **Neoporteria grandiflorens** *and below (16.25):* **N.villosa polyraphis** *are two of over 60 species of South American cacti that include some formerly classified as* **Pyrrhocactus, Horridocactus, Neochilenia** *and* **Islaya.** *Despite great confusion of names, they are attractively spined, almost hardy miniature cacti with small but numerous flowers. The majority can be grown easily from seed.*

is *N. nidus,* whose crown of interwoven, curling, bristle-like spines is fancifully compared to a bird's nest. The spines can be any shade from white through buff and bright yellow to black, and other hues. A pressing recommendation goes to *N. wagenknechtii* (16.26), which begins to open its rings of small but brilliant magenta blooms in October and continues for weeks: a fine splash of colour when few other cacti are performing. Typical *Neoporteria* flowers remain only half open; those of *Notocactus* open right out flat (rotate), and this genus also is differentiated by seed structure. It comes from Brazil, Uruguay and Argentina and has 30 species or more. The usually large yellow flowers appear near the centre of the crown; *N. uebelmannianus* has either yellow or purple blooms, and in *N. graessneri* they are lime green. To the old

favourites like *N. ottonis* and *N. leninghausii* have been added many marvellous recent discoveries: *N. magnificus, N. herteri, N. buiningii* and others.

Parodia (16.45) differs from the preceding in having some, at least, of the spines hooked, but there are exceptions. The seeds are very minute. All are beauties, but some have a tendency to lose their roots and need careful coaxing to get them started again. This is therefore a genus best left to the more experienced cultivator. *Frailea* and *Blossfeldia* are real miniatures—the latter is the smallest of all cacti. A *Frailea* flower is a rare sight; mostly the species are cleistogamous and all one sees is the relatively large fruit full of seeds. *Uebelmannia* is a new star gleaming bright in collections: it is credited with five or more species, of which the most remarkable is

U. pectinifera (16.27). The deep purple stems have many sharp ribs covered in silvery scales, and the areoles are so close together that the fine spines form a crest or comb along the ribs. Like *Parodia,* these are not plants for the beginner.

Cactinae

The two genera placed in this subtribe are not closely related. The stems are solitary and globose or flat-topped, and the flowers originate from a central cephalium. In *Discocactus* the flowers are quite large, white, beautifully moulded and with a delicate perfume, opening after dusk and wilted by the next morning. In *Melocactus* (16.28) the cephalium is much more prominent and hemispherical or even cylindrical. The flowers and fruits are like those of *Mammillaria,* quite small, and push out through the dense brush of

bristles that gives the genus the popular name of 'Turk's Cap'. Both genera are tropical and need all the warmth that they can get, but are not difficult from seed. In *Melocactus,* development of the cephalium terminates the growth of new green tissue, and imported adult specimens rarely survive for long.

Right (16.26): **Neoporteria wagenknechtii** *has the merit of blooming in autumn and early winter when few other cacti oblige, and the small but brilliant blooms last for several days.*

Below left (16.27): **Uebelmannia pectinifera,** *one of the most striking and sought-after novelties of recent years, is valued for its comblike spination and silver-scaled purple stems rather than the minute yellow flowers.*

Below right (16.28): *The 'Turk's Cap Cactus'* **Melocactus delessertianum,** *needs warmth, ample light and some water all the year round. Imported plants rarely live long, but seedlings make rapid growth.*

16: CACTACEAE

Echinocactinae

All 20 genera of this subtribe are esteemed by cactophiles, and the majority are solitary or form compact mounds of heads, and accommodate well to small pots in a glasshouse. Taking the largest-growing first, *Echinocactus* (6.11) and *Ferocactus* (2.1, 16.29) are the "barrel cacti", conspicuous features of the drier areas of Mexico and the southwest USA. But even though potted specimens need to be large before flowering, the plants are valued for the superb spines, often hooked in *Ferocactus* and marked with transverse bands; the colour intensifies on wetting. *F. fordii* and *F. viridescens* will bloom in a 12cm (5in) pot.

Thelocactus is an ill-defined genus but includes many desirable species such as *T. nidulans,* whose stout, grey, flaking spines surround the outside of the stem like a bird's nest (16.30). The obvious feature of all but one species of *Echino-fossulocactus* is the large number of very thin wavy ribs, which make it distinctive and readily recognizable. *Astrophytum,* composed of only four species, is a case of

"once seen, never forgotten". The stem branches only if damaged, and has a few deep, acute ribs more-or-less covered with white flecks, giving a snowy effect. Two species, *A. myriostigma* (16.31) and *A. asterias,* lack spines. *A. ornatum* is the largest-growing (16.32) and needs to be in a 15cm (6in) pot before flowering; the others flower more freely, and I have had *A. asterias* oblige in the second year from seed. *A. capricorne,* with soft curling spines, has the best bloom of all, fully 7cm (2¾in) across and bright clear yellow with a red throat. Propagation is by seed. The species are self-incompatible, and there are many intriguing hybrids.

Also distinctive at first sight is *Copiapoa cinerea,* with a greyish white, pruinose body contrasting with stout dark central spines. *Gymnocalycium,* with around 60 species from South America, is often made the subject of a specialist collection to itself (16.44): as with *Mammillaria,* the discerning eye can find endless pleasure in the subtle differemces of tubercle shape and spiralling, body colour, and number and disposition

of spines. Many of the flowers are a sombre off-white colour, but some are yellow (*G. andreae*), red (*G. baldianum*) or lilac (*G. horridispinum*). Characteristic features are a chin-like bulge to the tubercle below each areole, and the broad, rounded scales on the flower tube, without any hairs or spines.

Right (16.29): **Ferocactus acanthodes tortulospinus** *about 60cm (2ft) tall in Baja California. The long twisting spines are its most noteworthy feature.*

Far right (16.30): **Thelocactus nidulans** *also has a nickname: 'Bird's Nest Cactus' from the "nest" of grey fibrous spines that surrounds an old plant. The plant remains solitary and is propagated by seed.*

Below (16.31): The spineless **Astrophytum myriostigma** *in habitat in San Luis Potosi associated with bromeliads. The popular name is 'Bishop's Cap Cactus'. Astrophytums are typically covered in white flecks.*

Below right (16.32): **Astrophytum** *has only four species, but all are easily recognizable and have long been firm favourites in collections. This is the largest growing,* **Astrophytum ornatum,** *and one of the two species with spines.*

Leuchtenbergia principis (16.35) stands all by itself, with the longest of tubercles surmounted by long, flattened, papery spines. The impressively large yellow flower arises near the centre from the tip of a young tubercle. *Aztekium ritteri* is another oddity, in which the squat olive green stem is covered in horizontal creases giving the impression of great age. *Lophophora* is one of the few spineless cacti, its soft, grey, top-shaped body bearing a tuft of wool from each low, rounded tubercle. There is a single variable species *L. williamsii* (2.3, 16.34), although some botanists recognize a second, *L. diffusa*. The small white or pink flowers are self-compatible and set plentiful seed that is easy but slow to raise. This is the famous peyote (peyotl) of the Mexican Indians, and its ritual uses are discussed on page 18.

Ariocarpus looks even less like the conventional idea of a cactus. Its six species grow with the conical body buried in the ground, exposing only a flat rosette of tough, pointed or truncate incrusted tubercles (16.33). In habitat one can walk over them without either noticing or harming them. In cultivation it is wise to plant the body half way out of the soil to minimize the danger of rotting. From seed *Ariocarpus* is slow and takes many years to reach flowering size. Grafting can effect a remarkable growth acceleration, but produces a globular, untypical specimen. Contrary to earlier belief, *Ariocarpus* takes plenty of water in the summer, provided that it is well rooted

Below (16.33): **Ariocarpus retusus** *is hard to see in habitat, lying flush with the ground and partly covered in soil. The plant has a tuberous root and is very slow growing.*

Above (16.34): **Lophophora williamsii,** *the peyote or "L.S.D. cactus" referred to on page 18. In place of spines, the areoles produce a shaving brush of hairs.*

Right (16.35): **Leuchtenbergia principis** *differs from all other cacti in its triangular tubercles, which grow up to 10cm (4in) in length, and in its soft, papery white spines.*

and that sun and ventilation are maximal. Past losses have mainly arisen from damaged imported plants, which root slowly or not at all.

Epithelantha species and *Pelecyphora* (16.38) are neat miniatures of slow growth, covered in spiral tubercles with many short spines at each areole. In *Pelecyphora aselliformis* the body is grey and each areole is long and narrow with spines in two rows pointing in opposite directions—rather recalling a woodlouse viewed from above. *P. strobiliformis* has flat, incurved, overlapping tubercles like a pine cone. *Strombocactus* (taken here to include *Obregonia* and *Turbinicarpus*) and *Pediocactus* (embracing *Navajoa*, *Pilocanthus*, *Toumeya* and *Utahia*) include further collector's gems, mostly content with 7–9cm (3–3½in) pots and a cool, dry, light top shelf in winter. Those from the southwest USA are mostly difficult to keep and best left to specialists: *Pediocactus sileri*, *P. paradinei* (16.39) and *P. knowltonii*, for instance. Those from Mexico are more accommodating, trouble free, and among the earliest cacti to bloom in spring. *Strombocactus denegrii* (16.36) resembles an *Ariocarpus* in body form.

Neolloydia (16.37) from Mexico and *Escobaria* from further north into the USA comprise additional dwarf tuberculate plants having a conspicuous groove on the upper side of the tubercle leading

Right (16.36): **Strombocactus (Obregonia) denegrii** *never offsets and is raised only from seed. Notice the leaf-like tubercles and woolly crown. It comes from Tamaulipas in Mexico.*

Below right (16.37): **Neolloydia conoidea** *(syn.* **N. texensis***) from Texas and Northern Mexico eventually forms clumps. It thrives in full sun and flowers over several weeks.*

Below (16.38): **Pelecyphora aselliformis** *is readily recognized by the hatchet-shaped tubercles and comb-like spines. Plants rarely exceed 5cm (2in) in diameter.*

Above (16.39): **Pediocactus paradinei** *is rare in habitat and rarer in cultivation: a challenge for connoisseurs who like "difficult" species. This specimen is 4cm (1½ in) across the body.*

Left (16.40): **Coryphantha vivipara** *in habitat in Salida, Colorado. It is widespread in the USA and hardy, reaching almost to the northern limits of Cactaceae.*

from the areole to the axil. This is also clearly seen in the large genus *Coryphantha* (about 60 species), where the tubercles are large to very large. Although it is less free-flowering than some genera, the blooms are usually worth waiting for. *C. vivipara* (16.40) is frost hardy, and bears freely its eye-catching violet-magenta flowers followed by large, fleshy green berries.

Finally we come to *Mammillaria,* with over 225 species, second only to *Opuntia* in size and to none in popularity. From Mexico it extends north into the USA, east to the West Indies and south into northern South America. All are dwarf, solitary or clustering cacti with tubercles arranged in conspicuous spirals tipped by a group of spines. The main diagnostic feature is that innovations—new shoots or flower buds—arise from the base of the tubercle, not at its tip. The flowers are usually small but borne profusely in rings like a garland around the apex of the stem (16.42), and are succeeded by smooth, elongated, fleshy, usually red berries, which are a colourful sight in autumn (7.3). They are edible and have the native name "chilitos". Of spines, there seems no limit to variations (2.14): straight or hooked, variously angled, comb-like (pectinate) in *M. pectinifera*, feathered (plumose) in *M. plumosa* and *M. pennispinosa*, and so on. Some species exude drops of milky white sap when cut. Culturally they cover the whole range from easy-growing, almost hardy species such as *M. magnimamma* to others that are preserved with difficulty, usually as grafts, and hence keep the specialists on their toes. With so many desirable species a selection is almost too personal to venture. *M. guelzowiana* (16.41), *M.*

boolii (16.43) and other large-flowering species are favourites, especially when the plant body itself is very tiny *(M. theresae* and allies). *M. zeilmanniana* is mass-multiplied for the market for its profuse magenta flowers. *M. hahniana* and *M. plumosa* look as if wrapped in cotton wool.

Propagation is by seed, division of clumps, or cuttings. A few species seed themselves in the glasshouse, and under favourable conditions I have had *M. bocasana* in flower within a year of germination. It is no accident that

Mammillaria earned a society to itself, founded in the London area in 1960 and publishing a quarterly journal.

Right (16.41): **Mammillaria guelzowiana** *is treasured for its silky white hair and large blooms. But it needs careful watering.*

Below right (16.42): **Mammillarias** *appeal by their diversity of tubercle patterns, spination and flowers in rings round the stem.*

Below (16.43): Flat-topped and flush with the soil in habitat in Sonora, **Mammillaria boolii** *changes form when cultivated. The 5 cm (2 in) flower is one of the largest in the genus.*

16: CACTACEAE

Cultivation

A generous sampling of the cactus Family can be happily housed in a typical amateur glasshouse provided that it has ample light and ventilation and a minimum winter temperature of around 5°C (40°F). Occasional drops to freezing point will do no harm if the plants are dry. If no heat is available, the choice is much more limited, but not beyond hope. Certain groups of cacti need extra heat. There are the moisture-loving tropical pereskias and Hylocereinae, along with their hybrids, the epicacti. Collectors attracted by these, which mostly take up a lot of space, are usually willing to give them a house to themselves, although they consort well with orchids, bromeliads and some tropical African succulents such as *Kalanchoe*.

More xerophytic heat-lovers are the Cactinae and isolated species of other subtribes from the drier parts of Central America: some recent acquisitions from Brazil come within this category. The fancier of these plants has various ways of accommodating them. He can position them over the heat source, or he can build a polythene tent in a corner of the glasshouse, perhaps including his propagator as a heat source. Another possibility is to bring the plants into the home during the winter. A sunny windowsill in the lounge can be put to good use, if the temperature does not fall below about 10°C (50°F) overnight. If in doubt, cover the plants with newspaper in the evening, or move them away from the window and return them the following morning.

All Cactaceae can be treated as summer growers, irrespective of their origin north or south of the Equator. The only exceptions are a few that flower in the winter months and therefore appreciate a little water and extra warmth when the buds are forming: *Schlumbergera × buckleyi*, some *Rhipsalis* species, *Mammillaria plumosa, Neoporteria wagenknechtii* and a few others. After blooming, they should be kept dry and encouraged to rest.

Grafting is more practised in Cactaceae than in the other Families of succulents, and some extraordinary results have been reported, such as flowering *Ariocarpus* in the first year from seed. It is also possible to make novelties available in quantity for the market almost as rapidly as budded roses.

Overall, the majority of cacti are the least troublesome of all tender succulents to manage, which is doubtless a factor in their popularity. This tolerance of neglect and mismanagement has, however, often reacted to their disadvantage: whereas most plants die when maltreated, cacti linger on, and the terribly malformed, scarred survivors one often encounters serve to give the public the impression that all cacti are equally hideous. Nothing could be farther from the truth. If only the critics could be brought to see a really well-kept collection!

Right (16.44): Gymnocalycium *species in the research collection of an English specialist. Each specimen is documented for origin and locality — essential for studies on classification.*

Below right (16.45): Parodia mutabilis, *from Argentina, is but one of many handsome species available in cultivation. Note the hooked spines. Multiplication is by (very small) seed.*

Below (16.46): Most of the sixty or more species of Rhipsalis *have tiny blooms, but* R. rosea *is exceptional and almost as showy as* Schlumbergera.

The Didierea Family

This distinctive and isolated Family, endemic to southwest Madagascar, makes up for its small size by many features of botanical interest. Like the Cactaceae, to which it runs parallel in many ways, for a long time it resisted efforts to fit it into any system of classification, seeming to have no close allies. Now, however, anatomical features and the possession of the pigment beta-cyanin have sited it in Caryophyllales next to the Cactaceae, with which successful grafts have been made—an index of biochemical affinity.

The four genera are all heavily armed, thick-stemmed trees or shrubs of unique appearance, recalling cacti, tree euphorbias and *Fouquieria* (1.8) — another instance of convergent evolution. As in cacti, the spines are interpreted as modified leaves. Foliage leaves are also present, except in one species, *Alluaudia dumosa* (17.2). They are flat, scarcely succulent and simple in outline, and fall during the dry season. The flowers are tiny and unisexual, borne in bunches, but are rarely produced outside the habitat. Heidelberg University took the lead in the 1950s in introducing the riches of the Madagascan flora to Europe, and Prof. W. Rauh, the leading authority on the Family, reports three flowering species there.

Alluaudia produces long, thick stems with usually ascending branches up to 15m (49ft) tall, and has six species (17.2). The stems are covered in solitary or paired spines and small, leathery, almost circular leaves, sometimes turned into a vertical plane rather than borne horizontally.

Alluaudiopsis forms smaller shrubs up to 2m (6½ft) tall. There are two, very local species.

Decaryia consists of the single species D. *madagascariensis* (17.1), which in youth forms a compact shrub of singular appearance, the zigzag branches bearing a small leaf and two diverging spines at each node. In nature it eventually grows into a tree 8m (26ft) tall.

Finally, *Didierea* is the wonder of them all. Here the similarity to cacti is greater than in any other plant, the spines being borne in clusters from horny areoles at the tips of long tubercles (17.2). In D. *madagascariensis* there is a stout main trunk with a head of thick erect branches that somewhat recalls the saguaro of Arizona. The other species, D. *trollii* (17.3), is similar in old age, but for the early years looks quite different, with the branches growing prostrate on the ground.

Didiereaceae can be raised from seeds and from cuttings, although it must be

Below (17.1): **Decaryia** madagascariensis *brings novelty to any collection with its quaintly zig-zagging growth with a pair of spines at each joint. Cuttings will root.*

Below (17.2): A selection of Didiereaceae. From left to right, **Alluaudia dumosa, A.comosa** *(back),* **Decaryia madagascariensis, Didierea trollii** *and* D. madagascariensis.

added that neither, at present, is easy to obtain. They revel in warmth, and I have had *Alluaudia procera* for years on a sunny windowsill over a radiator, where it is watered throughout the year, although much less is given when the leaves drop—a wise precaution.

It may be asked why so tiny a Family— no more than 11 species in four genera— is given the honour of a chapter to itself. Their unique appearance—"the cacti of the Old World", as Werner Rauh puts it—and their sudden emergence from obscurity have excited much interest among both botanists and plantsmen. Plants are eagerly sought for; like pachypodiums, they have become status symbols for the connoisseur's collection and the exhibition table. But there is another reason why the Didiereaceae deserve extra publicity. They are all very limited in range in the wild and their habitats are rapidly being destroyed, so their preservation, at least in cultivation, is of special concern to conservationists.

Right (17.3): **Didierea trollii** *begins life prostrate but eventually throws tall vertical shoots like those of* **D.madagascariensis.** *Like all the Family, it must have warmth.*

18: APOCYNACEAE

The Periwinkle Family

A predominantly tropical Family, the Apocynaceae comprise about 180 genera and 1,500 species. They are mostly twining plants with a white milky sap *(latex)*. The flowers are often quite showy and some genera (such as *Allamanda*) are grown as glasshouse climbers. The shrubby *Plumeria* is the 'Frangipani', grown throughout the tropics for its scented blooms. Some growers of succulents have stretched the limits of their collections to include it on the strength of slightly fleshy branches. *Vinca,* the periwinkle, is a genus of hardy creepers. The flower parts are in fives but the internal structure is quite complex, approaching that of the Asclepiadaceae (Chapter 19).

Two genera are of interest to all who relish unusual succulents. *Adenium* has one widespread and variable species, or a few separate species, according to taste,

and spans Africa from the southwest through Kenya to Arabia. The habit varies from a low, caudiciform shrub with a massive gnarled trunk to tall erect stem succulents up to 4m (13ft) high. The thick stems are irregularly branched, smooth and unarmed, bearing at their tips flat, leathery, usually slightly shiny, dark green leaves up to 15cm (6in) long in loose spiral rosettes. They drop in the resting season. *Adenium* in full flower is one of the showiest of all African succulents (18.1). *A. obesum* is the 'Desert Rose' or 'Mock Azalea' (18.2) and its variety *multiflorum* is especially suited for small collections because it will bloom from 15cm (6in) rooted cuttings. It is much grown as an ornamental in Malaysia. The flower colour range is from intense red through pink to white with red margins. *Adeniums* are very tender and

thrive in a rich, porous soil, a bright warm situation and water in moderation all the year round.

Pachypodium (18.3–5) is distinguished from *Adenium* by possessing spines and by its seed, which has a tuft of hair at one end, whereas the seed of *Adenium* has a tuft at both ends. The 13 species occupy two discrete geographical areas: nine inhabit Madagascar and the other four South and South West Africa and Angola. The South African species include two that are best regarded as caudiciform. In my experience the toughest and easiest to grow is *P. lealii* ssp. *saundersii,* which

Adeniums have some of the showiest blooms outside of Cactaceae. **Adenium boehmianum** *(below, 18.1) is the 'Impala Lily' of South West Africa.* **Adenium obesum** *(right, 18.2) is East African. All species revel in warmth and will take ample water when in leaf.*

can be brought from seed to flower in five years. In habitat it is an extraordinary sight, with a massive gnarled trunk up to 1m (39in) thick at the base and erratically branched like *Adenium* but more cactus-like, being covered in stout spines in pairs with a third smaller one between them. The deciduous leaves are bright, glossy green and up to 8cm (3in) long. Attractive white flowers appear later in the season —often too late to expand properly in European cultivation. The 10cm (4in) fruits shed large numbers of parachute seeds. *P. namaquanum* is equally strange and distinctive (18.5): a conical, often unbranched, stem up to 2m (6½ft) tall, with a cabbage-like crown of foliage and spiral rows of tubercles bearing 5cm (2in) spines. In the rugged, moon-like landscape of its natural habitat along the banks of the Orange River one can well imagine being transported to another planet.

Two of the Madagascan species, *P. geayi* and *P. lamerei,* come close to *P. namaquanum* in general facies and have become more readily available during the past decade, even being offered by florists as house plants. With their robust erect stems (usually unbranched in cultivated specimens) and spirally arranged tubercles, each crowned with three long spines, they look extremely cactus-like. But the crown of long narrow leaves at once distinguishes them, and there is no felted areole or spine cushion. *P. geayi* is the more attractive because of its covering of grey felt on the young growth. An extraordinary cristate cultivar of *P. lamerei* has been kept going by grafting, and plants with variegated foliage also arise. These two species take plenty of water in the summer and are the most rapid growing.

Other choices are *P. densiflorum* (18.3) and *P. rosulatum* with orange to yellow flowers, and *P. baronii* with red ones. Like the *Adeniums, Pachypodium* likes warmth at all times, but plants can be brought into the home during winter and thrive on a light, sunny windowsill. When the leaves fall, this is a cue that a dry rest is needed. Both genera graft readily (6.25) but vegetative multiplication is rarely possible and the supply of imported seed hardly meets the demand for such striking and curious novelties.

Above right (18.3): Seedling of **Pachypodium densiflorum** *from Madagascar. The Madagascan species of the genus are more tender than those from South Africa.*

Right (18.4): **Pachypodium lealii** *in flower in Angola. This has an irregular lumpish, branching caudex up to 6m (20ft).*

Opposite (18.5) **Pachypodium namaquanum,** *one of the strangest and most cactus-like of African succulents, grows to 2m (6½ft).*

The Milkweed Family

The milkweed Family—so named after the common American weeds of the type genus *Asclepias*—is credited with 130 genera and around 2,000 species. They are mostly confined to the tropics and centred in Africa. The Family has been subdivided into six ill-defined Tribes, in all but one of which some form of succulence has evolved. Its closest ally is the Family Apocynaceae, from which it differs in a further floral specialization: the clumping together of pollen grains to form a *pollinium*, discussed below.

Raphionacme (page 214), *Fockea*, *Brachystelma* and some species of *Ceropegia* are caudiciform and will be found described in Chapter 21. *Cynanchum* and *Sarcostemma* are widely distributed genera of twiners or shrubs with somewhat fleshy rod-like stems, with or without small leaves. The *Cynanchum* illustrated on page 214 is interesting because of the curious, irregular, warty feel of the stems; the flowers are much more freely produced than in *Sarcostemma*.

Ceropegia (19.1–4) covers a range of life forms, some quite non-succulent, some stem-succulent, some fleshy leaved and some with long fleshy roots, or clusters of tubers, or a single large caudex. Jacobsen lists 66 species of interest to the grower of succulents. *C. dichotoma*, *C. fusca* and their allies form a distinctive little group from the Canary Islands. They bear stiffly erect, jointed, cylindrical succulent stems, and small, narrow leaves that soon drop. The remaining species grow prostrate or twine or are supported by shrubs. Although showy enough when displayed in a glasshouse, many *Ceropegias* in nature are inconspicuous, so that hunting them takes on the excitement of pursuing rare orchids. They tend to grow in isolation rather than as dense populations, and seek out the shade of the densest shrubs, so that even when in flower they easily escape detection. Some have been collected on only a few occasions, or are known from only one herbarium specimen. *Ceropegia* has the leaves opposite or (rarely) in threes, and usually stalked, but sometimes grass-like or reduced to scales. The flowers are tubular, narrow, and 2–12cm (¾–5in) long, and their diversity is amazing. At the top of the corolla tube the lobes separate but then usually unite again to form a canopy or umbrella over the top, sometimes with weirdly coloured hairs, spots or outgrowths that attract tiny insects (4.14). Sometimes the apex is drawn out into a spiral several centimetres long. The pollination mechanism is described on page 56.

A few ceropegias have developed highly succulent stems, which in *C. stapeliiformis* much resemble those of *Stapelia* although the tubular flower at once distinguishes it. The cristate cultivar defies description (19.1)! But even that is surpassed by *C. armandii*, a rather delicate rarity from Madagascar, which can best be compared to a lizard moulded from plastic.

A collection of ceropegias is rewarding because no two flowers are alike and their lantern-like appearance never fails to excite

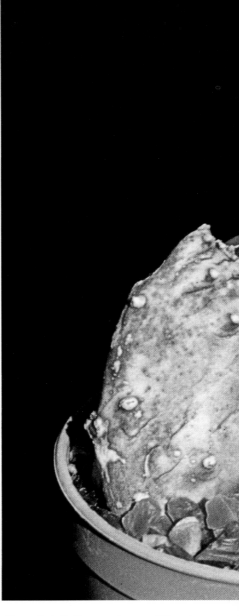

Above (19.1): **Ceropegia stapeliiformis cristata,** *a flowering crest of an already curious plant that looks all set for a part in a science fiction film. But it is real!*

Right (19.2): **Ceropegia ballyana** *has the "lantern" of petal tips extended and spirally twisted, sometimes enlarging the flower length to 10cm (4in) or more.*

Far right (19.3): **Ceropegia sandersonii x radicans,** *one of many curious hybrids arising from chance cross-pollination in cultivation. Such hybrids would rarely survive in nature through lack of a suitable pollinator.*

Left (19.4): **Ceropegia gemmifera** *from Ghana is quite at home ascending the prickly stems of a Brazilian* **Chorisia,** *a borderline succulent of the Family Bombacaceae.*

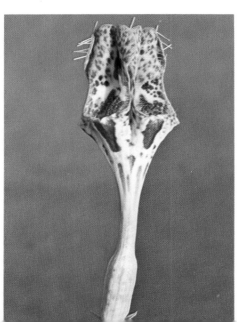

19: ASCLEPIADACEAE

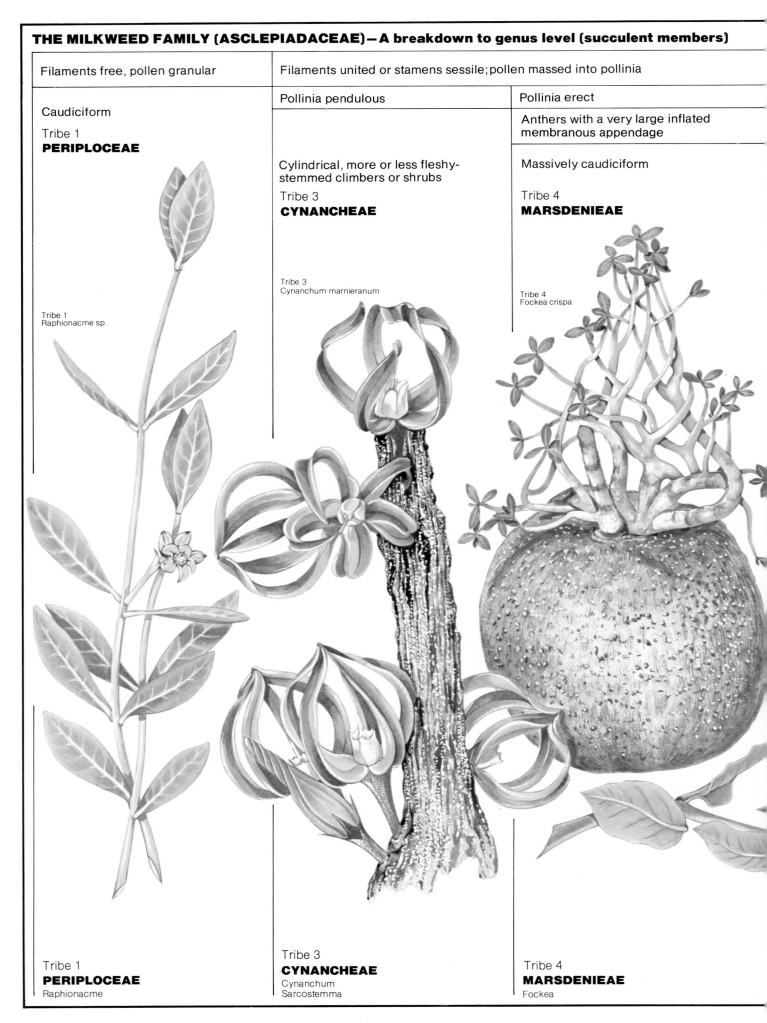

THE MILKWEED FAMILY (ASCLEPIADACEAE)—A breakdown to genus level (succulent members)

Filaments free, pollen granular	Filaments united or stamens sessile; pollen massed into pollinia	
	Pollinia pendulous	Pollinia erect
Caudiciform Tribe 1 **PERIPLOCEAE**		Anthers with a very large inflated membranous appendage
	Cylindrical, more or less fleshy-stemmed climbers or shrubs Tribe 3 **CYNANCHEAE**	Massively caudiciform Tribe 4 **MARSDENIEAE**

Tribe 1
Raphionacme sp.

Tribe 3
Cynanchum marnieranum

Tribe 4
Fockea crispa

Tribe 1
PERIPLOCEAE
Raphionacme

Tribe 3
CYNANCHEAE
Cynanchum
Sarcostemma

Tribe 4
MARSDENIEAE
Fockea

Anthers not so

| Corolla tube length more than twice its diameter midway, with the lobes usually united at the tips. | Corolla tube length less than twice its diameter midway, with free lobes |

| | Caudiciform with slender, non-succulent leafy shoots | Stem succulents with scale leaves or leafless (Exc. *Caralluma frerei*) |

Tribe 5
CEROPEGIEAE

Tribe 6
STAPELIEAE

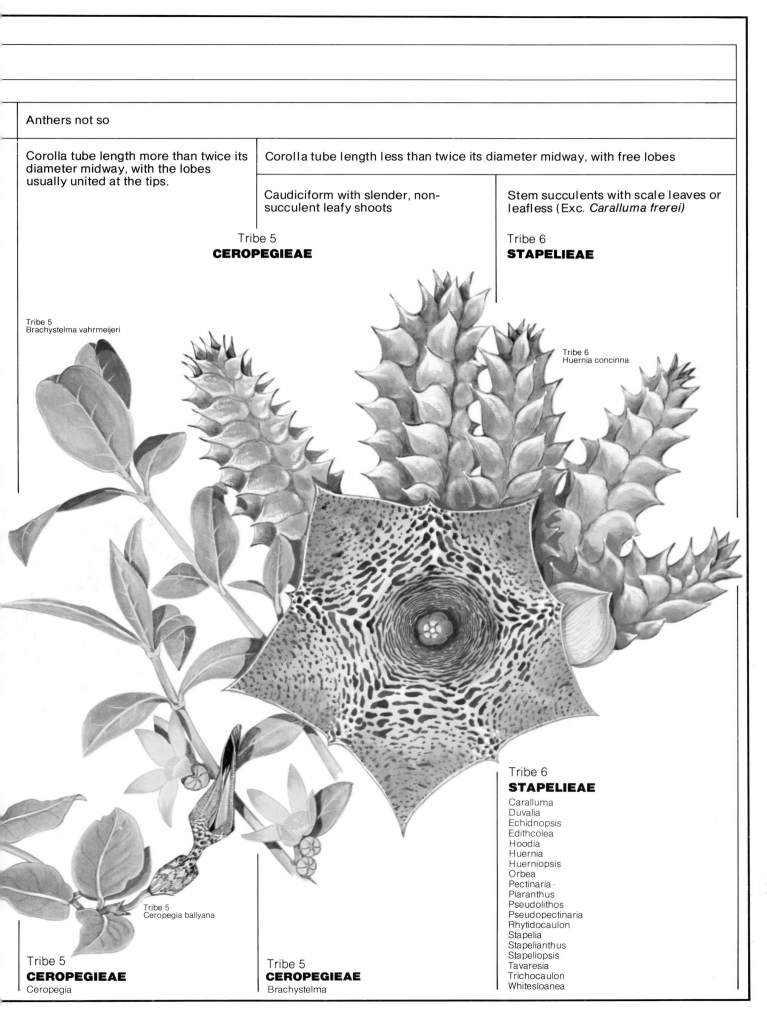

Tribe 5
Brachystelma vahrmeijeri

Tribe 6
Huernia concinna

Tribe 5
Ceropegia ballyana

Tribe 6
STAPELIEAE

Caralluma
Duvalia
Echidnopsis
Edithcolea
Hoodia
Huernia
Huerniopsis
Orbea
Pectinaria
Piaranthus
Pseudolithos
Pseudopectinaria
Rhytidocaulon
Stapelia
Stapelianthus
Stapeliopsis
Tavaresia
Trichocaulon
Whitesloanea

Tribe 5
CEROPEGIEAE
Ceropegia

Tribe 5
CEROPEGIEAE
Brachystelma

interest. But it is difficult to accommodate the long trailing stems in a small glasshouse. Some growers buy flower supports or make their own from sticks and wire. The resulting coils of stems look rather more like an electrician's workshop than a floral display, but the flowers make up for lack of charm in the rest of the plant. It is necessary to train the stems frequently, as they grow rapidly and plants may become entangled.

Stapelieae

The Tribe Stapelieae consists entirely of stem succulents with thick, often soft and juicy branches covered in low ribs or tubercles, often tipped with a scaly bristle which is all that remains of foliage. A superficial resemblance to cacti is to be found in several. One species from India, *Caralluma frerei* (19.6), retains flat, semi-succulent leaves, and is regarded as a pointer to the ancestral prototype from which the Tribe evolved. The main difference from the Ceropegieae is in the form of the flower, which is more open, with a shorter tube and free lobes not united at the tips. However, recent discoveries such as *Pseudopectinaria* have broken down these distinctions and some botanists combine both Tribes in one.

Flower structure and pollination. The flowers of the Stapelieae are structurally the most complicated in all succulents, and show a high level of evolution comparable to that of the orchids, with which this group shows certain evolutionary parallels. In explaining the structure of the commonest species, *Orbea (Stapelia) variegata* (19.7), it will help to have in view the diagram of a simple flower of *Crassula* (2.18) in order to understand the ways in which the consecutive whorls of floral parts have been transformed.

Beginning at the outside, the least altered organ is the calyx, made up of five small green sepals. Next comes the corolla, also of five petals, which are more or less united basally to form a saucer-like or cup-like tube. The Stapelieae come nearest to qualifying as plants with succulent flowers, for the texture is thick and leathery, and they are able to stay expanded in full sun for two days or more without unduly draining the plant's reserves of water. The corolla surface is smooth, sometimes glossy as if varnished, or covered in ridges, pimples or tiny bristles. The margins and even the surface may be covered in fine hairs, which wave to and fro in the slightest breeze and, combined with the purplish brown mark-

ings and rank odour, give an uncanny resemblance to fresh carrion, and this attracts the necessary agents of pollination (4.7). Some Stapelieae have an outgrowth of the corolla called an *annulus* ("little ring"), which surrounds the essential organs at the centre. In the genus *Huernia* it gives the popular name "lifebuoy huernias" to those species where it is prominently developed (19.9).

Instead of separate stamens, the Stapelieae have them fused into a hollow cylindrical body *(column)* that surrounds the two, free carpels. Viewed from above this column is seen to produce three different kinds of sterile outgrowths. First, lying close within the cup of the annulus are five tongue-like lobes known collectively as the outer corona — *corona* meaning 'crown'. Over and above them is the inner corona, which in *O. variegata* terminates in five inner horns and five

Right (19.5): A close up of the flower of **Orbea (Stapelia) maculata**. *Stapelieae have some of the most complicated and beautiful flowers, no two species being alike.*

Below (19.6): **Caralluma frerei** *(left), the "missing link" of the Stapelieae from tropical India, and the only species with leaves. Right, its hybrid with the leafless* C.europaea.

Flower structure of Stapelieae

*(19.7): A diagram showing flower structure of Stapelieae, based upon **Orbea variegata**. The five stamens are elevated and half sunken within a central column, which surrounds the two free carpels. The whole is adorned with inner and outer corona and a fleshy ringlike outgrowth of the corolla called the annulus.*

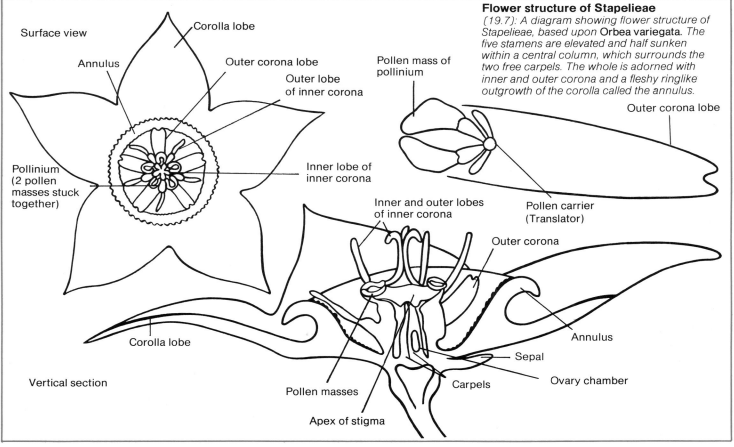

Surface view

Corolla lobe

Annulus

Outer corona lobe

Outer lobe of inner corona

Pollinium (2 pollen masses stuck together)

Inner lobe of inner corona

Pollen mass of pollinium

Outer corona lobe

Pollen carrier (Translator)

Inner and outer lobes of inner corona

Outer corona

Annulus

Sepal

Ovary chamber

Corolla lobe

Vertical section

Pollen masses

Apex of stigma

Carpels

outer horns, as shown in the diagram.

In a flower such as *Crassula,* each anther is two-lobed and splits vertically to shed a cloud of dust-like pollen on either side. This is not so in Stapelieae. The contents of each anther lobe remain stuck together, and each pair of pollen bodies is linked by a yoke bearing two wing-like appendages or carriers. We call such an organ a *pollinium,* and it has a counterpart in the orchid Family.

Finally we reach the centre of the flower where there are two separate (free) carpels, each containing numerous minute ovules. However, above the carpels is a solid disc of tissue that unites the tips of them to the column and immersed anthers.

How does pollination occur in Stapelieae? The full story has yet to be told—there are so many variations in flower form within the group—but a good introduction is given by Reese (1973). The strangely formed outgrowths of the two coronas are functionally guide barriers, which ensure that an insect randomly exploring the flower is eventually drawn to face the column at the centre. Unwanted visitors are excluded. There is a narrow vertical groove or cavity between the inner corona lobes. This groove—there are five to each flower—is the site of the receptive surface where the pollen mass has to arrive. The hairs on a leg or proboscis readily remove

the pollinium by its yoke, and a similar exploring by the insect of another flower of the same species results in the pollinium falling or being dragged off into the appropriate cavity, where pollen tubes grow inward towards the carpels. The mechanism is very specific, something like a key fitting into a lock, and is responsible for the rarity of hybrids even when different species grow side by side in the wild.

Following fertilization, the two free carpels grow out into a pair of slender, cylindrical fruits, which may be up to 20cm (8in) long. Each splits lengthwise (a *follicle,* in botanical parlance) to release a cloud of seeds, each with its own white parachute of hairs (19.8).

Classification. In the past, characters of the corona have been much stressed in dividing up the Family into genera. With more material now available, it is evident that considerable variation can occur, even within one species, and the classification of the Stapelieae is in the melting pot. The listing followed here is that of Larry Leach, who has devoted much study in field and herbarium to elucidating this difficult group. For identification of species, flowers are essential, although some genera may be recognized by their vegetative form. While hunting Stapelieae in South and South West Africa I realized

the impossibility of deciding the species, and even often the genus, unless blooms were to be found. One can only take a small sample of each large clump, grow them on and then examine blooms. Often what looks like a single population turns out to be made up of two or more separate species. This accounts for the disappearance and subsequent rediscovery of "Masson's lost Stapelieae" (page 96).

Overall there are from 400 to 450 species, of which about half belong to the two largest and most widespread genera, *Stapelia* and *Caralluma. Stapelia* (19.11, 12) is South African, with a thinning out northwards into tropical Africa; *Caralluma* reaches North Africa, Arabia and India and even ventures into Europe, the only native European stapeliad *(Caralluma europaea)* being found in southern Spain. The flower size ranges from only a few millimetres in some species to 30cm (12in) or more in *Stapelia gigantea* (19.11), among the largest of all flowers in the plant kingdom.

Right (19.8): Splitting follicles 10cm (4in) long of Stapelia *shed the numerous seeds, each with a parachute of hairs. The seeds germinate rapidly but soon lose viability.*

Below (19.9): Huernia zebrina, *4cm (1½in) across the bloom. The glossy "lifebuoy" rim and the small secondary tooth between each pair of corolla lobes is characteristic of the genus.*

Orbea (19.5) is very close to *Stapelia* and includes the longest and best-known of all this group, *O. variegata* (19.7). This species is also the most adaptable to European cultivation, coming from the Cape Town area, where the annual rainfall is quite high. There is a robust cristate cultivar, and many varieties differing in flower patterning are on record, as well as hybrids.

Duvalia, Huernia and *Piaranthus* are neat, compact-growing stapeliads that take up little room in collections and are worth having for their diversity of flowers. Those of *Huernia* have the distinguishing character of a tiny secondary lobe between each pair of the corolla lobes (19.9).

Stapelianthus comes from Madagascar and, not surprisingly, likes extra warmth. *Edithcolea* (19.10) is a real treasure from East Africa and Socotra. It has arguably the loveliest of all stapeliad flowers. I have seen flourishing clumps growing and blooming in California, but in Europe it is the despair of cultivators.

Hoodia (5.9, 19.13), *Tavaresia* and *Trichocaulon* belong to a distinct group with rather tough greyish or purplish glaucous stems with irregularly scattered tubercles, each often crowned with a bristle, and rarely arranged in ribs. They are intense xerophytes and extra sensitive to overwatering in cultivation. *Trichocaulon* has minute flowers, but those of *Hoodia* (flat and disc-like) and *Tavaresia* (deeply bell-shaped) are striking and unusual.

Somewhat similar in body form are *Pseudolithos* and *Whitesloanea*, rarities from East Africa (7.2), where the ill-fated flora has been so depleted by destruction of habitats. *Whitesloanea* is presumed extinct and *Pseudolithos cubiformis* is not known alive anywhere at the time of writing. *P. migiurtinus* lives on precariously in cultivation, although grafting on *Ceropegia* tubers is usually necessary to preserve it. These are most curious and fascinating plants: *Whitesloanea* is reminiscent of *Astrophytum myriostigma* (16.31). The world of succulents would be the poorer for their loss.

Cultivation

Some Stapelieae such as *Hoodia* (19.13), grow out in the full desert sun, and are extraordinarily resistant to drought. Most, however, seek out the shade, hiding like *Ceropegia* beneath shrubs, so that they often turn up when least expected. "Shrub lifting" becomes second nature to the field botanist in search of them. In cultivation they should all be treated as rather tender. Although some are almost as tough as *Orbea variegata*, which will thrive on a sunny windowsill or in a cool house in company with cacti, most seem generally happier with a winter minimum of about 10°C (50°F). They are more susceptible than most succulents to rot,

Above (19.10): **Edithcolea grandis** *from East Africa and Socotra produces a bloom about 10cm (4in) across. It prefers California sunshine to the cooler, moister climate of Europe.*

Below (19.11): **Stapelia gigantea** *has the largest bloom of all Stapelieae, ranging from 30-45cm (1-1½ft) across the tips of the petals. This one has an unusually pale flower.*

which is visible either as soft blackish patches or by a browning and drying up at the stem base, so that a clump is quickly reduced to a handful of cuttings. Regular inspection is needed. As soon as signs of rot are seen, the affected area should be cut back to green tissue, the surface dusted with flowers of sulphur or other fungicide in powder form, and the plant or cuttings left on a dry, airy shelf for the wounds to heal over. Some growers recommend regular overhead waterings with a liquid fungicide (Chinosol, Cheshunt Compound) or with a systemic fungicide during the growing season to discourage infection. Rarities are grafted on tubers of *Ceropegia woodii* for the same reason.

Seed raising is not too difficult if the same precautions are taken, and is the best way to raise *Hoodia, Tavaresia* and *Trichocaulon,* because cuttings are difficult to root and imported plants, when available, rarely re-establish. Seed can germinate in three or four days, and seedlings may be large enough to pot singly at the end of the first year.

Above (19.12): **Stapelia leendertziae** *has large bell-shaped blooms up to 8cm (3¼in) long. Its sombre beauty compensates for the scent of carrion found in Stapelieae.*

Below (19.13): **Hoodia gordonii** *in habitat in South West Africa. In contrast with the above, it has almost flat blooms. Unlike most Stapelieae, it grows out in the open in full sun.*

The Spurge Family

The Euphorbiaceae make up a large and cosmopolitan Family of plants of which the succulent element is but one of many facies. There are estimated to be 300 genera and over 5,000 species, of which one genus, *Euphorbia*, accounts for two fifths of the species. In the European flora the Family is known only by a handful of small annual or perennial weeds *(Euphorbia,* the spurges, and *Mercuralis,* the dog's mercury, for example). However, most are tropical woody shrubs and trees, including the economically important rubber-bearing genera *Hevea* and *Manihot* and the castor oil plant, *Ricinus.* A common feature of almost all species is a sticky white sap *(latex)* that exudes from any cut surface. It is generally poisonous and no doubt contributes to the protection of the plants from chewing and biting creatures: very few will touch Euphorbiaceae. The flowers (20.4) are always unisexual, small and simple in structure. The fruit is typically a three-lobed capsule that at maturity flies apart into three segments, each releasing one seed.

Turning now to the manifestations of succulence, *Jatropha,* least specialized florally, is discussed in its rightful place in the next chapter, being caudex-forming. This leaves us with five genera of the Tribe Euphorbieae, the most highly evolved in the Family.

Euphorbieae

Like the Compositae, the Euphorbieae have evolved an inflorescence that looks and functions like a single flower. Let us take a close look at one of the most familiar: the 'Crown of Thorns', *Euphorbia milii (splendens)* (20.6). The two red organs are not petals but coloured bracts, and each bears in its axil a dormant bud that can later grow out and add a new branch to the inflorescence. In the centre we find a single female flower reduced to one three-lobed ovary topped by a three-lobed style and set on a short stalk *(pedicel).* Surrounding it are what look like stamens of various ages: each is actually a single male flower reduced to the barest essentials—one stamen with two pollen-bearing anther lobes at the tip. This male flower stands on a tall pedicel with a constriction at the point where it detaches after shedding the pollen. The male flowers are interspersed with hairs and surrounded by a cup-like protective envelope, called an *involucre,* which bears fringes and nectar glands at the top. A "false flower" having this make-up is known as a *cyathium* (20.5). Even Linnaeus was deceived into treating it as a single flower, but by starting with the genus *Jatropha* with separate male and female flowers we can trace an evolutionary series showing progressive reduction of the flowers and their assembly

Below left (20.1): **Euphorbia** *has greater diversity of armature than any other succulents.* **E. neohumbertii** *shows a mixture of stiff spines and curious bristly fringes. Notice the broad scars, from which the flat deciduous leaves have fallen.*

Below (20.2): **Euphorbia cooperi,** *a tree species from Northern Transvaal. Each joint represents one year's growth. The paired spines are regarded as modified stipules.*

THE SPURGE FAMILY (EUPHORBIACEAE)—A breakdown to genus level (succulent members)

Inflorescence a dichasial thyrse; flowers separate, not enveloped by a common involucre	Inflorescence a cyathium, one female flower surrounded by several male flowers within a common involucre	
Tribe 3 **JATROPHEAE**	**Tribe 8** **EUPHORBIEAE**	
	Cyathium symmetrical about two axes, vertical and horizontal	Cyathium zygomorphic, symmetrical about one vertical axis only

Tribe 3
Jatropha ligarinthoides

Tribe 8
Monadenium coccineum

Tribe 8
Euphorbia milii

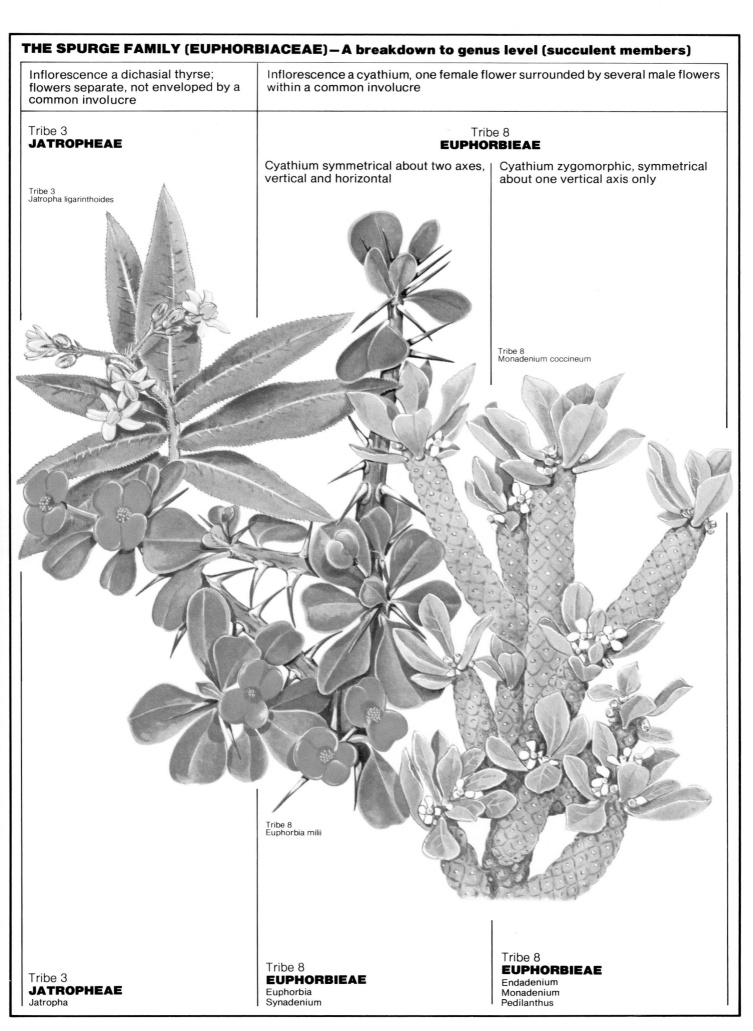

Tribe 3
JATROPHEAE
Jatropha

Tribe 8
EUPHORBIEAE
Euphorbia
Synadenium

Tribe 8
EUPHORBIEAE
Endadenium
Monadenium
Pedilanthus

into cyathia. The end product is unquestionably successful, having the same advantages as the capitulum of Compositae, and contributes to the wide distribution and protean diversity of the genus *Euphorbia*.

Only *Senecio* rivals *Euphorbia* in the variety of shapes and oddly diverse forms it offers, so both are ideal subjects for a collector wishing to specialize. The genus is estimated to include 2,000 species, distributed all over the world and ranging from tiny annual weeds through herbs, shrubs and trees of the tropics. Among the non-succulent species valued in gardens are many hardy foliage plants for the border, such as *E. characias* and *E. cyparissias,* and for the indoor window-sills *E. pulcherrima,* 'Poinsettia', with large red bracts. But it is in central and southern Africa that the genus comes into its own, with xerophytes of all sorts and cactus-mimics of all sizes: 463 species, according to Jacobsen (1975). A few are

Right (20.3): The curious cyathia of **Euphorbia globosa:** *what seem to be "petals" are the much enlarged, white encrusted, three-lobed glands of the involucre.*

Below (20.4): **Euphorbia horrida** *from the Karroos of South Africa effectively gives lie to the common belief that euphorbias have unattractive flowers.*

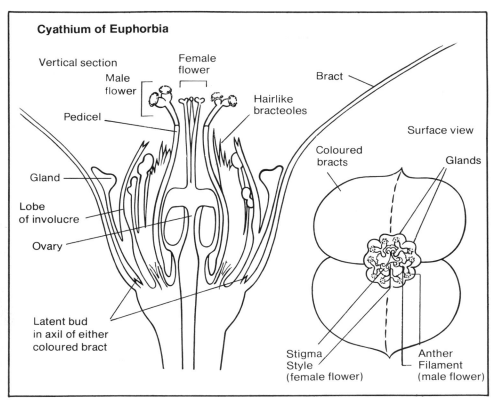

Cyathium of Euphorbia

Vertical section

Male flower

Female flower

Bract

Pedicel

Hairlike bracteoles

Surface view

Gland

Coloured bracts

Glands

Lobe of involucre

Ovary

Latent bud in axil of either coloured bract

Stigma
Style
(female flower)

Anther
Filament
(male flower)

caudiciform, the rest stem-succulent; leaf succulence, oddly enough, is restricted to one or two dwarf species, such as *E. cylindrifolia* and *E. decaryi* (20.7). Otherwise the leaves are flat, entire, more or less deciduous, and often reduced to grass-like blades or tiny scales.

Throughout all this diversity of habit, the cyathia remain constant to the plan described above, although varying greatly in the colour, shape and form of the involucral bracts. Some compare *Euphorbia* unfavourably to the cacti because of its smaller flowers, but collectively these can put up quite a display,

Left (20.5): The "flower" of a spurge is actually a whole inflorescence (cyathium) made up of a single central female flower (floret) reduced to three styles and a three-lobed ovary, surrounded by several male florets, each reduced to a single stamen. The whole is surrounded by bracts and bracteoles forming an involucre.

Below (20.6): Euphorbia milii, *the popular 'Crown of Thorns' from Madagascar, makes a good house plant and is rarely without flowers. A variety with yellow bracts is less popular.*

and last a good deal longer than cactus blooms. Some species are dioecious, and the grower who wants seed will need two plants, one a male and the other a female.

A long history. The latex of *Euphorbia* is carried in special branching latex tubes that circulate throughout the plant. Although they undoubtedly defend it against grazing animals, they have been blamed for the quick spread of disease and death of the plant once bacterial or fungal spores effect an entrance. This latex is responsible for taking *Euphorbia*

history back 2,500 years to the dawn of medicine, when Hippocrates, the father of medicine, is supposed to have known its properties. The popular name "spurge" comes from the same root as *purge* and *expurgate,* alluding to its properties if taken internally. Credit for discovering the first succulent *Euphorbia* on Mount Atlas (probably *E. resinifera,* 20.9) goes to King Juba II of Mauretania in the first century BC. He named it *Euphorbia* after his physician Euphorbus.

Euphorbia. Some euphorbias are un-

armed, but others have arms of the most diverse origins, and it is convenient to group the species according to whether they possess prickles, thorns or spines. So many are favoured by collectors that it is impossible to escape the charge of bias in choosing just a few here.

Beginning with unarmed species, *E. bubalina* is a good beginner's plant: quick-growing, with a thick upright green stem covered with low tubercles and lance-shaped leaves up to 10cm (4in) long in a terminal lax rosette. It eventually forms a small shrub, and is self-compatible,

Above (20.7): A gem for the lover of miniatures, **Euphorbia decaryi** *from Madagascar likes warmth at all times.*

Below (20.8): One of the 'Medusa Head' spurges, **Euphorbia woodii** *from Natal bears long branches from a club-shaped main stem.*

seeding itself if given the chance. Another long-lived, trouble-free species is *E. globosa*, with chains of walnut-shaped joints and long slender inflorescences with curious hand-like outgrowths from the involucres (20.3). In both these the dried inflorescence stalks persist and point to the way that thorns developed.

The 'Medusa Head' euphorbias get their name from the first discovered, *E. caput-medusae* from the Cape district of South Africa (5.6): a stout club-shaped trunk bears a head of thick, tortuous, snake-like branches. *E. woodii (flanaganii)*

is a smaller version very popular in collections (20.8) and it exists in two cristate cultivars, one with the main trunk fasciated and normal branches, the other grown from a cristate side branch, with no trunk.

E. bupleurifolia, obesa (symmetrica) and *suzannae* are much-esteemed dwarf globose dioecious species of which the first two never branch unless damaged, so seed is the only mode of propagation. *E. bupleurifolia* and *suzannae* are covered in tubercles, but *E. obesa* (20.10) is smooth and reddish brown with faint

striping, with eight low ribs, and fancifully compared to a football.

Turning to plants with surface prickles, we have a large group of bramble-like shrubs from Madagascar centred around *E. milii (splendens)*, already referred to. Whereas the large paired prickles could very well be modified stipules, others arise direct from the stem surface, as in the blackberry *(Rubus)*. *E. milii* (20.6) is a deservedly popular house plant, thoroughly at home in the hot dry atmosphere of centrally heated rooms, where it is in flower almost throughout the year. Its one disadvantage is its dropping of withered leaves.

Thorns in the euphorbias (2.13) can be recognized as the old, withered inflorescences in *E. meloformis (valida)*, where the remains of cyathia can still be seen. This is another dioecious species, long beloved of collectors and much like an *Echinocactus* at first glance. In *E. ferox*, *E. pentagona* and *E. mammillaris* the thorns are needle-like and bear only the tiniest, just discernible scales as evidence of their branch origin. Very curious thorn developments occur in *E. columnaris* (20.12), a rarity from northern Somalia, where each is divided into two, and in *E. stellispina*, where each thorn has four or more points arranged like a star.

A great many euphorbias have spines developed in pairs at the leaf base from modified stipules (20.2). Among these are tall trees such as *E. ingens*, a conspic-

Left (20.9): **Euphorbia resinifera** *forms shrubs that owe nothing to the topiarist for their compact, neatly trimmed appearance.*

Below (20.10): **Euphorbia obesa** *has the ultimate in surface reduction to a sphere, with attractive markings suggesting a football. It is dioecious; this is a female plant with seed pods.*

uous and unique feature of areas of South Africa, and medium to large shrubs such as *E. avasmontana* and *E. memoralis*. Where euphorbias can be bedded or grown permanently in the open, some of these arborescent species are essential: their appearance is unique, and there are many from which to choose. *E. candelabrum* var. *erythraea* is a favourite for its four-angled cereoid stems with slightly wavy margins. Specimens in large pots can be used to decorate annexes in office buildings that have plate glass windows facing the sun. But in a small glasshouse they take up too much room, and attention turns naturally to the smaller types, of which there are many. Special praise goes to *E. aeruginosa* for its dramatic patterning of stems, and to *E. tortirama* for the quaintly spiralled ribs. *E. grandicornis* excels in fierce spines, up to 10cm (4in) long, but it is a large grower and rather tender.

Finally, I must mention some curious Madagascan species in which the stipules are elaborated into fringes or crests running down the stems like ribs. Examples are *E. leuconeura* (20.14) and *E. neohumbertii*. Beautiful miniatures with a bonsai look are *E. francoisii* and *E. decaryi* (20.7). The demand exceeds the supply for these choice species, which are more suited to the experienced grower than to the beginner.

Other genera. *Synadenium* is a genus of two East African species of shrubs with cylindrical fleshy branches and large, thin, deciduous leaves. It makes a good house plant, but the sap is poisonous.

Pedilanthus also has cylindrical, unarmed, fleshy stems, usually grey and much branched, with tiny deciduous leaves. It is native to the warmer parts of America and has six species. The popular name is "slipper flower", referring to the shoe-like form of the highly zygomorphic cyathium, a feature also shown in the Old World genus *Monadenium* (20.11). This runs parallel to *Euphorbia* in many ways, and includes caudiciform species mentioned in Chapter 21. Coming from tropical and East Africa it requires considerable warmth and is rarely met with outside specialist collections. Nevertheless, the species include some real treasures, and some with notably showy flower heads (21.16).

Cultivation

The first thing to emphasize to all who fancy euphorbias as pets is to handle them, like lion cubs, with respect. The white latex that spurts from any cut surface is irritant and, in a few species, so poisonous that it is used for drugging fish and poisoning native arrows. Any that gets on the skin should be washed off immediately, and care should be taken

Above (20.11): **Monadenium coccineum** *from Tanzania shows the singular zygomorphic cyathia which distinguish this genus from* **Euphorbia**. *It is easy to grow and propagate.*

Below (20.12): **Euphorbia columnaris** *is one of the rarest spurges, with less than a hundred plants left in habitat in Northern Somalia. Notice the unique Y-shape thorns.*

when cutting a plant that it does not spurt into the eyes or lodge under the finger nails. Having said this, there is no reason to discourage the study of the genus: with normal care no danger is involved. An antidote to euphorbia poison I have seen recommended is the sap squeezed from the leaf of the *Aeonium lindleyi*.

Californians claim that Euphorieae are among the easiest succulents to cultivate, but elsewhere they make more demands on the grower than an equivalent collection of cacti, which is no doubt the reason for the wider popularity of the latter. A higher winter minimum temperature is advisable (minimum 10°C, 50°F), and the tropical and East African rarities will need it still warmer. Many will take plentiful water in summer, but they seem to have little natural resistance to rot infection, which runs through the plant quickly once it enters, so that it is difficult to save even cuttings. Hence the soil should be extra porous and the watering can used with restraint at all times, and not at all during adverse weather.

Propagation is from seed—never too freely available—and by cuttings, which may be slow and reluctant to root, so one needs patience and perseverance.

Euphorbias are no more difficult to graft than cacti. *E. mammillaris* makes a good stock. I find it best to work next to a running tap and not to place the two cut surfaces together until all the white latex has been washed away.

Several attractive hybrids of *E. obesa*, *E. meloformis* and others have been raised.

Above (20.13): **Euphorbia schizacantha,** *a rarity from Somalia and Ethiopia, shows another variation in armature, as well as attractive stem mottling.*

Below (20.14): **Euphorbia leuconeura** *from Madagascar is a relative of the 'Crown of Thorns' (20.6). The curious fringes to the stem angles are modified stipules.*

Caudiciform Succulents

"Plants differ greatly in their large or small size. in beauty and ugliness . . . Some plants verge on two very different classes. mallow. for example (since it is both a herb and a vegetable). and likewise beet. Some plants grow at first in the form of low bushes and afterwards become trees."

The common feature of plants grouped here is extreme differentiation between temporary food-forming organs (green leaves or shoots) formed during periods favourable for growth, and permanent, non-green, heavily protected water and food stores at or below ground level that enable the plant to endure long periods of desiccation. But the definition cannot be made more precise: if one fact emerges from a study of living organisms it is that they cannot be made to fit exactly into man-made categories. In the advance into drier and drier habitats, it was of little consequence whether water was stored in swollen leaves, stems or roots or partly in all three, and the grouping together of plants having a caudex is useful only in illustrating one of the three most successful strategies, and as an index to cultivation. It would be a mistake to insist on greater precision, as, for instance, by creating a class for caudiciform plants in a show schedule.

The caudiciform habit has evolved in varying degrees in many Families of flowering plants, and is not typical of any one. For that reason, no key is attempted here, and the choice of what to include in a succulent collection remains very much a personal affair. As a life form it is especially well adapted to flat, scrubby, semi-desert regions susceptible to periodic fires. Plants are modified in various ways to survive these, and the concentrating of their stored water and food at or below ground level is one such strategy.

Since 1946, when the word was redefined in the modern sense, something of a fashion for these weird and out-of-the-way plants has grown up and the thirst for more and yet more novelties remains unslaked. The result has been a source of consternation to cataloguers and show organizers, who now find it more difficult than ever to decide: "What is a succulent?" A large element of the world's flora in all climatic zones develops enlarged underground organs that can be revealed by planting above ground level in cultivation. Others can be induced to become temporarily caudiciform by giving them the "bonsai treatment": small pots, poor soil, little water and judicious pruning. About the only candidates that seem to be

Right (21.1): **Pachycormus discolor,** *endemic to Baja California, in a lunar landscape that dwarfs the botanist (Reid Moran) exploring it. Columnar* **Lophocereus** *and agaves can be seen in the foreground.*

ineligible are hardy types such as the bryonies *(Bryonia dioica, Tamus communis),* which in my experience are not xerophytic at all, and languish if the storage organ is planted above ground.

Anacardiaceae

This fairly large, mainly tropical Family includes the mango, *Mangifera,* and some hardy ornamental shrubs such as the sumach, *Rhus.* In the drier regions of Lower California, *Pachycormus discolor* gives an unearthly air of starkness and passivity to the landscape (21.1), with its swollen, gnarled trunks and tiny pinnate leaves that drop during the dry season. Small specimens (21.11), when obtainable, are beloved of bonsai collectors.

Apocynaceae

Two South African species of *Pachypodium* (Chapter 18) are best treated here because, like an iceberg, the greater part is hidden from view: a massive turnip-like caudex that penetrates deeply into the rocky substrate and is most difficult to dig out. The tangle of spiny shoots above ground is relatively inconspicuous. *P. succulentum* (21.4) has narrow-tubed flowers; in *P. bispinosum,* the most free-flowering of those I have grown, they are broad bells.

Asclepiadaceae

To the stem succulents described in Chapter 19 one must add at least four genera with caudices. *Ceropegias* are of diverse habit, but all merit attention for

Right (21.2): **Fockea crispa** *showing the massive basal caudex which is reported to reach 3m (10ft) in diameter in habitat. The foliage is attractively crisped at the margins.*

Below (21.3): **Ceropegia conrathii,** *a rare and intractable South African species reported from the Johannesburg area, but also found in Natal by the author in 1971.*

the tubular fly-trap flowers (21.3). In some the slender shoots die back to the caudex so that nothing is seen above ground during the resting period; in others they are more or less evergreen. Hardiest and most popular are *C. woodii* (4.14), with thick, rounded, grey and purple, short-stalked, ivy-like leaves, and its subspecies *debilis,* with linear leaves. These form new tubers along the creeping stems, which make them ideally easy to propagate. Large tubers are also excellent rootstocks on which to graft rare, delicate and cristate Stapelieae.

Brachystelmas are all caudex-forming, and differentiated from *Ceropegia* only by the shorter tube to the flower, which is commonly flat or saucer-shaped with free corolla lobes, not united at the tips. An exception is the most spectacular species, *B. barberae* (21.5), which produces a great ball, 8–12cm (3–5in) across, of sinister purple blooms with a smell that defies description in any polite terms.

Fockea and *Raphionacme* live to a great age and the underground caudex may weigh many kilograms. *F. crispa* (21.2) bears a tangle of twiggy, trailing shoots with small, thick, glossy green leaves attractively curled at the margins. It can be multiplied only by seed, but many of the others can be struck quite successfully from cuttings.

Above (21.4): **Pachypodium succulentum** *has the massive turnip-like caudex hidden below the soil in nature, and the twiggy branches are conspicuous only when the flowers open.*

Below (21.5): **Brachystelma barberae** *is the most showy of its genus, with a ball up to 12½cm (5in) in diameter of many curious lantern-like flowers. The scent is foul.*

21: CAUDICIFORMS

Burseraceae
Some species of *Bursera* (21.24) look almost as remarkable as *Pachycormus* and grow interspersed with them in the same areas. A parallel genus in Africa is *Commiphora*. Most plants of this Family are aromatic and some yield commercially useful resins.

Cochlospermaceae
This small Family of two genera of tropical trees and shrubs finds a place here solely because in youth the stems of some swell out, and seedlings make attractive bonsai succulents, such as *Cochlospermum hibiscoides*. The large thin leaves are usually lobed, and fall during the rest period. Propagation is from seed — if you can get it.

*Below (21.6): **Kedrostis africana**, a member of the cucumber Family, produces a massive caudex half-buried in the soil. This seedling's caudex is about 20cm (8in) across.*

Compositae
Having dealt with the leaf succulents in Chapter 9 and the stem succulents in Chapter 15, we are left with a number of dwarf, shrubby, intensely xerophytic caudiciform *Othonnas*. In some the swollen organ is almost or wholly below soil level; in others there are aerial branches. These are best thought of as connoisseur plants: not the easiest things to keep for long periods and all with rather over-familiar small yellow flower heads (red in *O. cakilefolia*). The most interesting are *O. euphorbioides* (21.12), with cactus-like clusters of often forking thorns, and *O. herrei*, a rarity with coral-like tubercled branches (21.10). *Othonnas* come into leaf about November in Europe and are best put on a light, warm, top

*Bottom (21.7): **Sedum rosea** in a rock crevice on the Isle of Skye, Scotland. Compare this with the robust garden-grown plant of 10.1. It is one of the most northerly succulents.*

shelf and watered from then onwards until after the flowers have finished at the turn of the New Year. For the rest of the year only light sprayings are needed to prevent excessive drying out of the roots.

Convolvulaceae
The bindweed Family, curse of gardens in temperate regions with such persistent weeds as *Convolvulus*, offers compensation with the showy large bell-flowers of the morning glories, *Ipomoea*. Some South African species of *Ipomoea* are perennials with large underground caudices, and fit in well with a succulent collection. *I. bolusiana* and *I. holubii* send up slender annual shoots and have large mauve funnel-shaped blooms from near the base of the stems in summer.

Crassulaceae
Although this Family (Chapter 10) is predominantly leaf-succulent, three of

the largest genera also exhibit trends to water storage in stems and roots. *Sedum rosea* (21.7) has already been referred to on page 116; it is native to the Northern Hemisphere up to the Arctic Circle, and hence the hardiest of succulents, as well as being one of the most variable. In the genus *Crassula,* the Section Tuberosae includes deciduous species such as *C. septas,* 'Cape Snowdrop' (21.9), that perennates with a cyclamen-like corm.

Cucurbitaceae

The Family that provides our gardens with marrows and cucumbers, melons

Left (21.8): The 'Elephant's Foot' Dioscorea (Testudinaria) elephantipes; *a 5-year old seedling showing the tessellated 10cm (4in) caudex and bryony-like foliage.*

Below (21.9): Crassula septas *in semi-shaded woodland on the slopes of Table Mountain. The plant dies down annually to a subterrranean cyclamen-like caudex.*

and pumpkins, is prolific in curiosities, and in the semi-desert regions of both Central America and southern Africa extraordinary caudiciform types occur. Jacobsen describes 19 genera, and others could be added. *Xerosicyos* we have already encountered as a leaf succulent (page 112). *Kedrostis* (21.6) is typical of the majority and one of the commonest: *K. nana* is native to the Cape Peninsula and is hence used to a fairly moist climate as in Europe. Succulent cucurbits are apt to produce yards and yards of climbing stems which occupy much space and need tidying up as the leaves drop. The flowers are little compensation, being small and unisexual, but the fruits are more showy, and it is worth the effort of hand pollinating. Some species are dioecious. In *Neoalsomitra* the caudex has long green prickles, somewhat like a chestnut burr, and the giant of the group is *Dendrosicyos*, endemic to Socotra, which is reported to grow 6m (20ft) tall in habitat.

Dioscoreaceae

The 'Elephant's Foot' *(Dioscorea* or *Testudinaria elephantipes)* is so oddly fascinating that I am tempted to use that overworn cliche "a must for every collection". Certainly, if only one caudiciform plant is to be allowed into a collection, this is it. The large, winged seed germinates to produce a 1cm (⅖in) spherical caudex the first year, with a single heart-shaped green leaf. Slender annual climbing shoots follow, like the black bryony, *Tamus,* its next-of-kin. As the sphere enlarges it develops corky polygonal warts (21.8) and in nature can reach a great age and size—over 1m (39in) across. Plants are dioecious and there are three other only slightly less marvellous species with the caudex more or less above ground. All the remaining species, of which there are about 600, have the storage organ below soil level and include the edible yams. It should be noted that the overground habit, as described above, has evolved independently in South Africa *(D. elephantipes, D. glauca* and *D. sylvatica)* and in Mexico *(D. macrostachya).*

The 'Elephant's Foot' is much less difficult to keep than was once thought, and there is no need to rob the habitat by importing plants when, under optimum conditions, superb football-sized show specimens can be reared from seed in 10–15 years. The aerial branches delight in full sun, but the caudex is best in shade beneath the staging, and takes continual watering during the summer or while carrying leaves; even in the rest period it should not be baked too dry.

Right (21.10): The rare **Othonna herrei**, *whose stems are covered in knob-like woody tubercles formed from leaf bases, is superficially like* **Cotyledon wallichiana**. *In cultivation,* **Othonnas** *are dormant during summer and need water only when leaves appear in late autumn.*

Above: (21.11): A seedling **Pachycormus discolor** *from the habitat seen on 21.1. The caudex grows fully above ground. Small plants are much in demand by lovers of bonsai. This plant is about 20cm (8in) high.*

Right (21.12): **Othonna euphorbioides,** *the most cactus-like of all succulent Compositae, bears branched spines derived from woody inflorescences. This plant, in a 10cm (4in) pot, has grown much taller than in nature.*

Euphorbiaceae

So diverse in life forms are the succulent spurges (Chapter 20) that it is not surprising to find the advantages of caudex formation exploited in several genera. In *Euphorbia* (21.25) there is *E. tuberosa* at the Cape, *E. trichadenia* from Angola to Rhodesia and *E. baga* in tropical West Africa, to quote but three. In *Monadenium* there is the miniature *M. montanum* and the even more attractive *M. majus* (21.16), a rare beauty with its modestly nodding cyanthia. *Jatropha* is a distantly related genus of 150 or more tropical shrubs, of which about a quarter qualify as caudiciforms (21.14). Botanically the genus is interesting for its simple unisexual flowers with a calyx and, in male flowers, a corolla too — very different from the advanced cyathia of the Euphorbieae (20.5). The above are all for experienced growers hardened to disappointments. *Jatropha podagrica* (21.15) grows rapidly from seed and is one of the easiest: it has large, stalked, lobed leaves, branching glandular stipules and flat heads of showy red flowers.

Fouquieriaceae

This tiny Family of one genus and eight species is endemic to Mexico. The plants are extremely xerophytic hard-wooded shrubs with a tendency to enlargement at the base that reaches a climax in the unique 'Cirio' or 'Boojum' of Baja California, *F. (Idria) columnaris* (21.13). The tall, mostly unbranched trunk looks like a huge inverted turnip, and bears wiry side branches with tiny short-lived leaves that leave a spine when they detach from the woody stalk. *F. columnaris* has proved long-lived and long-suffering in collections, although it is still far from common; it is a "show stopper" at any age or size. It likes ample space for the large roots (bedding out is ideal); growth is very slow in small pots. A winter minimum of 7°C (45°F) is recommended, but I have had plants down to freezing point for short

Near right (21.13): Flowers of **Fouquieria** (**Idria**) **columnaris**, *the cirio or boojum of Baja California. The darker seed pods of the previous year have shed their seeds.*

Far right (21.14): Some caudiciform Jatrophas: J. **berlandieri** (right), J. **texensis** (centre), and an unidentified species (left).

Bottom right (21.15): **Jatropha podagrica**, *a common shrub of tropical gardens, seen at its best in cultivation as small seedlings.*

Below (21.16): A treasure for the lover of miniatures: the scarce **Monadenium majus**, *a species producing an underground caudex.*

periods without loss. *F. fasciculata* and *F. purpusii* are equally commendable.

Geraniaceae

Growers of zonal and regal pelargoniums —the "geraniums" of the layman—may have little idea of the diversity of this large and versatile genus of over 250 species in the drier parts of South Africa. About the only thing all species have in common is an apparent indifference to neglect and hardships that would kill off anything but a superplant. *P. tetragonum* is truly stem-succulent, with three- or four-angled, jointed grey-green stems; *P. echinatum* has warty tubercles, and *P. gibbosum* a gouty swelling at each node. One or two come perilously near to being leaf succulents. But the majority have a caudex at or below ground level, bearing rosettes of deciduous leaves that are often much-lobed, pinnate or carrot-like (21.18). Flowers are far less showy than in the popular florists' cultivars, but not to be disregarded completely (4.5).

Sarcocaulon is a related genus of about a dozen species from South West Africa with thorny stems so rich in resin that long after they die the desert is littered with pipe-like fragments of the skeleton. The name 'Bushman's Torch' comes from the local custom of setting light to the stems, which burn like a torch.

All the succulent Geraniaceae come into leaf in late autumn, and are best accommodated on a high, unshaded shelf near the glass; give water only as long as they show green leaves.

Moraceae

Mulberries and figs are familiar household representatives of this Family which is related by its minute unisexual flowers to the hemp, hop and stinging nettle Families. A number of tropical figs, *Ficus,* have entered semi-desert areas and evolved grotesquely swollen, tapered trunks. Small specimens are occasionally to be found in succulent collections, valued for their bonsai appearance. *Dorstenia,* another widespread genus (170 species), has species in tropical and East Africa with a very fleshy caudex at or below ground level and thick branches covered in leaf scars. The bizarre flat or saucer-shaped inflorescences (4.19) that simulate a single flower have already been referred to on page 60. *D. foetida* (21.17) is the species most often seen in collections, although far from common, and seeds itself if given the chance. On

Right (21.17): **Dorstenia foetida** *from Southern Arabia, commonest and least demanding species of its genus in cultivation. The tentacled flower heads later expel the seeds explosively.*

Below (21.18): **Pelargonium carnosum** *from South West Africa. In habit the succulent pelargoniums display a wide variety of life forms ranging from fleshy stems to above- or below-ground caudices.*

21: CAUDICIFORMS

Socotra there is the unique endemic *D. gigas,* up to 1.2m (4ft) tall. *Dorstenias* need much warmth and can hardly be recommended to beginners.

Passifloraceae

Adenia could be thought of as a poor relative of the passion flowers, *Passiflora,* having none of the floral splendours of that genus. Of 92 species, 57 are African and a few of these are sufficiently oddly shaped to catch the eye of the succulent addict in search of novelty. Beginning with species where the trunk is extra thick and tapering *(A. glauca, A. fruticosa)* we find a massive more or less cylindrical caudex in *A. digitata,* spines on the aerial branches in *A. spinosa* and prickly tubercles in *A. aculeata* (21.19) and *A. globosa.* The caudex is attractively marked in pale and dark green in many, and in *A. globosa* is covered in warty outgrowths.

Pedaliaceae

Two small genera, *Pterodiscus* (21.20) with about ten species and *Sesamothamnus* with about five from southern and tropical Africa, need mention here. They are rare in cultivation but worth having for the large and sometimes scented flowers. In *Sesamothamnus* the branches are thick and thorny and the caudex is stated to exceed 2m (6½ft) in diameter.

Portulacaceae

Chapter 12 covers the leaf-succulent members of this Family and Chapter 15 those with fleshy stems. There are also a few species of *Portulaca* and *Talinum* (21.21) with swollen underground storage organs and more or less deciduous aerial parts. *Talinum caffrum* is noteworthy for its pleasant yellow flowers like small primroses, and grows rapidly from seed. But the greatest treasure, and quite unique among succulents, is *Anacampseros alstonii* (21.22), with a flat cake-like caudex up to 10cm (4in) or more in diameter covered with a white crown made up of hundreds of fine wiry branches, each packed with papery overlapping stipules concealing the minute green leaves below. By comparison with the branches that bear them, the pearly white flowers are gigantic — 2.5 to 3cm (1 to 1⅙in) across — and are freely borne in summer. Grown from seed, a pea-sized tuber is produced the first year.

Top right (21.19): **Adenia aculeata** *from Somalia is exceptional in having the caudex covered with prickles - an added attraction for the lover of cactus-like plants. The flowers are minute and unisexual.*

Right (21.20): **Pterodiscus speciosus** *from South and South West Africa forms a conical caudex up to 50cm (20in) tall. Both foliage and flowers are attractive, but plants rarely survive for long away from the habitat.*

Vitidaceae

The stem-succulent Vitidaceae are dealt with in Chapter 15; here belong a few species with massive caudices that were formerly included in the same genus *Cissus* but are now segregated as *Cyphostemma*. The thick, soft, greenish trunks are covered in peeling bark and bear large, fleshy, entire or three-lobed leaves that drop in the dormant season: one could equally class it with stem succulents, being intermediate in form. *C. cramerana* grows so large in South West Africa that I have climbed up among the branches and found a natural "armchair" near the top. *Cyphostemmas* grow rapidly from seed and adapt well to a summer growing season when they can take plenty of water, so they are among the easiest of caudiciform plants to manage. The tiny flowers are borne in broad, flat-topped inflorescences and are followed by small purple grapes (2.21).

Left (21.21): **Talinum paniculatum** *from Mexico and the Caribbean has small pinkish red flowers from a branching caudex.* **Talinum** *shows parallel variation in form to* **Portulaca,** *but few species are worthy of cultivation.*

Below (21.22): **Anacampseros alstonii,** *seen here filling a 7cm (2¾in) pot, is immediately recognizable, the flattened, potato-like caudex being covered in slender shoots.*

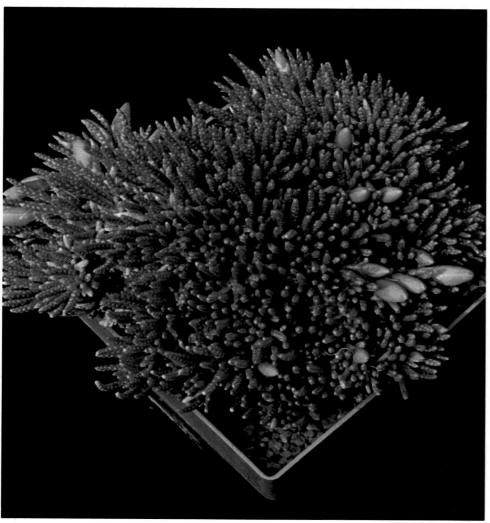

Cultivation

A feature common to all caudiciform plants is the need for alternating growing and resting seasons. The cycle is annual in cultivation, although in habitat the dormant periods may last longer and are determined by the erratic intervals between rains. During the rest period the temporary photosynthesizing organs die away or are at least reduced, so no watering is needed except the slightest damping to keep the roots from drying back too drastically. One species differs from another in the timing of the dormant season, and rather than go by the calendar it is better to gauge watering by the appearance of new growth or the dieback of old. Some, such as *Dioscorea,* seem to go their own way and may even resume growth on an old stem before it has died back completely.

As regards hardiness, caudiciform plants run the complete range from tropical and tender to the hardiest of all succulents, the circumpolar *Sedum rosea.* A beginner with an average cactus collection anxious to join the cult would be recommended to sample the following, which should thrive if the winter minimum temperature is set at 5°C (40°F): *Kedrostis, Cyphostemma, Pelargonium, Nolina, Pachypodium, Dioscorea, Fouquieria* and dwarf *Cotyledons.*

Right (21.23): A section of one glasshouse at Heidelberg University devoted to caudiciforms — perhaps the largest collection of them in Europe.

Below right (21.24): Bursera odorata, *like* Pachycormus, *(21.1, 11) is a grotesquely obese shrub in age, but small specimens, which are not easy to find, delight the lover of bonsai plants.*

Below (21.25): The caudex in Euphorbia silenifolia *is wholly below ground, although in cultivation it is usually planted at a higher level as a safeguard against waterlogging.*

A Final Thought

Although very few succulents qualify as economically useful plants, their popularity as ornamentals has never been greater. They are well suited to flourish in the typical small amateur glasshouse with its sharp temperature fluctuations and largely unobstructed light, and equally to sunny windowsills indoors where the dry air from central heating is inimical to mesophytes. In an age that seems to rejoice in reaction and the overthrow of conventions, the anarchistic look of a cactus is bound to appeal. Looking at it, one can imagine that its stark geometry, unfussy outlines and prime colour masses somehow harmonize with current fashion in decor, architecture and—dare I say—music and the other arts. Just why some people are "turned on" by succulents and others just as emphatically "turned off" is a subject for another book. But there is no doubt that there are different kinds of addiction: the urge to collect, the love of flowers, the love of the unusual, the rare, the costly, the near extinct or simply of what other people despise and reject—all come into it. And just as there are delights in exploring uncharted fields, so too there are dangers when the trees become too thick for the wood to be seen. Just as there are motorists who spend most of their lives tinkering with the engine, and hi-fi experts who somehow never get round to listening to a symphony, so there are collectors who mistake the means for the end and collect names rather than plants. This is hardly surprising when nurseries compete to offer the longest list, journals pour out descriptions of allegedly new species, and books champion X's classification while decrying those of Y and Z.

In this book I have purposely avoided long lists of species or emphasis on the often fine distinctions between them, preferring rather to stress the higher categories—genera, Tribes, subfamilies and Families—because the bird sees more than the worm, and usually lives longer. The aim has been all along to view succulents (perhaps 3-4 percent of all flowering plants) against the general background of the world flora and of their systematic grouping—a series of parallel lines of evolution from the most diverse and disparate of ancestors. By giving proportional treatment to each of the Families, I have endeavoured to give a balanced outlook, and to avoid the distortions that have abounded since H. Allnutt published his book *"The Cactus and other tropical Succulents"* in 1877.

A well-stocked cactophile's glasshouse is a phenomenon of our time: an Aladdin's cave crammed with rarities from all over the world. Here, for the first time, plants meet up with each other in serried ranks of little pots—a microcosm of vegetable wonders testifying to man's urge to explore the uttermost corners of the earth and to compress its treasures into a few square metres of his own back garden. If plants could talk, what tales of hardship and endurance some could relate, as could the collectors from days when travel in foreign parts was a lot less comfortable and safe than it is today! Viewed in this light, ownership of a rarity becomes a privilege rather than a right bought for cash. One commonly hears grumbles that this species won't grow, another doesn't flower, and a third fails to set seed. A visit to the habitat would send the grousers back full of wonderment that so many species do, indeed, acclimatize so well. That is the real eye-opener, and few other plants can match their adaptability.

As for the pursuit of the elusive True Species—a myth, anyway—it is best left in the hands of botanists equipped with a library, herbarium, laboratory and facilities for field studies. But this does not mean that the enthusiastic amateur is denied creative outlet if he wants to put his collection to a useful purpose. There are many neglected fields awaiting exploration. Which plants set fertile seed with their own pollen, and which do not? There is still no central bank of information. If wild collected seed is available, he could raise all the seedlings to maturity and investigate variability within the species. Better still, if space allows two or more populations to be raised, much could be learned from studying the degrees of overlap. The propagation of rare and endangered species is a top priority for the conservation-minded: unusual techniques, such as the taking of root cuttings or seedling grafting, are but two avenues for exploration. As Chapter 5 has shown, there is a wide-open field for the introduction of new hybrids, provided you have the strength of will to throw away everything that is not a real improvement.

A succulent collection can be anything from a mixed dozen on a windowsill to a botanical garden in miniature, drawing sightseers and specialists from afar. It can be dabbled in as an amusement for idle moments, or wallowed in so that it takes over your life: a plaything, or a tool for research, whichever you choose. And whether you wallow or play, there is something uniquely satisfying in the contemplation of nature: pass through one door and there are always more waiting to be opened.

Below: Most succulents, like this cactus, seed out the shade of rocks or other plants in the hot, dry regions where they grow.

References

References relating to Chapters 1–8 are arranged in the order in which they are cited in the text. Those for Chapters 9–21 begin with monographs and the works of broadest scope, and end with specialist works on single genera. The General Reading List is arranged alphabetically by author.

Chapter 1
1. BAUHIN, J. and CHERLER – *Historia Plantarum Generalis . . . Prodromus* Yverdon 1619.
2. BRADLEY, R. – *The History of Succulent Plants* London 1716–27.
3. BROWN, B. N. E. in *The Gardeners' Chronicle* Feb. 12, 1927: 116 and Apr. 9, 1927: 251.
4. HEYNE, B. in *Transactions of the Linnean Society 1814: 213–15.*
5. *JAMES, W. O. in Endeavour XVII: 90–95, 1958.*
6. TATE, J. L. *Cactus Cook Book* Cactus & Succulent Society of America, California: 1971.

Chapter 2
1. SPALDING, E. S. in *Bulletin of the Torrey Botanical Club* 32: 57–68, 1905.

Chapter 3
1. RUNDEL, P. W. in *Cactus & Succulent Journal of America* 48: 270, 1976.
2. SAUER, N. and I. in *Aloe* 14: 3–8, 1976.
3. CANNON, W. A. *The Root Habits of Desert Plants* Carnegie Institute of Washington Publication No. 131, 1911.
4. GLOVER, P. E. in *East African Agricultural Journal,* 16: 98–113, 1950.
5. BOWKER, L. H. in *Cactus and Succulent Journal of Great Britain* 37: 6–8, 1975.

Chapter 4
1. PERCIVAL, M. *Floral Biology* Pergamon 1965.
2. VOGEL, S. *Blütenbiologische typen als elemente der Sippengliederung* Botanischen Studien I. 1954.
3. MULLER, H. *The Fertilisation of Flowers* Macmillan, London 1883.
4. HAWORTH, A. H. *Observations on the Genus Mesembryanthemum* Chelsea 1794–95.
5. PROCTOR, M. and YEO, P. *The Pollination of Flowers* New Naturalist. Collins, London 1973.
6. RIDLEY, H. N. *The Dispersal of Plants throughout the World* Reeve, Ashford 1930.

Chapter 5
1. MENDEL, G. *Experiments in Plant Hybridisation* in *Journal of the Royal Horticultural Society* 26: 1–32, 1901.
2. BOOM, B. K. and ZEILINGA, A. E. in *Succulenta* 43: 122–24, 1964.
3. BENSON, L. *The Cacti of Arizona* (Edition 3) University of Arizona Press Tucson, Arizona 1969.

Chapter 6
1. PRUE, D. *Photoperiodism in Plants* McGraw-Hill 1975.
2. EDINGER, P. (Ed.) *Succulents and Cactus* Sunset Books, Menlo Park, California 1970.
3. DODSON, J. W. in *Cactus & Succulent Journal of America* 31: 3–5, 1959.
4. ATKINS, P. S. in *The Gardeners' Chronicle* June 29, 1966.

Chapter 7
1. JACQUIN, N. J. *Hortus Schoenbrunnensis* 4: 38, t. 475, 1804.
2. HERRE, H. in *Sukkulentenkunde 5:* 51–55, 1954.
3. *Register of Specialist Collectors of Succulent and Allied Plants in the United Kingdom* International Organisation for Succulent Plant Research, Kew 1975.
4. MELVILLE, R. *Red Data Book Vol. 5* International Union for the Conservation of Nature and Natural Resources, Morges 1970.

Chapter 8
1. STEARN, W. T. *Botanical Latin* Nelson, Edinburgh 1966.

2. STAFLEU, F. A. (Ed.) *International Code of Botanical Nomenclature* Utrecht 1978.

3. JEFFREY, C. *Biological Nomenclature* E. Arnold 1973.

4. GILMOUR, J. S. L. (Ed.) *International Code of Nomenclature of Cultivated Plants* Utrecht 1969.

5. ROWLEY, G. D. in *National Cactus and Succulent Journal 30: 17, 1975.*

Chapter 10

BERGER, A. *Crassulaceae* in ENGLER, A. and PRANTL, K. *Die Natürliche Pflanzenfamilien* (Edition 2) 18a, 1930.

HIGGINS, V. *Crassulas in Cultivation* Blandford, London 1964.

WALTHER, E. *Echeveria* California Academy of Sciences, San Francisco 1972.

CARRUTHERS, L. and GINNS, R. *Echeverias* Bartholomew, Edinburgh 1973.

HAMET, R. and MARNIER-LAPOSTOLLE, J. *Le Genre Kalanchoe* in *Archives du Muséum National d'Histoire Naturelle, Paris* 8: 1–110, 1964.

PRAEGER, R. L. *An Account of the Genus Sedum as Found in Cultivation* in *Journal of the Royal Horticultural Society* 46: 1–314, 1921.

EVANS, R. L. *A Gardeners' Guide to the Sedums* Alpine Garden Society, London 1971.

HART, J. A. and WRIGLEY, T. C. *Sedums* Succulent Plant Trust 1971.

PRAEGER, R. L. *An Account of the Sempervivum Group* Royal Horticultural Society, London 1932.

SMITH, A. C. *The Genus Sempervivum and Jovibarba* A. C. Smith, Kent 1975.

MITCHELL, P. J. *The Sempervivum and Jovibarba Handbook* Sempervivum Society, Burgess Hill 1973.

Chapter 11

HERRE, H. *The Genera of the Mesembryanthemaceae* Nasionale Boekhandel Ltd. Cape Town 1971.

SCHWANTES, G. *Flowering Stones and Midday Flowers* Ernest Benn Ltd. London 1957.

SCHWANTES, G. *The Cultivation of the Mesembryanthemaceae* The Garden Book Club, London 1954.

NEL, G. C. *Lithops* Stellenbosch University, Stellenbosch 1946.

COLE, D. T. *Lithops: a Checklist and Index* in *Excelsa* 3: 37–71, 1973.

NEL, G. C. *The Gibbaeum Handbook* Blandford Press, London 1953.

Chapter 12

ELLIOT, R. *The Genus Lewisia* Alpine Garden Society, 1966.

Chapter 13

BERGER, A. *Aloineae* in ENGLER, A. *Das Pflanzenreich 33, 1908.*

REYNOLDS, G. W. *The Aloes of South Africa* A. A. Balkema, Johannesburg 1950.

REYNOLDS, G. W. *The Aloes of Tropical Africa & Madagascar* Aloes Book Fund, Mbabane 1966.

NOBLE, W. C. *Aloes for Greenhouse and Indoor Cultivation* National Cactus and Succulent Society, Oxford 1976.

BAYER, M. B. *Haworthia Handbook* National Botanic Gardens of South Africa, Cape Town 1976.

PILBEAM, J. W. *The First Fifty Haworthias* Succulent Plant Institute, Morden 1970.

PILBEAM, J. W. *The Second Fifty Haworthias* Succulent Plant Trust, Essex 1976.

Chapter 14

BERGER, A. *Die Agaven* Jena 1915.

GENTRY, H. S. *The Agave Family in Sonora* United States Department of Agriculture, Washington 1972.

BREITUNG, A. J. *The Agaves* [of S.W. USA only] Abbey Garden Press, California 1968.

Chapter 16

BRITTON, N. L. and ROSE, J. N. *The Cactaceae* (Volumes 1–4) Carnegie Institute, Washington 1919–23.

BACKEBERG, C. *Die Cactaceae* (Volumes 1–6) Jena 1958–62.

BACKEBERG, C. *Cactus Lexicon* Translated by Lois Glass Blandford Press, Poole 1978.

HUNT, D. R. *Cactaceae* in HUTCHINSON, J. *The Genera of Flowering Plants* 2: 427–67, 1967.

BUXBAUM, F. *Morphology of Cacti* (Parts 1–3) Abbey Garden Press, California 1950–55.

BORG J. *Cacti* (Edition 2) Blandford, London 1951.

KRAINZ, H. *Die Kakteen* Stuttgart 1956 et seq.

BUXBAUM, F. *Cactus Culture based on Biology* Blandford, London 1958.

MARTIN, M. J., CHAPMAN, P. R. and AUGER, H. A. *Cacti and Their Cultivation* Faber & Faber, London 1971.

GINNS, R. *Gymnocalyciums* Succulent Plant Trust 1967.

PUTNAM, E. W. *A Synonymy of the Genus Gymnocalycium* Succulent Plant Institute 1969.

RAUSCH, W. *Lobivia* (Volumes 1–3) Vienna 1975–77.

CRAIG, R. T. *Mammillaria Handbook* Abbey Garden Press, California 1945.

MADDAMS, W. F. *Interesting Newer Mammillarias* Mammillaria Society 1973.

MACE, T. *Notocactus* National Cactus and Succulent Society 1975.

LEIGHTON-BOYCE, G. G. and ILIFF, J. *The Subgenus Tephrocactus* [of the Genus Opuntia] Succulent Plant Trust, Morden 1973.

BRINKMANN, K. H. *Sulcorebutia* [c.f. Rebutia] Steinhart KG 7820, Titisee 1976.

Chapter 17

RAUH, W. *The Didiereaceae* in *Ashingtonia* 2: 1–5, 9, 12, 1975.

Chapter 18

RAUH, W. *The Genus Pachypodium* in *Cactus & Succulent Journal of America* 44: 7–31, 1972.

Chapter 19

WHITE, A. and SLOANE, B. L. *The Stapelieae* (Edition 2, Volumes 1–3) Pasadena 1937.

LUCKHOFF, C. A. *The Stapelieae of Southern Africa* A. A. Balkema, Cape Town 1952.

LAMB, E. *Stapeliads in Cultivation* Blandford, London 1957.

HUBER, H. *Revision der Gattung Ceropegia* in *Memorias da Sociedade Broteriana* 12: 1–203, Coimbra 1957.

Chapter 20

WHITE, A., DYER, R. A. and SLOANE, B. L. *The Succulent Euphorbieae of Southern Africa* (Volumes 1–2) Pasadena 1941.

BREWERTON, D. V. *The Succulent Euphorbias* National Cactus & Succulent Society 1975.

BALLY, P. R. O. *The Genus Monadenium* Benteli, Berne 1961.

DRESSLER, R. L. *The Genus Pedilanthus, Contributions from the Gray Herbarium* 182, Cambridge, Massachusetts 1957.

General Reading List

BAILEY, L. H. and E. Z. *Hortus Third* Macmillan, New York and London 1976.

CHIDAMIAN, CLAUDE *Book of Cacti and Other Succulents* Doubleday, New York 1958.

GLASS, C. and FOSTER, R. *Cacti and Succulents for the Amateur* Blandford Press, Poole 1977; Van Nostrand Reinhold, New York 1977.

GRAF, A. B. *Exotica III* Scribner, New York 1975.

HAAGE, W. *Cacti and Succulents* Vista Books, London 1963; Dutton, New York 1963.

HIGGINS, V. *Succulents in Cultivation* St. Martins, New York 1960.

IVIMEY-COOK, R. B. *Succulents—A glossary of terms and definitions* National Cactus & Succulent Society, Oxford 1974.

JACOBSEN, H. *Handbook of Succulent Plants* (Volumes 1–3) Blandford, London 1960; Humanities, New York 1973.

JACOBSEN, H. *Lexicon of Succulent Plants* Blandford Press, Poole 1975; Humanities, New York 1975.

LAMB, E. and B. *Illustrated Reference on Cacti and Other Succulents* (Volumes 1–4) Blandford, London 1955–66; International Publications Service, New York 1955–69.

MARTIN, M. J. and CHAPMAN, P. R. *Succulents and Their Cultivation* Faber & Faber, London 1977.

RAUH, W. *Die grossartige welt der Sukkulenten* Hamburg 1967.

RAWE, R. *Succulents in the Veld* Howard Timmins, Cape Town 1968.

ROWLEY, G. D. and NEWTON, L. E. *Repertorium Plantarum Succulentarum* An annual index of all new names of succulent plants. Published for the International Organisation for Succulent Plant Research, 1960 et seq.

SHREVE, W. F. and WIGGINS, I. L. *Vegetation and Flora of the Sonoran Desert* (Volumes 1–2) Stanford University Press 1964.

STEARN, W. T. *Botanical Latin* Nelson, Edinburgh 1966; Lubrecht & Cramer 1966.

TATE, J. L. *Cactus Cook Book—Succulent Cookery International* Cactus & Succulent Society of America, California 1971.

WILLIS, J. C. *A Dictionary of the Flowering Plants and Ferns* (Edition 8 edited by H. K. AIRY-SHAW) Cambridge University Press, London and New York 1973.

Glossary

Words in *italics* refer to separate entries within the glossary.

Adj.=Adjective
cf.=compare
Pl.=Plural
V=Verb

Acicular Needlelike.
Actinomorphy Radial symmetry; said of a flower that can be divided into equal halves across many diameters. Adj. actinomorphic. (cf. *zygomorphy*).
Adventitious Said of roots that arise anywhere other than from a pre-existing root.
Allele One of two or more alternative states of a *gene*, and occupying the same site on a *chromosome*.
Anatomy The study of the microscopic structure of plants.
Androecium The male organs of the flower; collectively the *stamens*.
Anemophily Transfer of *pollen* by the agency of wind. Adj. anemophilous. (cf. *entomophily, ornithophily*).
Aneuploid Having a chromosome number that is not a regular multiple of the basic *(haploid)* number.
Annulus A ringlike outgrowth of the *corolla* in Stapelieae. Adj. annular.
Anthecology Floral biology; the functioning of flowers in relation to their pollinators.
Anther The top part of a *stamen* that contains the *pollen*.
Anthocyanin A widespread pigment in plants responsible for purplish-red as well as some blue shades.
Apetalous Lacking *petals*.
Arborescent Becoming tree-like.
Areole The spine cushion of a cactus; the organ from which arise wool, spines, leaf (when present), lateral branches and flowers.
Aril A fleshy or bony outgrowth of a *seed*. Adj. arillate.
Armature Plant defences: *prickles, thorns, spines*, etc.
Axil The upper angle between a stem and a leaf (or *tubercle*) arising from the stem. Adj. axillary.

Berry A fleshy *fruit* containing two or more *seeds*.
Betacyanin A nitrogenous pigment exclusive to members of the Caryophyllales and replacing *anthocyanin* in this Order.
Binomial The scientific name of a *species*, comprising a generic name followed by a specific *epithet*.
Biochemistry The study of the chemical substances within an organism; the chemistry of life.
Bisexual Said of a flower that includes both functional *stamens* and *carpels*. (cf. *unisexual*).
Bract A modified leaf at the base of a *pedicel* or *peduncle*.
Bracteole A small *bract* subtending a single *pedicel*, when the *bract* itself subtends a *peduncle*.
Bulb A usually underground storage organ comprising an enlarged bud of fleshy, sheathing leaves or leaf bases. Adj. bulbous.
Bulbil A small *bulb* borne above ground and functioning as a means of vegetative reproduction.

C₃, C₄ Symbols for variant pathways in the *respiration* cycle of certain plants, involving the intermediate formation of 3- and 4-carbon carboxylic acids respectively. (cf. *CAM.*).
Cactiform; Cactoid Having the general habit of globular cacti. (cf. *cereiform, cereoid*).
Cactophile A lover of cacti. Loosely applied to lovers of all succulents. (cf. *cactophobe*).
Cactophobe A hater of cacti. (cf. *cactophile*).
Cactus A member of the Cactaceae, the cactus Family. Pl. cacti; rarely cactuses.
Caespitose; Cespitose Forming tufted growth.
Callus The protective corky tissue covering a cut or bruised surface; to form such a layer.
Calyx The outermost envelope of the flower, made up of usually greenish, protective *sepals*.
CAM Symbol for Crassulacean Acid Metabolism, the unusual *respiration* cycle of most succulents. (cf. *C₃, C₄*).
Capitulum A flower head in which many small *sessile* flowers arise at the same level on a flattened axis surrounded by an *involucre* of *bracts*, the whole simulating a single large flower.
Capsule A dry *fruit* composed of two or more united *carpels*.
Carpel A modified leaf containing the *ovules* and with a *stigma* at the tip.
Caudex An enlarged storage organ at soil level, composed of a swollen stem base, or root, or both. Adj. caudiciform.
Caudiciform Having a *caudex*

and associated division of labour into a permanent water and food store and usually short-lived aerial *photosynthetic* organs; a plant of this nature.
Cell The basic unit or "brick" from which plant life is built. Each cell comprises a cell wall, the *cytoplasm*, the *nucleus* and various cell inclusions such as *chloroplasts*.
Cephalium A special crown of wool or bristles from which the flowers are borne in certain cacti.
Cereiform, Cereoid Having the general habit of columnar cacti. (cf. *cactiform, cactoid*).
Chlorophyll The green pigment of plants, located in *chloroplasts*.
Chloroplast Lens-shaped body located in the *cytoplasm* of the green tissue of plants and containing the *chlorophyll*.
Chromosome An elongated structure within the *cell nucleus* which carries the *genes* in linear sequence.
Ciliate Fringed with hairs like eyelashes.
Cladode See *phylloclad*.
Claw The tapered lower part of a *petal* (or *sepal*). (cf. *limb*).
Cleistogamy Ability of a flower to set viable *seed* without opening. Adj. cleistogamous.
Clone A group of genetically identical plants, such as those derived by vegetative propagation from one individual.
Connate Organically united with one another (cf. *Free*).
Convergence The phenomenon whereby unrelated organisms come to look alike in response to the same selection processes.
Cordate Heart-shaped.
Corolla The inner of the two *perianth* whorls, made up of usually coloured, attractive *petals*.
Corona An extra whorl of appendages in a flower, similar to a crown.
Corymb A flat-topped *inflorescence* in which the *pedicels* arise at different levels up the axis. Adj. corymbose. (cf. *umbel*).
Cotyledon The first leaf or leaf of a pair produced by a seedling.
Crest, Cristate A *fasciated* fanlike development of a stem. Adj. crested, cristate.
Crossing Cross-pollination; transfer of *pollen* between two genetically different individuals. (cf. *selfing*).
Cultivar a *taxonomic* group of cultivated plants

distinguishable by any characters that are stable and recognizable; a "cultivated variety".
Cuticle Varnish-like impervious coating of an *epidermis*. Adj. cuticular.
Cyathium The unique *inflorescence* of Euphorbieae in which a single female flower is surrounded by several males, the whole being enveloped in an *involucre* and simulating a single flower.
Cyme One of two basic types of *inflorescence* in which the oldest flower is at the centre and terminates the axis, subsequent growth being from branching beneath it. Adj. cymose. (cf. *raceme*).
Cytology The study of *cells*, in particular the *chromosomes* within them.
Cytoplasm The *cell* sap.

Decussate Crossed pairs, each pair of organs being at right angles to its predecessor up an axis.
Dehiscence The way in which a *fruit* or *anther* splits open at maturity. Adj. dehiscent. V. dehisce.
Desert A region averaging less than 25cm (10in) annual rainfall.
Dichasium A type of *cymose inflorescence* in which two side branches grow out from beneath the terminal flower. Adj. dichasial. (cf. *monochasium*).
Dicotyledon A plant having two *cotyledons*; one of two major subdivisions of flowering plants. (cf. *monocotyledon*).
Dimorphism Existence in two states. Adj. dimorphic.
Dioecious Having separate male and female flowers on different plants. (cf. *monoecious*).
Diploid Containing a double set of *chromosomes*, one from either parent, as in the non-reproductive *cells* of the plant body. (cf. *haploid, polyploid*).
Disc (1) The area surrounding the *ovary* in certain flowers when adapted for *nectar* secretion. (2) The flattened axis supporting the flowers in a *capitulum*. (cf. *ray*).
Discontinuous See *disjunct*.
Disjunct Occupying two or more separate areas; discontinuous in distribution.
Distichous In two opposite series.
Dominant Said of a *gene* which obscures the action of its *allele* when both occur in a hybrid. (cf. *recessive*).

Ecology The study of organisms in relation to their environment.

Endemism Occurence in a smaller than average area. Adj. endemic. (cf. *widespread*).

Entomophily Transfer of *pollen* through the agency of insects. Adj. entomophilous. (cf. *anemophily, ornithophily*).

Epicactus One of a range of hybrid cacti descended from *epiphytic* ancestors and grown primarily for the large and showy flowers.

Epidermis The surface layer of *cells* comprising the skin of a plant. Adj. epidermal.

Epigynous Having an *inferior ovary*. (cf. *hypogynous*).

Epiphyte A plant growing upon another for support only. Adj. epiphytic. (cf. *parasite*).

Epithet In *nomenclature*, the second word in a *binomial name*, also called the trivial name.

Evolution The process whereby all living things have descended from fewer and simpler ancestors.

F₁ The first filial generation following hybridization. F₂: the second generation, and so on.

Family A *taxonomic* grouping made up of related *genera*. Most Family names end in -aceae.

Fasciation An abnormal type of growth in which the stem apex broadens into a fan. Adj. fasciated.

Fertilization The fusion of male and female *gametes* in sexual reproduction.

Fibrous Thin and wiry, as in *lateral* roots.

Filament The usually threadlike base of a *stamen* that bears the *anther* above.

Floret A small flower, as found in the tightly packed *capitulum* of Compositae.

Fluctuation A non-heritable change brought about by nutrition or other environmental influence.

Follicle A dry *fruit* composed of a single *carpel* that *dehisces* longitudinally down one side.

Form A *taxonomic* subdivision of a *variety*; normally the smallest degree of differentiation considered worthy of a scientific name.

Free Separate from one another and not united. (cf. *connate*).

Fruit The *seeds* and their enclosing *ovary* at maturity, sometimes including also parts of the flower and axis.

Gamete A *haploid* sex cell that fuses with another gamete in sexual reproduction.

Gene The unit of inheritance, located on a *chromosome* at a specific site and able to reproduce itself.

Genetics the study of heredity and the mechanisms of inheritance.

Genus A *taxonomic* group composed of related *species*. Adj. generic. Pl. genera.

Glabrous With a smooth, hairless surface.

Glaucous With a fine waxy surface like a plum. (cf. *pruinose*).

Glochid The small, barbed, readily detached *spine* characteristic of *Opuntia*.

Gynoecium The female organs of the flower; collectively the *carpels*.

Halophyte A salt-tolerant plant, typically of maritime habitats and salt marshes, and showing usually a degree of *succulence*.

Haploid Containing a single, reduced set of *chromosomes*, as in the *gametes*. (cf. *diploid, polyploid*).

Herbarium A collection of preserved plants; the building in which such a collection is housed.

Hermaphrodite Possessing both male and female sex organs.

Hirsute Coarsely hairy.

Hispid Rough from short bristles or stiff hairs.

Homonym A name exactly duplicating that of another plant. In such cases the later name must be replaced by another. (cf. *synonym*).

Hygroscopic Able to change shape as a result of change in water content.

Hypocotyl The part of a seedling between the *radicle* and the *cotyledon(s)*; the transitional area between root and stem.

Hypogynous Having a *superior ovary*. (cf. *epigynous*).

Inbreeding Self-pollinating. (cf. *outbreeding*).

Indehiscent Not breaking open at maturity. (cf. *dehiscence*).

Inferior Growing below, as said of an *ovary* when the *perianth* arises from its apex. (cf. *superior*).

Inflorescence The axis bearing the flowers.

Internode That part of a stem between two *nodes*.

Involucre A circle of protective leaf-like organs, such as the *bracts*

surrounding a *capitulum*. Adj. involucrate.

Lamina The blade of a leaf.

Lateral On the side, as in the fine roots developed as branches from a *taproot*. (cf. *terminal*).

Latex White milk-like liquid that exudes from the cut surface of certain plants. That of euphorbias is often poisonous.

Leaf Succulent Having enlarged, fleshy, water-storing foliage; a plant of this nature.

Limb The broad expanded upper portion of a *petal* (or *sepal*). (cf. *claw*).

Lithophyte A plant that grows on the surface of rocks like a lichen.

Long-Day Plant A plant that flowers only in response to increasing day length. (cf. *short-day plant*).

Lumper A botanist who classifies into few, broadly conceived units. (cf. *splitter*).

Meiosis Reduction division; a special stage in the formation of *gametes* in which half the original total of *chromosomes* passes into each pollen grain or egg cell. Adj. meiotic.

Mendelian Ratio The mathematical ratio whereby, according to the laws of chance, the progeny of a cross will segregate for *dominant* and *recessive* factors. So called in tribute to Gregor Mendel.

Mericarp A part-fruit, made up of one or more *seeds* enclosed in an *ovary* segment and derived by the break-up of a *schizocarp*.

Meristem The mass of undifferentiated cells forming the growing tip of any organ.

Mesophyte A plant of average water requirements. (cf. *xerophyte*).

Metabolism The sum total of all chemical processes going on within a living organism.

Mimicry Natural camouflage; resemblance to the background, for whatever reason.

Mitosis That part of cell division in which each *chromosome* duplicates itself and an identical set passes to each of the two daughter *nuclei*. Adj. mitotic.

Monochasium A type of *cymose inflorescence* in which only one branch grows out from beneath the terminal flower. Adj. monochasial. (cf. *dichasium*).

Monocotyledon Having one *cotyledon*; one of two major subdivisions of flowering plants. (cf. *dicotyledon*).

Monoecious Having separate

male and female flowers on the same plant. (cf. *dioecious*).

Monotypic Having only one subordinate component; said of a *Family* containing only one *genus*, a genus containing only one *species*, and so on.

Monstrous In *succulents*, applied to a type of abnormal growth resulting from multiple growing points. (cf. *fasciation*).

Morphology The study of the form and development of parts of a plant.

Mutation A permanent genetic change; a sport. V. mutate.

Natural Selection The process whereby environmental forces select those individuals best adapted and eliminate the unfit.

Nectar The sugary secretion produced by a *nectary*.

Nectary A gland or secretory tissue that produces *nectar*.

Neoteny Arrested juvenility; the retention of youthful characters in an adult plant.

Node That part of a stem from which the leaf arises. (cf. *internode*).

Nomenclature A branch of *taxonomy* concerned with names and naming.

Nucleus The organizing body of a *cell*, largely made up of the *chromosomes*. Adj. nuclear.

Order A major *taxonomic* group made up of one or more related *Families*. Order names end in -ales.

Ornithophily Transfer of *pollen* by the agency of birds. Adj. ornithophilous. (cf. *anemophily, entomophily*).

Outbreeding; Outcrossing Cross-pollinating. (cf. *inbreeding*).

Ovary The central, female part of a flower made up of *carpels* containing *ovules*.

Ovule The "egg" of a plant which, on *fertilization*, develops into a *seed*.

Pachycaul Having a swollen base to the stem; an intermediate condition to the *caudiciform* habit.

Panicle A *raceme* of *racemes*. Adj. paniculate.

Papillate, Papulose Covered in minute, glossy, rounded, blister-like projections.

Parasite A plant that unites organically with another (the host) and derives nutriment directly from it. Adj. parasitic. (cf. *epiphyte*).

Pathology The study of diseases.

Pectinate Set with projections

like the teeth of a comb.

Pedicel The ultimate stalk supporting a single flower. Adj. pedicellate. (cf. *peduncle*).

Peduncle The secondary axis of an *inflorescence* that bears the *pedicels*. Adj. pedunculate.

Perianth The protective envelope of a flower, made up of uniform *tepals*, or of an outer *calyx* and an inner *corolla*.

Perigynous Halfway between *hypogynous* and *epigynous*, that is, with the *perianth* arising halfway up the *ovary*.

Petal One member of the *corolla*. Adj. petaloid.

Petiole The stalk of a leaf.

pH Mathematical notation for the degree of acidity or alkalinity. pH 7 is neutral, a soil with pH 8 is alkaline, and with pH 4 very acid. pH 6.5 suits most succulents.

Photoperiod The length of the daily exposure to light insofar as it effects plant growth and flowering.

Photosynthesis The process unique to plants whereby elaborate organic compounds (carbohydrates) are synthesized from carbon dioxide and water in the presence of light and *chlorophyll*. Adj. photosynthetic.

Phylloclad A flattened stem that looks and functions like a leaf.

Phyllotaxy The arrangement of parts on an axis, leaves in particular.

Phylogeny Race pedigree; the evolutionary history of a *taxon*. Adj. phylogenetic, phyletic.

Physiology The study of the life processes within an organism.

Placenta That part of an *ovary* bearing the *ovules*.

Pollen Dust-like grains produced by the *anthers* of flowering plants carrying the male *gamete* in *fertilization*. (cf. *pollination*).

Pollination The placing of *pollen* on the receptive *stigma* of a flower. (cf. *fertilization*).

Pollinium Pollen-mass; a structure comprising the contents of an *anther* packaged for transfer as one unit. Pl. pollinia.

Polygenes Linked *genes* which collectively determine the expression of a given character to different degrees.

Polyploid Containing three or more basic sets of *chromosomes* (cf. *haploid*, *diploid*).

Prickle A pointed, superficial outgrowth not linked to the *vascular* system of the plant.

Priority In *nomenclature*, the principle whereby the earliest validly published name takes precedence over others.

Proliferation Growth of buds that normally remain dormant. V. proliferate.

Protandry The maturing of *anthers* before *stigmas* in one flower. Adj. protandrous (cf. *protogyny*).

Protogyny The maturing of *stigmas* before *anthers* in one flower. Adj. protogynous. (cf. *protandry*).

Pruinose Having a pronounced white waxy coating. (cf. *glaucous*).

Pubescent Becoming downy.

Raceme One of two basic types of *inflorescence* in which the axis has unlimited growth at the tip, the oldest flowers being at the bottom. Adj. racemose. (cf. *cyme*).

Radical Arising from the root or at ground level.

Radicle The first root developing from a *seed*.

Ray A radiating organ, such as the outer ring of *florets* in Compositae. (cf. *disc*).

Receptacle The modified tip of the axis of a plant from which the floral parts develop.

Recessive Said of a *gene* whose action is obscured by its *allele* when the two are both present in a hybrid. (cf. *dominant*).

Relict A primitive survivor from earlier times; a "living fossil".

Respiration The reverse of *photosynthesis*, wherein some organic matter is broken down to carbon dioxide and water, with the release of energy.

Root Hairs Elongated cells from the surface of a root associated with absorption of salts in solution.

Runner A prostrate stem that produces a daughter plant at its tip.

Scape A conspicuous, almost or quite leafless *peduncle*.

Schizocarp A dry *fruit* that breaks up at maturity into two or more *mericarps*.

Scion The upper half of a graft. (cf. *stock*).

Seed The end-product of a fertilized *ovule*. The gardener accepts "seeds" in a less rigid sense, some being whole *fruits* or parts of fruits.

Self-compatible Able to set viable *seed* as a result of *selfing*; self-fertile. (cf. *self-incompatible*).

Self-incompatible Unable to set viable *seed* as a result of *selfing*; self-sterile. (cf. *self-compatible*).

Selfing Self-pollination; transfer of *pollen* to *stigmas* on the same plant. (cf.*crossing*).

Sepal One member of the *calyx*.

Sessile Lacking a stalk.

Short-Day Plant A plant that flowers only in response to shortening day length. (cf. *long-day plant*).

Shrublet A miniature shrub. (cf. *subshrub*).

Species A group of actually or potentially interbreeding plants more similar to one another than to the plants of any other species, with which they show some degree of intersterility. As the basic unit of classification systems, the species alone carries a *binomial* name. Adj. specific. P1. species.

Spike A *raceme* in which the flowers are *sessile*. Adj. spicate.

Spine A leaf or part of a leaf modified as a sharp pointed structure.

Splitter A botanist who classifies into many, finely divided units. (cf. *lumper*).

Sport See *mutation*.

Stamen The male organ of a flower, comprising a *filament* bearing an *anther* on top.

Staminode A barren *stamen* that may be modified to function as a *petal* or *nectary*.

Stem Succulent Having enlarged, fleshy, water-storing stems; a plant of this nature.

Stigma The receptive tip of the *style* on which the *pollen* alights.

Stipule One of a pair of lateral outgrowths from the base of a *petiole*, usually present as a scale, but spiny in euphorbias.

Stock The lower half of a graft, supplying the root system. (cf. *scion*).

Stoma The breathing pore of a plant. Pl. stomata.

Style Prolongation of the tip of a *carpel*, bearing the *stigma*.

Subshrub A smallish, soft-wooded shrub. (cf. *shrublet*).

Succulence Possession of *succulent tissue*.

Succulent Storing water in specially enlarged spongy *tissue* of the roots, stems or leaves; a plant of this type.

Sucker A shoot arising from below soil level close to the parent plant.

Superior Growing above, as said of *carpels* when they arise from the axis above the level of insertion of the *perianth*. (cf. *inferior*).

Synonym A surplus name, arising when one species has been given two or more names. (cf. *homonym*).

Systemic Said of pesticides that are absorbed by the plant and poison the cells against predators; a pesticide of this nature.

Taproot A stout, vertical, anchoring root developed from the *radicle*.

Taxon A *taxonomic* unit of any rank. Pl. taxa.

Taxonomy The study of classification, including *nomenclature*.

Tepal One member of the *perianth*. (cf. *petal, sepal*).

Terete Circular in cross-section.

Terminal At the end of the axis (cf. *lateral*).

Thorn Branch modified as a sharp, pointed structure, and containing *vascular tissue*.

Thyrse A *raceme* of *cymes*.

Tissue Aggregate of *cells* of similar form and function.

Transpiration Loss of water from plants by evaporation.

Tubercle Any conical or cylindrical outgrowth. Adj. tuberculate.

Tunicate Having two or more coats, as in *bulbs* with several concentric rings of leaf sheaths.

Type Specimen The actual plant, preserved, that served as the basis for a new name.

Umbel An *inflorescence* in which three or more *pedicels* arise from the same level. Adj. umbellate. (cf. *corymb*).

Unisexual Said of a flower that has *stamens* or *carpels*, but not both. (cf.*bisexual*).

Variegation Bicolour effect resulting from localized failure of development of pigment. Adj. variegated.

Variety A *taxonomic* subdivision of a *species*.

Vascular Provided with a conducting system made up of specialized *tissues* associated with the transport of fluid within the plant.

Widespread Having a wider distribution than average (cf. *endemic*).

Xeromorphic Preventing water loss, as in characters such as a thick *cuticle* or a surface covering of hairs in *xerophytes*.

Xerophyte A plant adapted to survive with less than average water supply. (cf. *mesophyte*).

Zygomorphy Symmetry about one plane only, which divides an organ (such as a flower) into two mirror-image halves. Adj. zygomorphic. (cf. *actinomorphy*).

Index

Figures in **heavy type** indicate an illustration in place of, or in addition to, a reference in the text. All generic names in common usage are listed; those regarded as synonyms are referred to accepted genera.

Picture Credits

The publishers wish to thank the following
photographers and organisations who
have supplied photographs for this book.
Photographs have been credited by page
number and position on the page: (B)
Bottom, (T) Top, (BL) Bottom left, etc.

Photographers

Heather Angel: 14(T), 22, 29(TL), 95,
165(T);
A–Z Botanical Collection: 54, 91, 105,
117, 124(T), 129(B), 184(T), 195(B),
239(B);
Pat Brindley: 138(B), 153;
Peter Chapman and Margaret Martin:
Contents page (6–7) (T), 20, 22(T), 64(B),
94, 121(BR), 122(L), 125, 126(T), 127(T),
130, 132, 133(B), 139(B), 141(B), 144(B),
145(T), 150, 163, 164(T), 187(BL),
190(B), 191(T), 192, 197(BR), 200(T,BL),
222 (L), 224(I), 225, 226(B), 227(R);
Eric Crichton: Half title(1), 75, 81, 83, 131,
176, 227(L);
Gerald Cubitt: 33, 48(T), 55, 136(T), 137,
157, 159, 161, 183, 208–9, 221(B);
Chester B. Dugdale:24(T), 133(T), 140,
145(B), 147(B), 210(T);
Dr. Donna Howell: 51;
George Kalmbacher: 108;
Heinz Klein: 202, 205(B);
Louise Lippold: 87, 121(T), 151(T), 160,
166, 184(B), 200(BR), 201(B), 203, 204,
207(T), 229(T), 233(B), 234(T), 241, 242,
243(T), 244, 245(B);

David Muench: 103;
Josef Muench: 177;
Department of Nature and Environmental
Conservation, Cape Province, South
Africa: 97;
L. E. Newton: 38
Dr. Edward S. Ross: Title page(2–3), title
verso page (5)(T), contents page (6–7)(B),
foreword (9)(T), 13, 19(T), 21, 27, 35, 39,
40(T), 44–7, 52, 56, 58(B), 69, 70, 100–1,
110–11(B), 148(B), 181, 182(B), 186,
197(TL), 210(B), 219, 220(B), 221(T),
222(R), 246–7;
Gordon Rowley: Endpapers, Title verso
(4–5)(B), foreword(8–9)(B), introduction
to part one (10–11)(B), 14(B), 15, 19(B),
23, 24(B), 25, 26, 28, 29(B), 30, 31, 32,
34, 36, 37, 48(B), 49, 50, 53, 58(T), 59,
60, 61, 63, 66, 67, 68, 71, 72, 73, 76, 77,
78, 79, 80, 82, 84, 85, 86, 88, 89, 92, 93,
98, 99, 102, 106, 107, 109, 111(T), 112,
113, 114, 120, 122(R), 123, 124(B), 126(B),
127(B), 128, 129(T), 136(B), 138(T),
139(T), 141(T), 142–3, 144(T), 146,
147(T), 148(T), 149, 151(B), 154–5, 156,
162, 164(B), 165(B), 167, 168–9, 170,
172–3, 175, 180, 182(T), 185, 187(T,BR),
188–9, 190(T), 191(B), 193, 194, 195(T),
197(TR), 198–9, 201(T), 205(T), 206,
207(B), 211–13, 216–18, 220(T), 224(B),
226(T), 228, 229(B), 231, 232, 233(T),
234(B), 235, 236–7, 238, 239(TL,TR),
240, 243(B), 245(T);
Philip W. Rundel: 41, 196;
B. Snoad: 64(T);
N. Taylor: 29(TR).

Artists

Copyright of the drawings on the pages
following the artists' names is the property
of Salamander Books Ltd.
Max Ansell (Temple Art Agency): 40, 43,
65
June Baker: 24–5, 31, 56–7, 91, 171
Pat Lenander (Temple Art Agency): 114,
118–19, 134–35, 152, 158, 174, 178–79,
214–15, 217, 223, 225
Glen Stewart (Bowen Davies Agency): 88,
90, 92

Acknowledgments

The "tree of Orders" diagram on pages
16–17 is based on TAKHTAJAN, A.
Flowering Plants, Origin and Dispersal
Oliver and Boyd, Edinburgh 1969. The
coding has been adapted and brought up
to date from HATCH, OSMOND and
SLATYER *Photosynthesis and
Photorespiration* 1971: 131.

The fog belt diagram on page 40 was
adapted from one appearing in an article
by Professor Philip W. Rundel of the
University of Irvine, California in *Cactus
and Succulent Journal of America* 48: 270,
1976, Editor, Charles Glass.

The rainfall maps of South Africa on page
42 have been adapted from N. and I.
SAUER in *Aloe* 14: 3–8, 1976.